MW00354648

THE WEDDING

Jesus Stands for His Bride in the Book of Revelation

"That He might present her to Himself, the church in glory,
not having spot, wrinkle, or any such thing; rather,
that she be holy and without blemish."
Ephesians 5:27

"Keep watch then at every season, praying that
you all may be deemed worthy to escape all
the things that will certainly take place,
and to stand before the Son of man."
Luke 21:36

"Now unto Him who is able to keep you from stumbling,
and to make you stand before the presence
of His glory without blemish
with exceeding joy."
Jude 24

SCOTT BURGESS

TEACH Services, Inc.
P U B L I S H I N G
www.TEACHServices.com • (800) 367-1844

World rights reserved. This book or any portion thereof may not be copied or reproduced in any form or manner whatever, except as provided by law, without the written permission of the publisher, except by a reviewer who may quote brief passages in a review.

The author assumes full responsibility for the accuracy of all facts and quotations as cited in this book. The opinions expressed in this book are the author's personal views and interpretations, and do not necessarily reflect those of the publisher.

This book is provided with the understanding that the publisher is not engaged in giving spiritual, legal, medical, or other professional advice. If authoritative advice is needed, the reader should seek the counsel of a competent professional.

Copyright © 2020 Scott Burgess
Copyright © 2020 TEACH Services, Inc.
ISBN-13: 978-1-4796-1138-6 (Paperback)
ISBN-13: 978-1-4796-1139-3 (ePub)
Library of Congress Control Number: 2020908781

Except where noted with the letters "KJV" (King James Version), all Bible verses are the author's own translation of the Hebrew and Aramaic Old Testament and the Majority Text Greek New Testament.

Published by

TEACH Services, Inc.
P U B L I S H I N G
www.TEACHServices.com • (800) 367-1844

TABLE OF CONTENTS

PRELIMINARY MATTER

LIST OF TABLES

ACKNOWLEDGMENTS

The following individuals are listed alphabetically for their role in bringing this project to completion:

NAME	HELP PROVIDED
Dr. Richard Davidson: Professor of Old Testament, Seventh-day Adventist Theological Seminary at Andrews University	Reviewed key areas of manuscript.
Charles & Sharon Ferguson: Pastor-and-wife team	Encouragement in getting started with this project.
Holly Joers: Active, soul-winning member of the Seventh-day Adventist Church	Encouragement to employ TEACH Services, Inc. as publisher.
Brenda Nieves: English teacher, Ouachita Hills College	Sundry formatting/style pointers.
Magda Rodriguez: President of Ouachita Hills College, Ph.D. candidate	Granting time to work on manuscript.
David Sydnor: Book reviewer, former pastor	Proofread manuscript thoroughly and swiftly.
Dr. Karl Tsatalbasidis: College instructor, pastor, author	Sharing insights while writing his Ph.D. dissertation.
Matthias Urbatzka: Master's student, completed his practicum teaching English at Ouachita Hills College	Reviewed opening chapters for writing mechanics.

READER REACTIONS

Pastor Charles Ferguson, D.Min., Carolina Conference of Seventh-day Adventists
We have long anticipated Scott Burgess's *THE WEDDING: Jesus Stands for His Bride in the Book of Revelation*. It was worth the wait. Burgess brings the same freshness to *THE WEDDING* that he brought to his previously published companion book *THE STAND: Jesus in the Book of Daniel*. As with *THE STAND* Burgess uses the tools of a trained biblical theologian. Yet the author has fresh insights into this ancient book of the Revelation of Jesus. Burgess is a gifted writer possessing the ability to make the complex comprehensible. He draws you into the story line. It is captivating. Laity and scholar alike will benefit from *THE WEDDING*.

Scotty Mayer, Founder Little Light Studios
This is one of the most amazing and beautiful illustrations of God's love for us. Such a timely and important message for anyone longing to see their Bridegroom coming in the clouds. The level of detail in this study is unprecedented. It will greatly enrich your understanding of the depth of God's love for us, but it will also reveal the passion He has for His bride. Once you start in you won't be able to put it down. It is a must read for the remnant church!

Edwin de Kock, M.A., Dip. Theo.

THE WEDDING: Jesus Stands for His Bride in the Book of Revelation by Scott Burgess is deeply Christ-centered, like his other work, *THE STAND, Jesus in the Book of Daniel*. As an interpreter of Bible prophecy, this author is clearly a Historicist. He rejects Catholic Preterism and Futurism as well as Dispensationalism, its Protestant derivative. In this book, too, he draws on the most up-to-date and varied research as well as the time-tested work of Uriah Smith. He is well acquainted with Koinē Greek, the original language of the New Testament, as well as different manuscript traditions. Among other things, this helps him to vindicate the *Vicarius Filii Dei* interpretation of the number 666 in Revelation 13:17, 18. He also shows that the third-century Chester Beatty papyrus, which antedates all other manuscripts, makes it clear that the mark and the number of the Beast should not be confused with each other. While both refer to the papacy, they are distinctly different. The mark of the Beast is Sundaykeeping, which will yet be enforced by legislation. But the number is the notorious 666. It not only provides the correct gematria for *Vicarius Filii Dei*, but is vindicated by copious historical examples of how various Popes for centuries boosted their power and authority by using that title. While there may be some points of prophetic interpretation where I differ, I do indeed recommend *THE WEDDING* as a valuable resource.

INTRODUCTION

The Bible was written for and meant to be understood by everybody. To that end, the present work employs Scripture's own simple method of exegesis: "precept must be upon precept, precept upon precept; line upon line, line upon line; here a little, and there a little" (Isa. 28:10, KJV). The present work walks the reader through the author's own thought process, teaching the reader *how to uncover truth for oneself*. Once one masters how to apply this skill prayerfully, *any* Scripture may be understood, no matter how difficult.

The principal theme traced throughout this commentary on Revelation is the wedding theme. According to Matthew 22:1–14, Jesus marries those who not only accept His invitation, but also, upon investigation, show themselves to be clothed only in His righteousness. Thus, Jesus' wedding is in fact the judgment to which all of Scripture points. This investigation is necessary, for Christ will present His bride "to Himself, the church in glory, not having spot, wrinkle, or any such thing; rather, that she be holy and without blemish" (Eph. 5:27).

The good news is that Jesus strengthens His bride, enabling her to meet His perfectly righteous standard. Of special interest are the 7 times Jesus stands for His bride throughout the book. To draw attention to this, **bold print** is employed in the translation of Revelation whenever Jesus **stands**.

This work follows the historicist method of prophetic interpretation, permitting history to confirm the prophecies of Revelation. The preterist, futurist, and idealist schools of interpretation are all rejected, as they 1) spiritualize away historically verifiable realities and 2) fail to identify Satan's earthly agent.

The present author also has a passion for numbers, and this work on Revelation is unique in its emphasis upon the use of numbers that saturate the book. Certain passages *cannot* be fully appreciated without due attention to the numbers employed. This is not to be confused with numerology (e.g., the Jewish *Kaballah*), which gives to biblical numbers mystical meanings not supported by the text.

The author has intentionally gone contrary to the rule of spelling out numbers, instead printing them numerically (e.g., "7," "62," "490"). Ordinal numbers (e.g., "first," "second," etc.) are spelled out. Numerically written numbers are simply easier to read, write, and locate on a page.

This commentary supplies its own translation, as the author has been trained in the original, biblical languages and passionately studies the Scriptures daily in them. Revelation was written in Greek, but it draws all of its imagery from the Old Testament, and much of its wording comes from the Septuagint (Greek Old Testament). Hence, the author, at times, translates words and phrases by their underlying Hebrew Old Testament equivalent. For example, "candlestick" is replaced by "menorah" (see Exod. 25:31) and "Lord God Almighty" by "*Yahweh*, God of hosts" (see Hosea 12:5).

May the reader prayerfully take up the study of this most challenging end-time book of books. Further, may this commentary shed light on the prophecies therein, that the reader may be enabled to stand with the Lamb on Mount Zion in the judgment hour of earth's history. May it serve to kindle a fire in the reader's heart to prepare other souls to stand with their Bridegroom—the Lord Jesus.

Scott Burgess
February 2020

ABBREVIATIONS

BOOKS OF THE BIBLE AND 1 MACCABEES

ABBREVIATION	BOOK	ABBREVIATION	BOOK
1 Macc.	1 Maccabees	Jonah	Jonah
Gen.	Genesis	Mic.	Micah
Exod.	Exodus	Nah.	Nahum
Lev.	Leviticus	Hab.	Habakkuk
Num.	Numbers	Zeph.	Zephaniah
Deut.	Deuteronomy	Hag.	Haggai
Josh.	Joshua	Zech.	Zechariah
Judges	Judges	Mal.	Malachi
Ruth	Ruth	Matt.	Matthew
1 Sam.; 2 Sam.	1 or 2 Samuel	Mark	Mark
1 Kings; 2 Kings	1 or 2 Kings	Luke	Luke
1 Chron.; 2 Chron.	1 or 2 Chronicles	John	John
Ezra	Ezra	Acts	Acts
Neh.	Nehemiah	Rom.	Romans
Esther	Esther	1 Cor.; 2 Cor.	1 or 2 Corinthians
Job	Job	Gal.	Galatians
Ps.	Psalms	Eph.	Ephesians
Prov.	Proverbs	Phil.	Philippians
Eccles.	Ecclesiastes	Col.	Colossians
Song of Sol.	Song of Songs	1 Thess.; 2 Thess.	1 or 2 Thessalonians

ABBREVIATION	BOOK	ABBREVIATION	BOOK
Isa.	Isaiah	1 Tim.; 2 Tim.	1 or 2 Timothy
Jer.	Jeremiah	Titus	Titus
Lam.	Lamentations	Philemon	Philemon
Ezek.	Ezekiel	Heb.	Hebrews
Dan.	Daniel	James	James
Hosea	Hosea	1 Peter; 2 Peter	1 or 2 Peter
Joel	Joel	1 John; 2 John; 3 John	1, 2 or 3 John
Amos	Amos	Jude	Jude
Obad.	Obadiah	Rev.	Revelation

BIBLES CITED

ABBREVIATION	BIBLE
BYZ	*The New Testament in the Original Greek: Byzantine Textform 2005* ("Majority Text")
CJB	*Complete Jewish Bible*
EBR	*Rotherham's Emphasized Bible*
ESV	*The Holy Bible, English Standard Version*
HCSB	*Holman Christian Standard Bible*
KJV	*King James Version*
LXX	*Septuaginta (Old Greek Jewish Scriptures)*
MIT	*The Idiomatic Translation of the New Testament*
NAB	*New American Bible, revised edition*
NET	*The NET Bible (New English Translation)*
NJB	*New Jerusalem Bible*
NKJV	*The New King James Version*
NRSV	*New Revised Standard Version*
NTG	*Novum Testamentum Graece* ("Critical Text" or "Eclectic Text")
RSV	*Revised Standard Version of the Bible*
TR	*Textus Receptus* ("Received Text")
YLT	*Young's Literal Translation of the Holy Bible*

REFERENCE WORKS

ABBREVIATION	AUTHOR/EDITOR	TITLE
AA	Ellen G. White	*The Acts of the Apostles*
ANLEX	Friberg, Friberg, and Miller	*Analytical Lexicon of the Greek New Testament*
BDAG	Bauer, Danker, Arndt, and Gingrich	*A Greek-English Lexicon of the New Testament and Other Early Christian Literature*
CG	Ellen G. White	*Child Guidance*
CT	Ellen G. White	*Counsels to Parents, Teachers, and Students*
COL	Ellen G. White	*Christ's Object Lessons*
DA	Ellen G. White	*The Desire of Ages*
1888	Ellen G. White	*The Ellen G. White 1888 Materials*
Ev	Ellen G. White	*Evangelism*
EW	Ellen G. White	*Early Writings*
GC	Ellen G. White	*The Great Controversy*
GELNT	Joseph Henry Thayer	*A Greek-English Lexicon of the New Testament*
GELNTBSD	Louw, Nida, Smith, and Munson	*Greek-English Lexicon of the New Testament Based on Semantic Domains*
GSG	Conybeare and Stock	*Grammar of Septuagint Greek*
LSJ	Liddell, Scott, Jones, and McKenzie	*A Greek-English Lexicon* (Oxford: Oxford University Press, 1843)
MB	Ellen G. White	*Thoughts from the Mount of Blessing*
xMR	Ellen G. White	*Manuscript Releases*, Vol. x
PK	Ellen G. White	*Prophets and Kings*
PP	Ellen G. White	*Patriarchs and Prophets*
RH	Ellen G. White	*The Review and Herald*
1SAT	Ellen G. White	*Sermons and Talks*, Vol. 1
ST	Ellen G. White	*The Signs of the Times* (Seventh-day Adventist periodical)
xT	Ellen G. White	*Testimonies to the Church*, Volume x
TM	Ellen G. White	*Testimonies to Ministers and Gospel Workers*
VGNT	Moulton and Milligan	*Vocabulary of the Greek New Testament*

THE STRUCTURE OF REVELATION

The structure of Revelation gives enormous insight into its meaning. Table 1 provides a simplified structure of the book:

Table 1: Simplified Structure of Revelation

SECTION	REFERENCE	SUBJECT	SUBJECT	REFERENCE	SECTION
1	1:1–8	Judgment wedding to begin soon.	Judgment wedding to end soon.	22:6–21	1'
2	1:9–20	The Son of man.	The bride.	21:2–8	2'
	2 and 3	Son of man's call to conquer sin.	Bride has conquered sin.	21:9–22:5	
3	4:1–8:1	Pre-advent judgment: Throne, scroll, saints stand.	Post-advent judgment: Throne, scrolls, wicked stand.	20:11–21:1	3'
4A	8:2–6	Jesus intercedes.	Jesus no longer intercedes.	15	4A'
	8:7–11:19	7 trumpets: Wedding coming.	7 last plagues: Wedding over.	16	
4B	12	Dragon persecutes.	Dragon destroyed.	20:1–10	4B'
	13	Sea beast, land beast, and wisdom riddle.	Whore, scarlet beast, and wisdom riddle.	17:1–13	

(*continued*)

Table 1: Simplified Structure of Revelation (*continued*)

SECTION	REFERENCE	SUBJECT	SUBJECT	REFERENCE	SECTION
	14:1–5	The Lamb and the 144,000.	Those with the Lamb.	17:14	
	14:6–13	Proclamation of 3 angels' messages: To everyone sitting on earth. Give Him glory. Judgment hour has come. Worship Maker. Babylon fallen. Wine of fornication. Nations intoxicated. Cup of retribution. Fiery torment. Smoke ascends forever. Endurance of holy people. God's commandments. Jesus' faith. "Blessed are the dead," says the Spirit.	Result of 3 angels' messages: Whore sits on everyone. Give Him glory. Judgment came in 1 hour. Creatures worship. Babylon fallen. Wine/ fornication. Nations fallen. Her cup. Burned up with fire. Smoke ascends forever. Righteous ways of holy people. God's reign. Lamb's wedding. Blessed are those called … spirit of prophecy.	17:15–19:10	
	14:14–20	14:14–16: Son of man harvests earth. Seated on white cloud. Golden crown on head.	19:11–16: Son of man comes for bride. Seated on white horse. Many diadems on head.	19:11–21	

(*continued*)

Table 1: Simplified Structure of Revelation (*continued*)

SECTION	REFERENCE	SUBJECT	SUBJECT	REFERENCE	SECTION
		14:17–20: Earth's vintage trampled. Angel exits temple, calls with loud cry. Vine cast into winepress, winepress trampled.	19:17–21: Wicked killed. Angel stands in sun, calls with loud voice. Beast and false prophet cast into lake of fire, winepress trampled.		

Table 1 reveals an elegant literary structure for Revelation, but what are we supposed to learn from it? To answer, work your way down the two central columns labeled "SUBJECT," noting how the columns present matching trains of thought. Each column ends with the second coming of Jesus as Bridegroom for His beleaguered bride.

The grand theme of Revelation is Jesus' wedding with His bride. How perfectly fitting, then, that the very structure of Revelation points to Jesus' return for His bride as its climax!

1:
JESUS' WEDDING
TO BEGIN SOON

REVELATION 1:1–8: PRE-ADVENT JUDGMENT TO BEGIN SOON

1 [1]The revelation of Jesus Christ which God gave Him, to show His servants those things which must transpire in the near future; He encoded it in symbols, sending it via His angel to His servant John, [2]who attested the Word of God and the testimony of Jesus Christ, as much as he saw. [3]Blessed is he who reads aloud, and those who hear the words of this prophecy, keeping the things written therein—for the appointed time is near.

[4]John, to the 7 churches, those in the Roman province of Asia:

Grace unto you and peace from God—He who is, He who was, and He who is coming—and from the 7 spirits which are before His throne, [5]and from Jesus Christ, the faithful Witness, the Firstborn of the dead, the Ruler of the kings of the earth. Unto Him who loves us and has washed us from our sins by His blood, [6]and made us a kingdom, priests unto God, even His Father—unto Him be glory and dominion forever and ever. Amen. [7]Behold: He is coming among the clouds! Every eye will see Him, notably those who pierced Him; all tribes of the earth will beat their breasts on His account. Indeed, amen.

[8]"I AM is the Alpha and the Omega," says *Adonai Yahweh*—He who is, He who was, and He who is coming—the God of hosts.[1]

---

[1]Greek: "Lord God, He who is, He who was, and He who is coming, the Almighty." The LXX (Septuagint) routinely substitutes the title "Lord" for the divine name "*Yahweh*" and "Lord God" for "*Adonai Yahweh*." English translations almost universally follow suit, rendering "*Yahweh*" as "LORD" and "*Adonai Yahweh*" as "Lord GOD." The LXX reads, "Lord God Almighty" for the Hebrew

COMMENTARY

The opening verse makes clear the point of the book: to reveal Jesus Christ. Revelation centers on Jesus' work as High Priest during the Day of Atonement—the day of judgment (see Lev. 16; 23:26–32). God made mankind in His own image and likeness (see Gen. 1:26, 27), but with Adam and Eve's fall into sin (see ch. 3), this image became tarnished and has grown steadily worse over the last 6,000 years. The astonishing message of Revelation is God's pledge to restore His image and likeness *in you*!

Daniel and Revelation are companion books. Just as Daniel is couched in symbols, and God sent His angel Gabriel to communicate with Daniel (see 8:16; 9:21), so Revelation was communicated by God's angel Gabriel to his servant John.[2] Revelation concerns the Word of God and the testimony of Jesus Christ. This is an example of hendiadys, which means that the Scriptures *are* the testimony of Jesus Christ. To properly understand Revelation is to recognize Jesus in every verse of Scripture. "Search the Scriptures ... they [the Scriptures] are those which testify about Me" (John 5:39).

God pronounces a blessing on both the person who reads the message to others, as well as those who hear it read. What constitutes this blessing? According to Revelation 1:3, the blessing is found in *keeping*, or following, what is written in the book. What are we called upon to keep? The key to answering that question lies in understanding the explanatory phrase, "for the appointed time is near."

The vision of Jesus that John sees in 1:12–16 matches that which Daniel saw at the close of his book (see Dan. 10:5, 6), indicating that John's vision picks up where Daniel's vision left off. It follows that this "appointed time"

"*Adonai Yahweh*, God of hosts" in Amos 3:13. Revelation 1:8 is identical, but with the explanatory phrase "He who is, He who was, and He who is coming" inserted after "God." This phrase points back to Exodus 3:14, where God introduces Himself to Moses as the great "I AM," the covenant-keeping *Yahweh*. In keeping with the Hebrew mindset of Revelation, it is best to translate Revelation 1:8 as "*Adonai Yahweh*—He who is, He who was, and He who is coming—the God of hosts."

[2]"Of Gabriel the Saviour speaks in the Revelation, saying that 'He sent and signified it by His angel unto His servant John.'" (White, *DA*, p. 99).

is none other than the period spoken of in the last verse of Daniel as "the end of the days," namely, the end of the 2,300 evening-mornings, at which time the heavenly sanctuary was to be "restored to its righteous condition" (8:14). This cleansing of the heavenly sanctuary is none other than the pre-advent judgment—the Day of Atonement—that immediately precedes Jesus' second coming. The Day of Atonement is indeed one of the "appointed times" of the sacred calendar (see Lev. 23:4, 27).

This end-time day of atonement also necessitates a cleansing of the hearts of God's faithful remnant, to be identified explicitly later in this commentary. For now, understand it to refer to those who surrender *fully* to God's control in their lives, in both thought and deed, as they experience the fulfillment of the *new covenant*: their old stony heart is removed, God's law is written in the new heart of flesh, and they are completely filled with the Holy Spirit (see Ezek. 36:26, 27; Jer. 31:31–34). This is the very covenant made with Abraham in Genesis 15–17.

Hence, the phrase "appointed time" in Revelation 1:3 refers to the end-time day of atonement, the final judgment, when the new-covenant experience is fully realized in the lives of God's remnant people as He cleanses both their hearts and the record of their sins in the heavenly sanctuary. Jesus refers to this judgment hour in the parable of the 10 virgins in Matthew 25:1–13. In this parable, the midnight cry marks the announcement that the final judgment is about to commence and the Bridegroom (Jesus) is soon to come for His expectant bride.

Thus, Revelation opens with an invitation to Jesus' wedding! Those who keep the things written therein enter by faith with Jesus into the Most Holy Place. When He pronounces them fully clean, they are prepared to be eternally wed to Him. At His second coming, they go with Him to the marriage supper of the Lamb (see Rev. 19:9).

In 1:4, reference is made to the 7 churches in the Roman province of Asia. The 7 churches in John's day typify the 7 stages of church history outlined in chapters 2 and 3 under the baleful influence of imperial—and later papal—Rome. "The names of the seven churches are symbolic of the church in different periods of the Christian Era. The number 7 indicates completeness, and is symbolic of the fact that the messages extend to the end of time, while the symbols used reveal the condition of the church at different periods in the history of the world" (White, *AA*, p. 585).

Revelation refers to the Roman church as spiritual Babylon (see Rev. 14:8; 16:19; 17:5; 18:2, 10, 21). Peter confirmed this, a fact acknowledged in Roman Catholic Bibles: "The chosen one: feminine, referring to the Christian community (*ekklesia*) at Babylon, the code name for Rome in Rev 14:8; 17:5; 18:2" (NAB, comments on 1 Peter 5:13). The message of Revelation is not simply a message for those living in a Roman province in John's day; it is for everyone throughout history who, no matter their church membership or profession of faith in Jesus as Savior, may be living contrary to God's will by following the teachings or practices of spiritual Babylon. Indeed, one aspect of Jesus' purifying work as High Priest during the end-time day of atonement is to explicitly identify spiritual Babylon, pleading with His people to come out (see Rev. 14:8–11; 18:2–4). As our brother's keeper (see Gen. 4:9), we are each called to direct our fellow human beings into the truth.

The text goes on to state that God offers grace (the ability He imparts to remain faithful) and peace. He identifies Himself as "He who is, He who was, and He who is coming," a clear reference to the covenant name of God—*Yahweh*. The name *Yahweh* is a form of the Hebrew verb "to be" and points to God's existence from eternity past to eternity future. When *Yahweh* established the everlasting covenant with Abram, He promised him that his seed, though afflicted 400 years, would be brought out (see Gen. 15:13–16). When the 400 years were up, *Yahweh* introduced Himself to Moses as the God of the fathers with whom He cut the Abrahamic covenant, informing him that the time of deliverance had come (see Exod. 3:6, 8, 14).

Just as God kept covenant with the Hebrews of old and delivered them when the 400 years appointed them concluded, so the appointed time for the end-time judgment in Revelation 1:3 is a time of deliverance. While the world fears to be judged by a perfectly just and holy God, His people are to rejoice, confident that He will deliver them from the power of sin, enabling them to walk perfectly in His royal law, the law of liberty (see James 1:25; 2:8, 12).

Twice in the introduction, *Yahweh* refers to himself as "He who is coming." John uses this same description in reference to Jesus' incarnation, identifying Jesus as *Yahweh*:

> John 1:9: The true Light, which illuminates every man, was about to come into the world.
>
> John 6:14: They were saying, "This is truly the Prophet who is to come into the world."
>
> John 11:27: She said ... "I believe that you are the Messiah, the Son of God, the one who is to come into the world."
>
> John 12:13: They were crying out, "Blessed is He who comes in the name of *Yahweh*, the King of Israel!"

We are further introduced to "the 7 spirits which are before His throne." Grace and peace come from the 7 spirits, as also from the Father and Son, implying that these 7 spirits must also be God. Does this imply some 9-headed monstrosity? Certainly not. Jesus prayed for perfect unity among His disciples, not just in His day, but *for all time* (see John 17:11, 20–23), and this unity is accomplished by the Holy Spirit (see Eph. 4:3). Just as Revelation 2 and 3 divide the history of the true church from John's day until the second coming into 7 periods, so the Holy Spirit would strive with the church during all 7 periods.

The introduction of the Holy Spirit at the very outset of Revelation points to the crucial significance of His role in the heavenly trio.[3] While

---

[3] "The Comforter that Christ promised to send after He ascended to heaven, is the Spirit in all the fullness of the Godhead, making manifest the power of divine grace to all who receive and believe in Christ as a personal Saviour. There are three living persons of the heavenly trio; in the name of these three great powers—the Father, the Son, and the Holy Spirit—those who receive Christ by living faith are baptized, and these powers will co-operate with the obedient subjects of heaven in their efforts to live the new life in Christ" (White, *Ev*, p. 615).

it was imperative that the Father send Jesus to die in our place—to make the atoning sacrifice on our behalf for the remission of sin (see Heb. 9:22; Lev. 16:8, 9.)—there is another aspect of atonement that many overlook: the *application* of Jesus' blood to one's life, which purifies and restores the sinner in God's image. The life of all flesh is in the blood, but God's Spirit is also life to the soul (see Lev. 17:11; Gen. 2:7; Job 27:3). As Jesus ministers His blood for us, the Holy Spirit simultaneously works in our hearts "both to will and to do concerning His good pleasure" (Phil. 2:13).

The text resumes its focus on Jesus, whose continuing love for us was demonstrated in that He "has washed us from our sins by His blood." While this is an accomplished fact, we are also told that those who experience the fulfillment of God's covenant in their lives are those who have "washed their robes and whitened them with the blood of the Lamb" (Rev. 7:14). Thus we see that the righteousness given us involves 1) a washing on the part of Jesus that involves nothing on our part (justification, made possible by Jesus' perfect atoning sacrifice, which cleanses our sinful past) and 2) a washing on our part, a cooperation with God as we allow Him to cleanse our very being (sanctification), that the indulgence of sin (not the sinful nature itself) may be forever eradicated from the life. To this end, the exercise of faith, both in the sacrifice He has already accomplished at Calvary and the soul-cleansing He longs to accomplish in our lives right now, is critical. Scripture is plain that we are saved by grace through faith alone (see Eph. 2:8, 9); at the same time, faith without works is dead (see James 2:20, 26). The resolution to this seeming paradox is that true, saving faith itself works through love (see Gal. 5:6).

We must note that the text refers to Jesus as "Firstborn of the dead," i.e., preeminent among those raised from the dead. We should take great comfort from this! We all have sinned, and the wages of sin is death (see Rom. 3:23; 6:23). However, Jesus became sin for us and therefore died on the tree in our behalf (see 2 Cor. 5:21; 1 Peter 2:24). Of course, the Father who raised Jesus from the dead has granted Him the right to have eternal life within Himself (see Gal. 1:1; John 5:26). Therefore, Jesus may say

He is "the resurrection and the life" (John 11:25). If we remain faithful, He will raise us from the dead, should we die before He returns.

Having just referred to Jesus as "Ruler of the kings of the earth," the text goes on to clarify God's view of kings: God's kingdom is composed of His priests. His kings are not autocrats, as in many nations of today; rather, they are those who are privileged to judge with Jesus, the Judge of judges (see Rev. 20:4–6). This kingdom of priests points back to Exodus 19:6, just before God proclaimed the 10 Commandments from Mount Sinai. The 10 Commandments are the words of God's covenant (see Exod. 34:28; Deut. 4:13; 1 Kings 8:9, 21), but they are also the basis of the end-time judgment (see Eccl. 12:13, 14). Once again, the introduction to Revelation blends covenant and judgment. Hence, those whom Jesus judges faithful *before* His second coming will in turn judge the unfaithful *after* His second coming.

The glimpse of the second coming in Revelation 1:7 pictures Jesus as Judge at the close of the pre-advent judgment, as confirmed by comparison with Daniel 7:9–14, in which Jesus comes to His Father, the Ancient of Days, at the *commencement* of the judgment "with the clouds of the heavens." How is it that "every eye will see Him" at His second coming when there are two distinct resurrections: that of the righteous at the beginning of the 1,000 years and that of the wicked following the 1,000 years (see Rev. 20:5; John 5:25–29)? Comparison with Daniel 12:2 reveals that it is the righteous people of ages past who awaken to everlasting life, along with a *select* group of the wicked, those who most actively participated in Jesus' death ("those who pierced Him"), who awaken "to reproaches, to everlasting abhorrence" at the second coming. In other words, all who are alive when Jesus comes will see Him.

The introduction closes with God's assurance that He is the Alpha and the Omega. This reference to the beginning and ending of the Greek alphabet makes clear that Jesus is the Creator of all things (see John 1:3; Heb. 1:2; Col. 1:16). Again, Jesus is the Author and Finisher of our faith, and the end goal of our faith is our salvation (see Heb. 12:2; 1 Peter 1:9). "He which hath begun a good work in you will perform it until the day of Jesus Christ" (Phil. 1:6, KJV). As the Alpha and the Omega, primary emphasis is given to Jesus as Creator and Deliverer from sin, the very reasons cited by the fourth commandment as the reason He is due worship (see Exod. 20:11; Deut. 5:15). This theme is developed extensively throughout Revelation.

The section closes by once again identifying Jesus as "He who is, He who was, and He who is coming"—*Yahweh*, the covenant-keeping God. In the next section, this same covenant-keeping Jesus extends to everyone an invitation to His wedding—an invitation to become part of His faithful bride.

PART 1: THE KEY POINTS

REVELATION 1:1–8: JESUS

Revelation reveals Jesus. Jesus is the Messiah, the Son of God, and He is fully God. Jesus is *Yahweh*, the God who keeps covenant. Jesus rose from the dead, giving promise of the resurrection to *all* faithful believers. He is Alpha and Omega: our Creator and Deliverer from sin.

Jesus appeared to Moses as *Yahweh* because it was time to fulfill the *everlasting* covenant established with Abraham (see Gen 15:13–18; Exod. 2:24; 3:8). Of course, marriage is a covenant (see Mal. 2:14), and since God hates divorce (see Mal. 3:16), marriage is a picture of God's everlasting covenant. Hence, Jesus is the divine Bridegroom.

REVELATION 1:1–8: GOD THE FATHER

God is presented as *Yahweh*, the covenant-keeping God who delivers His people via the judgment.

REVELATION 1:1–8: THE HOLY SPIRIT

The 7 spirits is a reference to the Holy Spirit. The Holy Spirit has been at work throughout the 7 periods of church history outlined in Revelation 2 and 3, wooing God's people to faithfulness.

REVELATION 1:1–8: THE WEDDING THEME

Revelation is especially concerned with the appointed time of the end-time judgment—the day of atonement. During the judgment, Jesus cleanses us from our sins by *applying* His shed blood to our lives and filling us with the Holy Spirit. With our characters purified, we are then qualified to also serve with Him as judges. Judgment culminates with the second coming of Jesus to take His faithful bride home.

As Jesus makes plain in the parable of the 10 virgins (see Matt. 25:1–13) and the parable of the wedding garment (see Matt. 22:1–14), the end-time judgment is the wedding between Jesus and His corporate bride—His faithful followers. John heard that the "appointed time" for the end-time judgment—God's wedding—was near. In fact, the end-time judgment—the wedding—is in session *right now*.

REVELATION 1:1–8: DECISION QUESTION

The Bridegroom, Jesus, is coming soon to take home His faithful bride, those who by God's grace have become one with Him in character.

Do you choose to live with God forever? Let Him begin the necessary work of character perfection in you today, that you may be fully ready to meet Him at the second coming and serve Him faithfully throughout eternity.

2:
JESUS PROPOSES TO MARRY HIS BRIDE

REVELATION 1:9–20:
THE SON OF MAN

1 ⁹I, John, your brother and partner in the tribulation, kingdom, and perseverance in Christ Jesus, came to be on the island called Patmos on account of the Word of God and on account of the testimony of Jesus Christ. ¹⁰I came to be in [the] Spirit on the Lord's day; I heard a voice behind me, loud like a trumpet, ¹¹saying, "What you see, write upon a scroll, and send to the 7 churches: unto Ephesus, unto Smyrna, unto Pergamos, unto Thyatira, unto Sardis, unto Philadelphia, and unto Laodicea."

¹²There I turned to see the voice that was speaking with me; when I turned, I saw 7 golden menorahs, ¹³and among the 7 menorahs one like the Son of man, wearing an ankle-length robe and bound at the chest with a golden sash. ¹⁴Now, His head and hairs were white as white wool, like snow; His eyes were like a fiery flame; ¹⁵His feet were like purified bronze, as though refined in a furnace; His voice was like a voice of many waters; ¹⁶He was holding in His right hand 7 stars; from His mouth a sharp double-edged sword was proceeding; His appearance was like the sun shining in its intensity.

¹⁷When I saw Him, I fell at His feet like a dead man. He placed his right hand upon me, saying, "Do not fear. I AM is the First and the Last, ¹⁸and He who lives. I was dead, yet behold, I am living forever and ever. Amen. I hold the keys of death and the grave. ¹⁹Therefore write out those things you see—both those which are, as well as those which must take place afterward.

20"The mystery of the 7 stars which you saw upon[4] my right hand, and the 7 golden menorahs: the 7 stars are the angels of the 7 churches; the 7 menorahs are [the] 7 churches."

COMMENTARY

John identifies himself with his readers as a brother, one suffering tribulation, yet clinging to the hope of the kingdom and the perseverance to be found only in Christ Jesus. His experience typifies that of believers throughout history. In Revelation 6:9, it is prophesied that believers would be persecuted centuries later by the papacy for their testimony of the Scriptures and Jesus Christ.[5] John's use of the word "tribulation" identifies his experience with that of the faithful remnant in the end-time persecution (see Rev. 7:14; Dan. 12:1, LXX). Serving as a model for the end-time remnant, John perseveres in spite of circumstances.

John is now relegated to Patmos, having already been cast into a pot of boiling oil, in which his life was miraculously preserved, akin to the three Hebrews of Daniel 3.[6] Patmos is a rocky island in the Aegean Sea, a fitting place for his receipt of the Revelation. Indeed, John could there best appreciate Jesus as his *Ebenezer* ("Stone of help," 1 Sam. 7:12). The reason given for his banishment is his adherence to the Word of God and the testimony of Jesus. This further identifies John with the end-time remnant, those who "keep God's commandments and have the testimony of Jesus" (Rev. 12:17).

John relates that he came to be in the Spirit, meaning God gave him the grand vision that we know as the Revelation. This occurred on

---

[4] Greek επι (genitive case) usually = "upon." Comparison with εν = "in" (e.g., v. 16) shows that here, επι is equivalent to "in."

[5] See, for example, Wylie, *Protestantism in the Waldensian Valleys*, and Foxe, *Actes and Monuments* (*Foxe's Book of Martyrs*).

[6] "John was cast into a caldron of boiling oil; but the Lord preserved the life of His faithful servant" (White, *AA*, p. 570).

the "Lord's day." Revelation is saturated with references to the Old Testament, and the Septuagint (Greek Old Testament) routinely substitutes the Greek κυριος ("Lord") for the divine name *Yahweh*. For this reason, the phrase κυριακος ημερα in 1:10 is best understood as "*Yahweh's* day" rather than "the Lord's day."

Modern Greek employs the phrase κυριακη ημερα to designate Sunday, hence many conclude that John had his vision on Sunday. Indeed, it is not uncommon in some Sunday-keeping Christian circles for a church elder or pastor to begin the weekly service with a "Welcome to God's house this Lord's day." However, this is reading into Scripture from modern experience; the Christian is to interpret experience in light of Scripture. Consider the following:

> Isa. 58:13: If you turn away your foot from the Sabbath (i.e., from doing your own pleasures on My holy day) and call the Sabbath a delight, *Yahweh's* holy day, worthy of honor, then you will honor it by not doing your own ways, finding your own delights or speaking [your own] matter. Then you will take delight in *Yahweh*; I will cause you to ride upon the high places of the earth; I will feed you with the inheritance of your father Jacob, for the mouth of *Yahweh* has spoken.

> Mark 2:27, 28: The Sabbath came into existence for man, not man for the Sabbath. Therefore, the Son of man is κυριος ["Lord"] also of the Sabbath.

The foregoing verses provide a *biblical* definition of the Lord's day: it is *Yahweh's* holy day, the Sabbath, the seventh day of the week. The remainder of the book of Revelation is replete with references to the Sabbath, confirming that the "Lord's day" in verse 10 is indeed His holy seventh day. It is reasonable to ask why John doesn't simply say "Sabbath" instead of "Lord's day." His vision of Jesus in verses 12–16 points one to the Day of Atonement, which was considered an annual convocation, holy like the weekly Sabbath (see Lev. 23:3, 27, 32). Hence, John's use of "Lord's day" is a compact way of referring to *both* the weekly Sabbath and the Day of Atonement. Both relate to the wedding theme in Revelation: as already noted, the end-time day of atonement is the end-time judgment, which is Jesus' wedding; as will be shown in remarks on chapter 4–7, the Sabbath is the seal of the everlasting covenant, meaning it is Jesus' pledge to marry His people.

He hears behind him a voice "loud like a trumpet." This points back to the initial mention of "trumpet" in the Bible: the giving of God's holy law, the 10 Commandments, at Sinai. Amid the thunderclaps and lightning flashes came "the voice of a trumpet exceedingly loud," just prior to God's pronouncement of His holy law (see Exod. 19:16, 19; 20:18).

Another observation on the trumpet-like voice is in order. *Yahweh* gives the command to "lift up your voice like the trumpet, and declare to my people their rebellion, to the house of Jacob their sins" (Isa. 58:1). Paul and James make plain that the way to recognize sin is by looking at God's law (see Rom. 7:7; James 1:22–25). The last three verses of Isaiah 58 draw attention to the Sabbath, the capstone of God's law. The giving of the law at Sinai and God's call for repentance in Isaiah 58 each draw attention to His downtrodden law, particularly His Sabbath. This is no mystery, for the 10 Commandments are called His covenant (see Exod. 34:28; Deut. 4:13; 1 Kings 8:9, 21), and of these commandments, the Sabbath alone is styled as the everlasting covenant (see Exod. 31:16; Isa. 56:6). Both God's law and Sabbath figure prominently throughout Revelation. Indeed, *repentance* is critical, for the book centers around the judgment, the end-time day of atonement, in which God's people are called to repent (see Lev 16; 23:26–32).

Again, Joel speaks of blowing the trumpet in Zion in preparation for "the day of *Yahweh*" (Joel 2:1, 15). The chapter as a whole speaks of an invading army from the north unlike any other in history. The day of *Yahweh* is so overwhelming that the question is asked in verse 11, "who can endure it?" Thus, *Yahweh* calls His people to turn to Him in complete repentance, that He may protect them during this excruciating time. During the end-time day of atonement, Jesus' work is to reproduce

His character in His people. Of course, the 10 Commandments are a transcript of his character, so we are again pointed to Sinai.

One final point on the trumpet-like voice: Jesus says that His voice wakes the dead (see John 5:25–29), and Paul confirms this, equating it with the voice of the archangel (Michael, who is Jesus, see comments on Revelation 12) and the trumpet of God (see 1 Thess. 4:16). This is especially fitting, for John "fell at His feet like a dead man," needing to be resurrected, as it were. Further, the law was ordained unto life (see Lev. 18:5; Gal. 3:12), the 10 Commandments open with a reminder that God is Israel's deliverer (see Exod. 20:2), and the Sabbath commandment reiterates this point (see Deut. 5:15). Those who are resurrected unto life are those who have been delivered from sin via the new covenant, which writes the law in the heart (see Jer. 31:31–34; Ezek. 36:26, 27).

Hence, Jesus' trumpet-like voice weaves together several related themes: the proclamation of the law at Sinai, warning others of their sins, proclaiming the Day of Atonement, and the resurrection.

At this point, John is directed to write the contents of the vision in a scroll, just as Daniel had written his matters in a scroll and sealed it (see Dan. 12:4). The scroll is to be sent to the 7 churches in the Roman province of Asia, referring not just to 7 churches in John's day, but the church throughout all time. Daniel's scroll was *sealed* until the end time; John's vision is an apocalypse, an unveiling, a revelation—the very key to unlock Daniel's scroll during the end time.

Naturally, John turns to see the source of this trumpet-like voice, and he sees 7 golden menorahs. The Greek word literally means "lampstand," leading one to envision a stand with a single candle upon it. However, the Septuagint uses this word routinely to translate the Hebrew "menorah," the 7-branched candlestick of the wilderness sanctuary (see Exod. 25:31). Why does John see 7 such menorahs, as the wilderness sanctuary had a single menorah? All difficulty is removed when we recall that the wilderness sanctuary was later replaced by Solomon's temple, which had 10 menorahs before the Most Holy Place (see 1 Kings 7:49; 2 Chron. 4:7). In fact, our study of Revelation will show that the heavenly sanctuary corresponds more exactly to Solomon's temple than it does the wilderness sanctuary, which was a simplified structure suited for portability. Hence, in Revelation 1, John's attention is focused upon the heavenly sanctuary, specifically the Holy Place.

In Revelation 1:13, John sees Jesus as the Son of man, a reference to Jesus in connection with the judgment (see Dan. 7:13). He is dressed in a ποδηρης ("ankle-length robe"), used in the Septuagint for the robe of the high priest, and he has a sash about his chest, as does the high priest (for both, see Exod. 28:4). The color of the sash is not given in Exodus 28, but Daniel 10:5–6 describes Jesus' loins as "girded with fine gold of Ufaz." In the visions of Daniel and John, Jesus' costume lacks the remaining elaborate articles of Exodus 28, conforming to the plain linen attire worn by the high priest as judge on the Day of Atonement (see Lev. 16:4). Hence, Jesus' attire confirms Him as High Priest and Judge in the end-time day of atonement.

Jesus' hair is "white as white wool, like snow," corresponding to the Ancient of Days, whose "garment was white as snow" and "the hair of His head like lamb's wool," as He sat at the commencement of the judgment (Dan. 7:9, 10). Though distinct beings, this confirms that Father and Son are both involved in the end-time judgment. Jesus confirms that the Father "has given all judgment to the Son" (John 5:22). God refers to cleansing His people from sin as being made "white as snow" and "like wool" (Isa. 1:18). Hence, the work of judgment introduced in Revelation 1 is about purifying His people, freeing them from the controlling power of sin. His people retain their sinful natures until they are changed in the twinkling of an eye at the second coming (see 1 Cor. 15:51, 52), yet their *characters are purified beforehand*, for during the judgment hour, God works in their lives until the divine nature keeps the carnal nature in submission continuously (see 2 Peter 1:4; Rom. 8:4). "What we make of ourselves in probationary time, that we must remain to all eternity. Death brings dissolution to the body, but makes no change in the character. The coming of Christ does not change our characters; it only fixes them forever beyond all change" (White, *5T*, p. 466).

The phrase "like a fiery flame" points primarily to the commencement of judgment, for the throne of judgment is described as a "fiery flame" (Dan. 7:9). Further, this very phrase is used of the burning bush when *Yahweh* met with Moses, declaring that the end of the 400 years of Egyptian affliction was at hand (see Exod. 3:2, 6–10). *Yahweh* was now to fulfill His covenant with Abram, providing the deliverance He had promised (see Gen. 15:13, 14). God's work of judgment is a work of *deliverance*, for in Daniel 7:22, the Ancient of Days concludes the end-time judgment *in favor* of the holy people, those who have allowed Jesus to give them victory over sin. Hence, when Revelation 1:3 says that the appointed time is near, it means that the time for freedom from the indulgence of sin is near (and just beyond that, the second coming).

Jesus' feet are described in the same manner as are the feet of the 4 living creatures, the cherubim, of Ezekiel 1:7. The faces of these living creatures are described as those of a man, lion, ox, and eagle (see v. 10), matching the phases of Nebuchadnezzar's conversion,[7] precisely matching the working out of God's covenant in his life (see Lev. 26:14–19; Dan. 4:23). The phrase "refined in a furnace" points to Jesus' purifying work in the lives of believers (see Mal. 3:2, 3; Prov. 17:3). Jesus walked with the Hebrew worthies in the fiery furnace (see Dan. 3). His purifying work may not be pleasant for us, as purified bronze requires the tremendous refining heat of the furnace, but Jesus promises to walk *with us* as He fulfills His covenant *in us*.

Jesus' voice is described as a voice of many waters. This may conjure up a peaceful image of a babbling brook, or waves rolling in and receding, but this is not the intent. The sound of Jesus' words is "like the voice of a multitude" (Dan. 10:6). The "many waters" upon which the Babylonian whore sits are explicitly identified as the multitudes following Babylon (Rev. 17:1, 15). Jesus has His own multitude, in number as the stars of heaven and the sand of the sea, their voice like many waters (see Gen. 15:5; 22:17), the 144,000, in whom is fulfilled God's everlasting covenant with Abraham (see Rev. 14:2; Gen. 17:7).

---

[7] Nebuchadnezzar became like an ox, with hairs and nails like an eagle (see Dan. 4:32, 33); he is described as a lion with eagle wings who is then given a man's converted heart (see 7:4).

Jesus holds in His right hand 7 stars, defined in verse 20 as the angels (those with a message to, and hence the leaders of) the 7 churches. It is comforting to know that Jesus has control over the church at the highest levels, especially in those times when it may appear to human sight otherwise. The sharp double-edged sword is an interesting expression. At one level, it points us to the Scriptures, which are indeed double-edged, being called the Law and the prophets (see Matt. 5:17). However, the descriptions of the Word of God as the "sword of the Spirit" (Eph. 6:17) and "sharper than any double-edged sword" (Heb. 4:12) are translations of an entirely different Greek word, better rendered a "saber."

The double-edged sword of verse 16 points most directly to the sword *Yahweh* God placed with the cherubim at the east of the Garden of Eden to protect the way of the tree of life (see Gen. 3:24). To be sure, the cherubim and sword prevented Adam and Eve from returning to the garden at will.[8] Nevertheless, they were to come and offer sacrifice there, as indicated in Genesis 4:3.[9] With this in mind, we can understand that it was never God's intention to keep humanity away from the Garden of Eden and its tree of life *permanently*; however, they must be kept away until they should learn the way of life *properly*. The Garden of Eden was a representation of the sanctuary (e.g., note its sole entrance facing the sunrise). The lesson that Revelation teaches concerning the sanctuary is how to come to God and be restored in His image, that we *can* live forever in peace and joy, not in a state of wretchedness and sin. In fact, Jesus holds out a promise of being granted access once more to the tree of life in the Eden paradise of God (see Rev. 2:7).

---

[8] "After man's fall, holy angels were immediately commissioned to guard the tree of life. Around these angels flashed beams of light having the appearance of a glittering sword. None of the family of Adam were permitted to pass the barrier to partake of the life-giving fruit; hence there is not an immortal sinner" (White, *PP*, p. 60).

[9] "The Garden of Eden remained upon the earth long after man had become an outcast from its pleasant paths. The fallen race were long permitted to gaze upon the home of innocence, their entrance barred only by the watching angels. At the cherubim-guarded gate of Paradise the divine glory was revealed. Hither came Adam and his sons to worship God. Here they renewed their vows of obedience to that law the transgression of which had banished them from Eden" (White, *PP*, p. 62).

The intensity of Jesus' appearance is like the sun shining. Elsewhere, Jesus is called the "Sun of righteousness with healing in His wings" (Mal. 4:2). This is an apt description for the High Priest, whose work during the end-time day of atonement positively *cures* all who are willing of their indulgence of sin. As noted earlier, He does not remove the sin nature (the possibility of being tempted), but He *does* give complete victory over indulgence of sin (see 1 Cor. 10:13). There is an irony here: Revelation is full of admonitions to keep the Sabbath and decries the *dies solis*, the pagan day of the sun, yet Jesus Himself shines like the sun in its brilliance. At His second coming, His glory is so awesome that He is pictured as standing in the sun (see Rev. 19:17).

John is so awed by this vision of Jesus that he "fell at His feet like a dead man." This illustrates the humility with which we should see ourselves in relation to Jesus' purity: we should realize the reality that "the wages of sin is death." Praise God, though, because "the gift of God is eternal life through Jesus Christ our Lord" (Rom. 6:23, KJV). Jesus has the power to remove death from our experience—the second, eternal death, as well as the first death for those who are translated at the second coming—but of course, this necessitates a removal of sin from the life. This was the experience of Enoch and Elijah, neither of whom tasted death, for they had been "pleasing to God." The only way to please God is via the exercise of faith (see Heb. 11:5, 6), the reward of which is the impartation of His righteous character, and with that, eternal life (see Rom. 6:16).

It is worthwhile to compare John's experience in Revelation 1:17 with that of Daniel in Daniel 10. Daniel was "unconscious upon [his] face, and [his] face was toward the ground" (verse 9), while John "fell at his feet like a dead man." Daniel was awakened by the touch of Gabriel's hand, John with the touch of Jesus' hand. Together, these passages affirm the biblical truth that the first death is, in fact, deep, unconscious sleep, while the second death is truly eternal death. This truth, while repudiated by many professing Christians, is solidly biblical.[10] In Revelation 1:17, we have a

---

[10] See, for example, John 11:11–14; Ps. 146:4; 115:17; Eccl. 9:5; Job 14:10–15.

miniature illustration of Jesus' power over death, for He "resurrects" John, as it were.

In verse 19 appears a statement that seems almost unworthy of notice, but it is profoundly important. John sees things that "are," as well as those that "must take place afterward." What things "are" now, and what marks the time that qualifies as "afterward"? Since verse 3, Revelation has focused on the coming judgment. John lived in the time preceding the judgment; for him, that was the time period of the things that "are." Events following the commencement of the judgment are those that "must take place afterward." This observation will prove helpful when we come to Revelation 4.

The last verse of this chapter is really an introduction to chapters 2 and 3. Jesus provides definitions for previously used imagery: He walks among His 7 churches and holds their messengers in His hand. Those with messages to the church are its teachers and ministers.[11] The representation of the 7 churches as 7 golden menorahs indicates that Jesus' goal has always been for His church to be full of the Holy Spirit. Recall from our study of verse 4 that the 7 Spirits before God's throne corresponded to the Holy Spirit who has been at work in all 7 periods of church history. Recognize further that each of the 7 menorahs have 7 lamps, hence a total of 49 lamps, the number of jubilee (see Lev. 25:8, 9). Hence, the representation of the church throughout history as 7 menorahs indicates that the conclusion of the seventh church period ushers in its long-awaited *deliverance* (see v. 10), the very goal of the Day of Atonement.

Why are the 7 angels and 7 menorahs referred to as a mystery? In Revelation 10:7, the mystery of God is said to be finished in the days of the seventh (last) trumpet. It will be shown that this finishing of the mystery of God is the complete restoration of His character in those individuals who, while fallen like all of us are, surrender *everything* to Him. This absolute

---

[11] "'These things saith He that holdeth the seven stars in His right hand.' Revelation 2:1. These words are spoken to the teachers in the church—those entrusted by God with weighty responsibilities. The sweet influences that are to be abundant in the church are bound up with God's ministers, who are to reveal the love of Christ" (White, *AA*, p. 586).

surrender permits the Holy Spirit to completely fill them, and so mankind will once again reflect God's image as in the beginning (see Gen. 1:26, 27). This is what the Bible calls the "mystery of godliness," the "mystery of His will," and the "mystery of the gospel" (1 Tim. 3:16; Eph. 1:9; 6:19). Of course, the book of Revelation reveals that the enemy of all righteousness has his mystery as well, the mystery of Babylon, the "mystery of lawless-ness" (see Rev. 17:5; 2 Thess. 2:7).

REVELATION 2 AND 3:
SON OF MAN'S CALL TO
CONQUER SIN IN JUDGMENT

Ephesus

2 ¹"To the angel of the church in Ephesus, write:

'Thus says He who holds fast the 7 stars in His right hand, He
who walks among the 7 golden menorahs:

²"I know your deeds, your wearing labor, your perseverance,
that you cannot tolerate evildoers, so you tested those claiming
themselves to be apostles (though they are not) and found them
liars. ³You have perseverance, have tolerated [much] on account
of My name, and did not grow weary. ⁴Nevertheless, I have this
against you: you let go your first love. ⁵Therefore, remember
whence you have fallen and repent, i.e., do the first deeds; otherwise, I am coming to you quickly and I will remove your menorah from its place—unless you repent. ⁶But this you have: you
detest the deeds of the Nicolaitans, which [deeds] I, too, detest.

⁷"He who has an ear, let him hear what the Spirit is saying to
the churches: to the one who conquers, I will grant permission
to eat from the tree of life which is in the garden [of Eden] of
My God."'

Smyrna

[8]"To the angel of the church in Smyrna, write:

'Thus says the First and the Last, who was dead, yet lived:

[9]"I know your deeds, tribulation, and poverty—though you are rich; also, the blasphemy of those who claim themselves to be Jews, yet are not—but are the synagogue of Satan. [10]Fear none of the things which you are about to suffer. Behold, now: the devil is about to throw some of you into prison, that you may be tested; you will have tribulation for 10 days. Be faithful unto death, and I will give you the crown—life.

[11]"He who has an ear, let him hear what the Spirit is saying to the churches: he who conquers will by no means be hurt[12] by the second death."'

Pergamos

[12]"To the angel of the church in Pergamos, write:

'Thus says He who has the sharp double-edged sword:

[13]"I know your deeds and where you dwell—where the throne of Satan is. You are holding fast My name, and did not deny My faith in the days in which Antipas was My witness—the faithful [witness]—who was killed among you where Satan dwells. [14]Nevertheless, I have a few things against you: you have there those holding fast the teaching of Balaam, who taught Balak to cast a stumbling block before the sons of Israel, both to eat those things which have been sacrificed to idols, and to commit fornication. [15]Further, you have also those holding fast the teaching

---

[12] In Revelation, the Greek αδικεω is often better translated "made unrighteous, corrupted" in keeping with the overall theme of character perfection.

of the Nicolaitans as well.[13] [16]Therefore, repent; otherwise, I am coming to you quickly, and I will contend with them with the sword of My mouth.

[17]"He who has an ear, let him hear what the Spirit is saying to the churches: to him who conquers, I will give of the concealed manna, and I will give him a white stone, and upon that stone a new name written, which no one knows except the recipient."'

Thyatira

[18]"To the angel of the church in Thyatira, write:

'Thus says the Son of God, who has eyes like a fiery flame and whose feet are like purified bronze:

[19]"I know your deeds—your love, faith, service, and perseverance—and your latest deeds exceed the first. [20]Nevertheless, I have something against you: you tolerate that wife of yours, Jezebel, who proclaims herself a prophetess, even as she is teaching and misleading My servants to commit fornication and eat things sacrificed to idols. [21]I granted her time so she might repent, but she does not want to repent of her fornication. [22]Behold, I am about to cast her upon a bed, and those committing adultery with her into great tribulation—unless they repent of her deeds. [23]I will kill her children with death[14]; then all the churches will know that I AM is the one who scrutinizes minds and hearts. I will give each of you according to your deeds. [24]But I say unto you—those who remain in Thyatira, all who do not

---

[13] BYZ and NTG read ομοιως ("as well"), while TR has ο μισω ("which I hate"). These are nearly identical in pronunciation—"oh-me-os" versus "oh-me-so." No doubt one of these readings involves a transposition of letters. TR may in fact be correct.

[14] To "kill with death" is often synonymous with "deadly pestilence/disease" (see Ezek. 5:12, 17), in which the LXX uses "death" to translate the Hebrew *dever* = "pestilence." In this context, though, "death" refers to the final, second death.

hold to this teaching, who have not known 'the depths of Satan,' as they say—I will not cast upon you another burden; 25however, that which you *do* have, hold fast until I come.

26"The one who conquers, keeping My deeds unto the end, I will grant him authority over the nations 27('He will shepherd them with an iron rod—like ceramic vessels, they will be shattered'15) as I, too, have received [authority] from My Father. 28I will also give him the early morning star. 29He who has an ear, let him hear what the Spirit is saying to the churches.'"

Sardis

3 1"To the angel of the church in Sardis, write:

'Thus says He who holds the 7 spirits of God and the 7 stars:

"I know your deeds, that you have a name as though you live, though you are dead. 2Become watchful, and establish the remaining deeds which you are about to cast aside,16 for I have not found your deeds to be complete before my God. 3Therefore, remember how you have received and heard—keep [your garments],17 and repent! For should you not watch, I will come upon you as a thief—and there is no way you will know what hour I will come upon you. 4But you have a few names in Sardis which have not defiled their garments; these will walk with Me in white garments, for they are worthy.

5"The one who conquers, he will be clothed in white garments; there is no possibility I will wipe away his name from the scroll of

---

15 See Psalm 2:9; referenced also in Revelation 12:5 and 19:15.

16 TR and NTG read, "the remaining deeds which are about to die."

17 Note "garments" in verse 4. Also, compare Revelation 16:15, which mentions "thief," "watches," "guards," and "garments."

life; rather, I will declare his name before My Father and before His angels. [6]He who has an ear, let him hear what the Spirit is saying to the churches."'

Philadelphia

[7]"To the angel of the church in Philadelphia, write:

'Thus says the Holy One, He who is true, "who holds the key of David, who opens, and no one will shut it except He who opens, nor will anyone open [it except He who shuts]":[18]

[8]"I know your deeds (behold, I have placed before you an open door which no one is able to lock), that you have little power, yet you kept My word and did not deny My name. [9]Behold, I decree that those of the synagogue of Satan—those who claim themselves to be Jews, yet are not, but are lying—behold, I will cause them to come and prostrate themselves at your feet, and they will recognize that I have loved you. [10]Because you kept My word about perseverance, I also will keep you from the hour of testing which is about to come upon the entire world, to test those dwelling upon the earth. [11]I am coming quickly. Hold fast what you have, that no one take your crown.

[12]"The one who conquers I will make a pillar in the temple of My God; there is no possibility he will leave anymore. I will write upon him the name of My God; the name of the city of My God—New Jerusalem—which comes down out of heaven from My God; and My new name. [13]He who has an ear, let him hear what the Spirit is saying to the churches."'

---

[18] See Isaiah 22:22.

Laodicea

[14]"And to the angel of the church in Laodicea, write:

'Thus says the Amen, the faithful and true Witness, the Initiator[19] of God's creation:

[15]"I know your deeds, that you are neither cold nor hot—how I wish you *were* cold or hot! [16]Therefore, since you are lukewarm, and neither hot nor cold, I am about to vomit you out of My mouth. [17]Because you say, 'I am rich, I have amassed wealth, and I have need of nothing,' yet you do not know that *you* are the one wretched, the one pitiful, poor, blind, and naked, [18]I counsel you to buy gold from Me refined by fire, that you may be rich; white garments, that you may be clothed and the shame of your nakedness not be exposed; and eye salve, that it may anoint your eyes so you may see. [19]As many as I love, I convict and discipline; therefore, be zealous, and repent! [20]Behold: I am **standing** at the door, and knocking; if anyone hears My voice and opens the door, then I will come in to him, dine with him, and he with Me.

[21]"He who conquers, I will grant to sit with Me upon My throne, as I, too, conquered, and sat with My Father upon His throne. [22]He who has an ear, let him hear what the Spirit is saying to the churches.""'"

COMMENTARY

The letters to the churches each begin with the phrase ταδε λεγει ("thus says"), followed by a description of Jesus taken from Revelation 1.

---

[19] The Greek word αρχη, in its most elementary sense, signifies primacy, whether in time or position. As the "Initiator" or "Source" of God's creation (see John 1:1–3), Jesus is also its Ruler.

Of the 348 times this phrase appears in the Septuagint, 324 of them read ταδε λεγει κυριος ("Thus saith the LORD," KJV). Once again, Revelation teaches that Jesus is "the LORD" (better, *Yahweh*), the covenant-making and covenant-keeping God. This observation refutes the belief of groups such as Jehovah's Witnesses, who hold that Jesus is created by God, and not fully God.

Ephesus

The letter opens with Jesus walking *among* the churches, holding *fast* the teachers and ministers, indicating His supreme regard for His church. It has always been Jesus' intention to walk among us, and for us to dwell with Him: "I will walk among you. I will be your God, and you will be My people" (Lev. 16:12); "Abide in Me, and I in you" (John 15:4). Jesus walks among His people in order to deliver them from their enemies (the greatest of whom is Satan; see 1 Peter 5:8), hence He is calling them to put any uncleanness (sin) outside the camp (the church body) and be holy. If sin is retained, He will turn away from walking among His professed people (see Deut. 23:14).

In verse 2, the words "you" and "your" are singular, indicating Jesus is addressing the angel of the church (i.e., its leader).[20] He begins by commending this leader's deeds. Salvation is by grace, not any works we perform, yet we are judged by our works (see Eccles. 12:13, 14). Our works are the evidence of the genuineness of our profession, proof that the Holy Spirit dwells within us. No one will enter heaven *because* of good works, yet it is equally certain that no one will enter heaven *without* them.

The angel is commended for thoroughly examining all who seek membership in the church. While some claimed to be sent with a message from on high as apostles, examination proved them to be liars. Liars are

---

[20] Of course, the angel is expected to share the message with all the members. The principle of a leader standing for all the people is established in Daniel 2:38–39 and 7:17 and 23, in which "king" and "kingdom" are used interchangeably.

explicitly barred from heaven (see Rev. 21:8; 22:15), and conversely, the 144,000 have no lie in their mouth (see 14:5). The angel is likewise commended for his perseverance, a characteristic of God's faithful people in the very last days (see v. 12).

In spite of this, something is lacking: namely the initial *love* that drove the angel and his church. Note what Scripture says in its first mention of "love": "Take now your son, your *only* [son], whom you love—Isaac. Go to the land of Moriah and offer him there as a burnt offering" (Gen. 22:2). True love for God is unreserved in the extent to which it is willing to make a sacrifice.

The charge is given to repent, which will be manifest in reformation, a return to one's first deeds—not merely a prayer for forgiveness. Jesus' call for the church leadership to reform is serious: if reformation is not forthcoming, the menorah—the church—will be removed from the angel's oversight.

While the Ephesian angel's zeal could stand to be warmed by the Holy Spirit, the angel is commended for detesting the bad deeds of the Nicolaitans. Comparison with verses 14 and 15 suggests that the Nicolaitans hold to the teaching of Balaam, meaning they condone sexual misconduct and eating that which has been offered to idols. Idolatry is routinely characterized as fornication (see Ezek. 23:30; Rev 14:8, 9), and eating that which is offered to idols would be to condone the idolatry itself.[21]

Just as each letter opens with a description of Jesus matching His description as High Priest and Judge from Revelation 1, so each letter closes with a message from the Holy Spirit—a message to conquer sin. Coupled with each admonition to conquer sin is a promise of what the conqueror will inherit. Thus, the 7 letters to the churches are an expression of the will and testament associated with God's everlasting covenant

---

[21] "A portion having been offered to idols, the food from the king's table was consecrated to idolatry; and one partaking of it would be regarded as offering homage to the gods of Babylon. In such homage, loyalty to Jehovah forbade Daniel and his companions to join. Even a mere pretense of eating the food or drinking the wine would be a denial of their faith. To do this would be to array themselves with heathenism and to dishonor the principles of the law of God" (White, *PK*, p. 481).

(see Heb. 9:15–17). This will was contingent upon Jesus' death, provided for an inheritance for the heirs, notably the promised land (see Gen. 15:18; 17:8). The letter to Ephesus points to the true, heavenly promised land with its mention of the tree of life in the restored Garden of Eden.

As mentioned in the remarks on Revelation 1:16, the Garden of Eden was a model of the heavenly sanctuary. By sin, Adam and Eve forfeited the Garden of Eden, their earthly sanctuary. It was in that garden that marriage was first instituted (see Gen. 2:24; Mal. 2:14–16). It is God's mission, in working out His everlasting covenant in His people, to restore them to that garden, and hence, a sound marriage with Him. That accomplished, His people will once again eat from the tree of life and experience eternal life.

The historical period associated with the church of Ephesus is from Jesus' death until the close of John's ministry toward the end of the first century.

Smyrna

The second letter is addressed to the angel (and by extension, the members) of Smyrna, an area whose name is the same Greek word translated "myrrh," the perfume used to anoint Jesus' body at his death (see John 19:39). Appropriately enough, the letter opens with a message from Him "who was dead, yet lived." Victory over death is a major theme in Revelation, culminating in the resurrection of the righteous (see Rev. 20:6). Of course, since it is sin that brings death (see Rom. 6:23), victory over death necessitates a victory over sin in the life of the believer. Indeed, this is the very aim of Jesus' work during the end-time day of atonement, the fulfillment of His everlasting covenant. How fitting, then, that the letter closes with a promise that the second death will not touch him who conquers in the battle with sin!

The church has continued to persevere, but Satan has ensured that progress is not easy, supplying tribulation, poverty, and no lack of false professors to dishearten believers. Jesus does not measure wealth by earthly standards, so he assures Smyrna that while their earthly means may be scant, their character shows them to be rich in godliness. If they stay faithful, they will win the greatest of crowns—eternal life.

Jesus does not remove the prospect of suffering from the lives of those in Smyrna, for all who live godly will suffer persecution, and His followers are not to be removed from trials, but rather preserved through them (see 2 Tim. 3:12; John 17:15). Jesus assures the church that their trial will be short, only 10 days. This hearkens back to Daniel 1, in which God appointed a 10-day trial for Daniel and his 3 companions. In both cases, Satan sought to vanquish the faithful, but God *permits* persecution so that the character of His faithful ones may be proven—investigated, as it were. The book of Revelation is symbolic, so 10 days refers to a 10-year period, using the prophetic year-day principle (see Num. 14:34; Ezek. 4:6). This also allows us to identify the historical event marking the close of this period: the conclusion of the bloody, 10-year persecution begun on February 24, AD 303 under Emperor Diocletian and Augustus (co-emperor) Maximian, ending with the Edict of Milan issued by Emperors Constantine and Licinius in February, AD 313.[22]

The allusion to Daniel 1 suggests that the church emerged from this trial unsullied by compromise with sin. Recall from Daniel 1 that the 10-day trial was sufficient for an investigative judgment to determine that Daniel and his friends manifested obedience to God's 10 Commandments, and so it is here. The church proved faithful unto death, its members choosing rather to suffer for the sake of Jesus and His truth than compromise principle. Indeed, Jesus says, "whoever seeks to save his life will forfeit it, but whoever forfeits it will preserve it" (Luke 17:33). To this end, the church of Smyrna typifies the end-time church, whose members are to experience the fullness of God's everlasting covenant, willingly yielding their own lives rather than bringing reproach upon God and His cause by indulging in sin (see Rev. 12:11). Note that Jesus does not reprimand Smyrna for any sin.

The letter concludes by reinforcing this assurance of victory over death: the conqueror "will by no means be hurt by the second death."

---

[22] "Edict of Milan," Wikipedia, https://1ref.us/13k (accessed February 18, 2020).

The Greek uses its most emphatic form to express this promise. As the conqueror *par excellence*, Jesus was not hurt by the second death. He experienced the soul anguish of separation from His Father as the sins of the world began to roll upon Him in the Garden of Gethsemane, but He could not be overcome by the second death; He conquered it. Conversely, Satan, his angels, and all who cling to sin will die and *not* overcome the second death in the lake of fire (see Rev. 20:10, 15; 21:8).

The letter to Smyrna opens by introducing the resurrected Jesus. He goes on to promise the conquerors that, should they die, they will be resurrected as well, for they have partaken of His divine nature which cannot sink and die—they have become one flesh with Him. With the strong emphasis on death and resurrection in this letter, it is illuminating to note that the popular conception among Christians that each person has an immortal soul that, at death, goes immediately to heaven or hell began to creep into the church during the historical period that this letter covers.

Ancient pagan religions all had some notion of life after death. For our purposes, it is critical to note that the Greek philosopher Socrates (470–399 BC) went to Egypt to learn its ideas on the immortal soul. This in turn was passed on to his illustrious pupil Plato (428–348 BC). In his *Phaedo*, Plato plainly asserts that "Death is merely the separation of soul and body." From here, the thought moved into Hellenistic Judaism through Philo (circa 20 BC–AD 47). Perhaps the most influential thinker in developing the notion of an immortal soul for each person was Greek philosopher Plato. In the historical period covered by the Ephesus church (from Jesus' death until the close of John's life), the biblical teaching that God *only* is immortal and humanity is asleep, knowing nothing in death, was held steadfast by Christians.[23] However, through the persistence of Satan, Christian writers eventually adopted this view as well. The earliest ones of influence were Tertullian (AD 155–240) and the notoriously allegorical Origen (AD 185–254).[24] It is just such deceivers that compose "the synagogue of Satan."

---

[23] See 1 Tim. 1:17; 6:16; John 11:11–14; Eccl. 9:5; Ps. 146:4; 115:17; Job 14:12–15.

[24] The synopsis presented here follows Bacchiocchi, *Popular Beliefs Are They Biblical?* pp. 46–54. For an extensive historical survey, see Froom, *The Conditionalist Faith of Our Fathers*, vol. 1, pp. 703–802.

This letter covers church history from the close of John's life (history confirms that he ministered in Ephesus after returning from Patmos), up through the close of the 10-year persecution with the Edict of Milan issued by Emperors Constantine and Licinius in March, AD 313.

Pergamos

The letter to Pergamos opens with a description of Jesus as having the "sharp double-edged sword," i.e., the Scriptures, which point to the sanctuary and its outline of salvation. As the letter to Pergamos makes clear, there is a hardness of heart on the part of some, yet Jesus seeks by the cutting truths of His Word to circumcise their hearts.[25]

Jesus notes that their lot is difficult, remarking that they dwell where Satan himself is enthroned. It will be remembered that the 7 churches were located in the Roman province of Asia, hence the throne or seat of government is Rome. Just as Jesus has His throne in the heavenly city, Jerusalem, so Satan has set his throne in the worldly city, Rome. In the historical periods of Ephesus and Smyrna, the Roman empire's seat was Rome itself; during the time of Constantine, the seat of the empire was moved to Constantinople, and the Western Roman Empire saw its demise. Both were necessary for setting up the papacy to rule for its 1,260 years in the time of Thyatira.

In spite of this hard lot, Pergamos has those who hold fast to Jesus' name, being faithful unto death. This solidity of character stems from more than a mental assent *to* or a mere belief *in* or *about* Jesus; they possess "My faith," i.e., Jesus' faith. He was faithful unto death when all hope was (apparently) lost. Likewise, He gives such faith to those who need it.

Reference is made to the witness of Antipas, who was faithful unto death. Antipas is apparently a contraction of the Greek *anti* ("in the place

---

[25] Zechariah 7:12 refers to the heart of Israel as flint or adamant, a rock noted for 1) hardness, hence its appropriateness to describe Israel's heart hardened against the Torah and prophets, and 2) sharpness, hence its use in covenant circumcision.

of," "against") and an abbreviated form of *patros*, "father" (GELNT, entry on *Antipas*). This takes on greater significance when it is recognized that the word "pope" is Middle English, from Old English *pāpa*, Late Latin *papa*, Greek *pappas, papas*, a title of bishops, literally, "papa."[26] Hence, Antipas signifies "against/in the place of the Roman bishop" just as antichrist (see 1 John 2:18, 22; 4:3; 2 John 7) means "against/in the place of Christ." Thus, the conflict between the Roman bishop and the martyr Antipas typifies the later conflict between papal Rome and the tens of millions who were martyred at her hands during the Dark Ages.

As the professing Christian church and the pagan Roman government united, compromise with paganism crept in, leading to that syncretistic blend of nominal Christianity and paganism, the Roman papacy. In commending Antipas, Jesus commends all who stand against compromise with paganism.

Jesus goes on to make His case against Pergamos. Some in Pergamos advocated eating what has been sacrificed to idols, as well as fornication— the very tools Balaam used to ensnare God's people. Hired by Balak to curse God's people, Balaam could not utter a curse, so he resorted to stratagem: he sought to corrupt the Israelites by *association with pagan idolaters*. God's people joined the pagans in their heathen rites and consorted with their women, bringing God's wrath upon themselves (see Num. 22–25; 31:16).

While there is no reason to doubt the historicity of this event in the church at Pergamos in John's day, the thrust here is its spiritual application to the period following AD 313. When Jesus directs us to eat His flesh and drink His blood (see John 6:53), He refers to internalizing Scriptural truth, partaking of His atoning sacrifice and ministry on our behalf. In like manner, eating what is sacrificed to idols refers to the church's adoption of *pagan customs* in a vain effort to win over pagans in the empire, sanctifying or baptizing such practices, as it were. Fornication is another representation of the infidelity of God's people in adopting idolatrous customs.

---

[26] "Pope," *Merriam-Webster's Dictionary*, https://1ref.us/137 (accessed, June 17, 2019).

As noted in the comments for Ephesus, the Nicolaitans are yet another representation of infidelity to God. He is a jealous God, satisfied with nothing less than complete allegiance (see Exod. 20:4–6).

The chief agent of compromise in the history covered by the church of Pergamos is Emperor Constantine. He made a profession of Christianity, though apparently for the temporal interest of gaining the support of Christians in his realm. In order to avoid alienating the pagans in the empire, he enacted the first national Sunday law on March 7, AD 321. Such a law appealed to pagans who already kept the "venerable day of the sun." While Rome might have seemed to offer the advantages of imperial and military support, the loss of the purity of the church was incalculable, for pagans were permitted to continue their heathen worship practices and live unholy lives.

Hence, Jesus calls for true repentance—reformation—lest He contend with the nominal Christians with the sword of His mouth—His Word—which points people to true salvation accomplished in His sanctuary. The Spirit calls the church to conquer sin, holding out precious promises, each dealing with the heart problem.

First, He promises the concealed manna, referring to the manna God fed His people for 40 years in the wilderness. In Exodus 5:1, Moses informs Pharaoh that he is to let the Hebrews go, that they may worship *Yahweh*; in verse 5, Pharaoh objects, noting that Moses and Aaron are leading the people out to make them cease [literally, "keep Sabbath"] from their work. After leading His people out of Egypt, *Yahweh* gave them a test of fidelity to His law *before* uttering the 10 Commandments at Sinai: they were to observe the Sabbath day as Moses and Aaron had been teaching them prior to their departure.[27] They were to gather the heavenly manna each day, gathering a double portion on the sixth day so that they might not gather any on the Sabbath (see Exod. 16:4, 5, 23).

---

[27] "In their bondage the Israelites had to some extent lost the knowledge of God's law, and they had departed from its precepts. The Sabbath had been generally disregarded, and the exactions of their taskmasters made its observance apparently impossible. But Moses had shown his people that obedience to God was the first condition of deliverance; and the efforts made to restore the observance of the Sabbath had come to the notice of their oppressors" (White, *PP*, p. 258).

As a perpetual reminder of God's provision for His people in their wilderness sojourn, as well as the sacredness of the Sabbath day (the heart of the 10 Commandments), He directed that an omer (a tenth of an ephah) be placed in a pot before *Yahweh* (see Exod. 16:32–36). When the sanctuary and its furnishings were later built, the manna was placed in the ark, along with the 10 Commandments (see Heb. 9:4).

The 10 Commandments are the words of God's covenant (see Exod. 34:28; Deut. 4:13; 1 Kings 8:9, 21), of which the Sabbath is the especial token (see Exod. 31:16–18), so the concealed manna points to God's everlasting covenant. In Daniel 7 (as well as the trumpets of Revelation 8–11) is revealed a special, historical fulfillment regarding the concealed manna during the Pergamos period of church history (see *THE STAND*, remarks on Daniel 7). Faithful believers held to the true Sabbath, notably the North African Vandals, Italian Ostrogoths, and Heruli. It was prophesied that the horn from insignificance would uproot 3 horns (see Dan. 7:8, 20, 24) on its quest for dominance: the North African Vandals, Italian Heruli, and Ostrogoths. The Roman Catholic Church disparaged these groups as Arian, while the real reason for their persecution was more likely that they held to the Sabbath while Rome was pushing for Sunday observance (see de Kock, *Christ and Antichrist in Prophecy and History*, pp. 287–308, particularly pp. 289, 290). In stamping out these faithful people groups, the papacy sought to conceal true Sabbath observance—the concealed manna.

The Sabbath is God's appointed antidote for idolatry. Of the 10 Commandments, the second (image worship forbidden) and fourth (Sabbath observance enjoined) are the longest and similar in their references to creation (mankind not to make likenesses of things in heaven or earth, for *Yahweh* made the heavens, earth, sea, and all that is in them). The link is especially clear in Leviticus 26, the chapter on covenant blessings and curses. In verse 1, idolatry is forbidden, and in verse 2, the Sabbath is to be kept, and the sanctuary reverenced. Hence, the concealed manna is the cure for Balaamite and Nicolaitan idolatry.

Second, the white stone is promised. Speculation abounds as to the significance of this stone, many supposing it represents a voting pebble, for voting was sometimes done by means of white and black pebbles, black representing negative votes; white, positive. However, the Bible explains the matter plainly. A simple search for the word translated "stone" in verse 17 shows that its first appearance refers to the sharp stone Zipporah used to circumcise her son by Moses (see Exod. 4:25). Circumcision is the sign of the everlasting covenant (see Gen. 17:13), the physical practice thereof pointing to true *heart* circumcision (see Lev. 26:41; Deut. 10:16; 30:6; Jer. 4:4; Rom. 2:29). This makes evident why the stone here in verse 17 is white, for God's covenant creates in those who submit to heart circumcision a *pure* heart, free from *all* idolatry (see Ezek. 36:25–27; Ps. 51:10).

Third, a new name is written in that stone. New names stand for changes in one's life experience (e.g., Abram to Abraham; Sarai to Sarah; see Gen. 17:5, 15) or character (e.g., Jacob to Israel; see 32:28). In the case of Abraham, the name change is explicitly linked with the establishment of the everlasting covenant (see 17:1–9). How appropriate, then, is the sharp, double-edged sword at the opening of the letter: the white stone points to the sharp instrument for circumcision, and the new name requires a sharp instrument to engrave it. All three promises to Pergamos serve as pledges on God's part to enter His everlasting covenant—marriage with His people.

Pergamos covers church history from the time of Constantine up to the fortification of the papacy in AD 538, which, as a crowning event, inaugurates the history of Thyatira.

Thyatira

The letter to the angel of the church in Thyatira is the longest. Pergamos has been increasingly compromised by numerous pagan errors, and by AD 538, the papal leadership of Satan's *counterfeit* church (which embraces and teaches all such pagan errors) is firmly established as high priest (see *THE STAND*, remarks on Daniel 7 and 8, for historical details and the date AD 538). Jesus pointedly seeks to protect His precious, true church from further compromise and consequent ruin.

Before examining this letter, which deals with God's true church during the historical period in which the papacy reigns supreme, it is critical to understand that the papacy purports to have at its head a man who is both God and His vicegerent or vicar:

> We define that the Holy Apostolic See and the Roman Pontiff holds the primacy over the whole world, and that the Roman Pontiff himself is the successor of the blessed Peter, prince of the apostles, and the true vicar of Christ, the head of the whole church, the father and doctor of all Christians; and that to him, in the person of blessed Peter, was given, by our Lord Jesus Christ, full power to feed, rule, and govern the universal church, as is contained also in the acts of the ecumenical councils, and in the sacred canons. (Decree of the Council of Trent; recorded in Labbe and Cossart, *The Most Holy Councils*, vol. 13, col. 1167).

> The Pope is of so great dignity and so exalted that he is not a mere man, but as it were God, and the vicar of God. (Ferraris, *Prompta Bibliotheca*, vol. 6, article "Papa," p. 17)

> The Pope is as it were God on earth, sole sovereign of the faithful of Christ, chief king of kings, having plenitude of power, to whom has been entrusted by the omnipotent God direction not only of the earthly but also of the heavenly kingdom. (Ferraris, *Prompta Bibliotheca*, vol. 6, article "Papa," p. 18)

> The Pope can modify divine law, since his power is not of man but of God, and he acts as vicegerent of God upon earth with most ample power of binding and loosing his sheep. (Ferraris, *Prompta Bibliotheca*, vol. 6, article "Papa," p. 19)

> We hold upon this earth the place of God Almighty. (Pope Leo XIII, *The Great Encyclical Letters of Pope Leo XIII*, "The Reunion of Christendom," p. 304)

> For thou art the shepherd, thou art the physician, thou art the director, thou art the husbandman; finally, thou art another God on earth. (Oration of Christopher Marcellus before the pope in the fourth session of the Fifth Lateran Council (1512); recorded in Labbe and Cossart, *History of the Councils*, vol. 14, col. 109).

> Peter and his successors have power to impose laws both preceptive and prohibitive, power likewise to grant dispensation from these laws, and, when needful, to annul them. It is theirs to judge offenses against the laws, to impose and to remit penalties. This judicial authority will even include the power to pardon sin. (*The Catholic Encyclopedia*, Vol. XII, art. "Pope," p. 265)

Returning to the letter, Jesus' eyes are described as a "fiery flame," hearkening back to the throne of judgment upon which the Ancient of Days sat (see Dan. 7:9). Hence, Jesus is presented as both *divine* and the Son of *man*. This establishes that He is fully God and man, contradicting the papal fallacy that the *pope* is God on earth as a man. God's only "vicar" on earth is Jesus. Following His ascension to heaven, the Holy Spirit is His means of continuing in this role (see John 14:16, 26; 15:26; 16:7).

As noted in the remarks on Revelation 1:15, His feet like purified bronze point to the fact that Jesus walks with us during times of great trial (the furnace of affliction), just as He did with the Hebrew worthies in the fiery furnace of Daniel 3. This is a key promise for the period of this letter, for the papacy, during the Dark Ages, was responsible for the deaths of countless millions.

The letter continues with what seems like a flattering compliment: the angel (i.e., teachers and ministers of the true church) is full of good deeds, with the latest ones exceeding the first. This would appear to answer Jesus' admonition to Ephesus in Revelation 2:5: "repent, i.e., do the first deeds." However, in spite of any "love, faith, service, and perseverance," what follows is a scathing indictment of the angel's lack of watchfulness, for he has permitted a counterfeit to infect the ranks, a woman referred to as Jezebel.

God's characterizes His people, His church, as a woman (see Jer. 6:2; 33:16). It is imperative that one recognize that Jesus is *not* calling the church in Thyatira Jezebel, which would be to say that she is irretrievably fallen. Rather, He asserts that *another* woman, termed Jezebel, has been permitted to come in and influence the church of Thyatira.

The Greek word translated "wife" is often rendered "woman," the context indicating which idea is to be understood. The reference to Jezebel, the wife of King Ahab, suggests the reading "wife."[28] Ahab's wife was the daughter of Ethbaal, king of the Sidonians (see 1 Kings 16:31). History informs us that Ethbaal, as his name suggests, was the high priest of Baal. His daughter Jezebel followed in his footsteps, influencing her husband Ahab to make idolatry ubiquitous in Israel:

> Eth-baal—Identified with the Ithobalus of Menander, who reigned in Tyre, probably over all Phoenicia, within 50 years of the death of Hiram. This Ithobalus, whose name means "With him is Baal," was originally priest of the great temple of Astarte, in Tyre. (Barnes, *Notes on the Old Testament*, comments on 1 Kings 16:31)

> Taking to wife Jezebel, "the daughter of Ethbaal king of the Zidonians" and high priest of Baal, Ahab "served Baal, and worshiped him. And he reared up an altar for Baal in the house of Baal, which he had built in Samaria." (White, *PK*, p. 114)

In John's day, the angel of the church in Thyatira was married, and like Ahab of old, he permitted his wife to teach the church members to fornicate and eat things sacrificed to idols. These are the very crimes noted in Jesus' rebuke to the angel of Pergamos and suggested by Balaam to heathen king Balak to seduce Israel into idolatry, thereby forfeiting God's protection and blessing (see Rev. 2:14). In the historical period

---

[28] BYZ reads, "woman/wife of yours"; TR and NTG read, "woman/wife." The pronoun "yours" suggests "wife" is the correct understanding.

corresponding to this letter (the Dark Ages commencing in AD 538), the leaders of the true church permitted a degree of interaction with representatives of the papal (Jezebel) system:

> She had her name from לבֹז, "Zebel", "dung", to which Elijah has reference in 2Ki 9:37; the Ethiopic version calls her "Elzabel". By her is meant the apostate church of Rome, comparable to Jezebel, the wife of Ahab; as she was the daughter of an Heathen, so is Rome Papal the daughter of Rome Pagan; and as she was the wife of Ahab, and therefore a queen, so the whore of Babylon calls herself; and as Jezebel was famous for her paintings, so the church of Rome for her pretensions to religion and holiness, and for the gaudiness of her worship; and as she was remarkable for her idolatry, whoredoms, witchcrafts, and cruel persecution of the prophets of the Lord, and for murder, and innocent blood she shed; so the church of Rome, for her idolatrous worship of images, for her whoredoms, both in a literal and spiritual sense, and for the witchcrafts, magic, and devilish arts many of her popes have been addicted to, and especially for her barbarities and cruelties exercised upon the true professors of Christ, and for the blood of the martyrs, with which she has been drunk; and as Jezebel stirred up Ahab against good and faithful men, so has this church stirred up the secular powers, emperors, kings, and princes, against the true followers of Christ: and the end of both of them is much alike; as scarce anything was left of Jezebel, so Babylon the great, the mother of harlots, shall be cast into the sea, and be found no more at all: compare 2Ki 9:7 with Rev 17:1. (Gill, *Exposition of the Old Testament*, comments on Rev. 2:20)

Of those who resisted the encroachments of the papal power, the Waldenses stood foremost. In the very land where popery had fixed its seat, there its falsehood and corruption were most steadfastly resisted. For centuries the churches of Piedmont maintained their independence; but the time came at last when Rome insisted upon their submission. After ineffectual struggles against her tyranny, the leaders of these churches reluctantly acknowledged the supremacy of the power to which the whole world seemed to pay homage. There were some, however, who refused to yield to the authority of pope or prelate. They were determined to maintain their allegiance to God and to preserve the purity and simplicity of their faith. A separation took place. Those who adhered to the ancient faith now withdrew; some, forsaking their native Alps, raised the banner of truth in foreign lands; others retreated to the secluded glens and rocky fastnesses of the mountains, and there preserved their freedom to worship God. (White, *GC*, p. 64)

It is very evident from history, as well as from this verse in Revelation, that the church of Christ did suffer some of the Papal monks to preach and teach among them. See the history of the Waldenses [reference to Wylie's work]. (Miller, *Miller's Works*, Vol. 2, p. 142)

In 1489, Prince Charles II promised the Vaudois (the Waldensians) that they would not be persecuted in the future. While he was able to prevent further persecution by crusaders, he was not able to prevent a stealthier assault: that of papal missionaries and inquisitors who jailed the Waldensian "heretics." Centuries of persecution were taking their toll on the Waldenses, who began to decline in their fortitude. The desire for peace led to outward compromise with the Church of Rome. They accepted certificates from the Romish priests that declared them to be papists. To procure these certificates, it was required of them "to attend the Romish chapel, to confess, to go to mass, to have their children baptized by the priests." These dishonest compromises troubled their consciences, so as they entered a Roman church, they said, "Cave of robbers, may God confound thee!" (Wylie, *Protestantism in the Waldensian Valleys*, ch. 4, par. 1).

Coincident with the Waldensians' decline in piety and willingness to compromise in order to avoid temporal persecution, the Reformation was gaining ground in Western Europe. Getting wind of this, the Vaudois, in 1530, dispatched George Morel and Pierre Masson to visit the Reformers in Switzerland and Germany to see if they were proclaiming the same truths that the Waldensians had held for centuries prior. In October of 1530, they met with Oecolampadius of Basel, who welcomed them as brethren and confirmed that their doctrines were in common, though he did rebuke them:

> We are informed that the fear of persecution has caused you to dissemble and to conceal your faith ... There is no concord between Christ and Belial. You commune with unbelievers; you take part in their abominable masses, in which the death and passion of Christ are blasphemed. ... I know your weakness, but it becomes those who have been redeemed by the blood of Christ to be more courageous. It is better for us to die than to be overcome by temptation. (Wylie, *Protestantism in the Waldensian Valleys*, par. 6)

To their everlasting credit, the Waldenses humbly took such rebuke to heart. They convened a synod on October 12, 1532 to discuss whether or not to accept the reforms advocated by their Protestant brethren. All the Waldensian churches sent representatives, as did the Albigenses to the north of the Alps and the Vaudois churches of Calabria. Further, William Farel and Anthony Saunier, from French Switzerland, attended. Following 6 days of deliberation, they produced a "Short Confession of Faith," which essentially confirmed their more ancient version in 1120. The greatest result of this synod was that the Waldenses no longer sought peace by compromise with Rome; they stopped attending mass and no longer recognized Romish priests as ministers of Christ. Further, they began rebuilding their own churches, for their own public worship had all but ceased in the Waldensian valleys. They also produced a translation by Robert Olivetan of the entire Scriptures into French, printed by Pierre de Wingle (also known as Picard) in 1535 (see Wylie, *Protestantism in the Waldensian Valleys*, paras. 7–17).

Hence, the letter to the church in Thyatira covers the period from the installation of papal supremacy (AD 538) until the Waldenses were reinvigorated in the 1530s—roughly 1,000 years.

In verse 21, Jesus, in His mercy, gave the apostate papal church a chance to repent. Of course, being the Adversary's counterfeit of all things true, she does not wish to repent of her idolatry. With fitting irony, Jesus promises to "cast her onto a bed," indicating that from that point on, He will leave her to her wicked ways ("cast" in Revelation often refers to a close of probation; see Rev. 8:5; 12:9; 14:16; 18:21). Like Pharaoh of old, she is so hardened in sin as to be beyond redemption (see Exod. 4:21–14:8). In His end-time call to leave Babylon, Jesus confirms the papacy's completely fallen condition (see Rev. 18:1–5).

In His great prophetic discourse, Jesus spoke of the papacy's reign as a time of great tribulation for the true church (see Matt. 24:21). In the message to the angel of Thyatira, He warns that the false church, Jezebel, and all who fornicate with her, will come out on the losing end of the [ultimate] great tribulation, culminating in the seventh plague just before the second coming (see Rev. 7:14; 16:17–21; 19:17–21).

Jesus speaks of Jezebel's children. Offspring is of the same kind as is the parent (see Gen. 1:11, 24), so as a corrupt church, Jezebel gives birth to more corrupt churches. For much of the history of the Dark Ages, there existed but two churches: Jezebel (Roman Catholicism) and the church in Thyatira (the persecuted church of the wilderness, exemplified by the Waldenses, Albigenses, and Lollards). With the Protestant Reformation of the 1500s, new churches arose. While they began nobly, they did not continue to grow in a knowledge of truth beyond that of their founders. As a result, they eventually fell prey to papal error and are designated as her children. This same identification is made in Revelation

17:5: papal Babylon is a harlot (Jezebel) with harlot daughters (i.e., fallen Protestant churches).

The time is coming when all who hold to the false churches will face the second death spoken of in verse 23; then it will be known that nothing is hidden from Jesus' searching eyes. The ultimate fulfillment of casting Jezebel upon a bed, as well as those who commit adultery with her into great tribulation, and killing her children with death occurs in the lake of fire. The false papal and Protestant churches are cast there at the second coming (see Rev. 19:20), and the individual sinners comprising those churches are cast in the lake of fire (the second death) after the 1,000 years (see 20:13–15; 21:8).

Jesus encourages the faithful remnant, those who have thus far resisted idolatry, to hold fast the truths they have. He who keeps His deeds unto the end will be granted the privilege of ruling the nations with Him.

Jesus also promises the early morning star. In the midst of the spiritual blackness pervading the centuries of papal oppression, Jesus raised up John Wycliffe, herald of the Protestant Reformation.[29] While it is true that Protestant churches have imbibed papal error, the work of Wycliffe and his successors began to open up the Word of God to people's understanding, and ultimately, this will result in a purified remnant church on this earth.

While the morning star does refer to John Wycliffe in a limited sense, ultimately it refers to Jesus, as He himself states (see Rev. 22:16). The morning star is associated with the initial glimmers of morning, which grow brighter as midday approaches (see Prov. 4:18). Jesus' light will shine fully in those who are faithful.

The letter concludes with promises to the conqueror, followed by the admonition to hear what the Spirit is saying to the churches, exactly the reverse found in the first three letters. Those initial letters acknowledged

---

[29] "In the fourteenth century arose in England the 'morning star of the Reformation.' John Wycliffe was the herald of reform, not for England alone, but for all Christendom. The great protest against Rome which it was permitted him to utter was never to be silenced. That protest opened the struggle which was to result in the emancipation of individuals, of churches, and of nations" (White, *GC*, p. 80).

but one church; the latter four deal frankly with God's true church and Satan's counterfeit churches.

Sardis

The letter opens with a description of Jesus holding not only the 7 stars (the angels of the churches), but also the 7 Spirits of God. Again, this shows that the one Holy Spirit has been dealing with God's one true church throughout all 7 ages of church history. Jesus desires to fill the leaders of the churches, and by extension, the churches themselves, with His Spirit. This is indeed the grand hope of Scripture just prior to the second coming (see Joel 2:28, 29).

Like the prior letters, this letter continues with "I know your deeds." However, Jesus presents no compliments. He is very blunt in informing the angel of the church that he has "a name as though you live, though you are dead." The irony is palpable, for Jesus presented Himself in the letter to Smyrna as He "who was dead, yet lived." The angel of the church in Sardis is warned that he is on a path (and as such, is leading others to take the same path) that is the exact opposite of Jesus' example.

Life came to Adam when God breathed into him the breath of life (see Gen. 2:7). In the very last days, God breathes His Spirit into His lifeless church (see Ezek. 37:9, 10). Jesus charges the angel of Sardis with lacking God's Spirit, being spiritually dead—mere dry bones. The Protestant churches started off well in rejecting papal error, but they did not advance beyond the reforms of their founders. Hence, they have stagnated and lost God's Spirit.

The critical and *Textus Receptus* Greek texts indicate that the remaining deeds are about to die, while the Majority Text indicates a note of personal responsibility, in that the angel of the church is told that *he* is "about to cast [the remaining deeds] aside." It is one thing to be neglectful and unaware; it is yet worse to knowingly cast aside truth. This personal responsibility in one's relation to truth harmonizes with the overall message of Revelation, suggesting the Majority reading is correct.

With the church in this condition, God sees that Satan will continue on until every last bit of truth is cast aside. It behooves us to re-examine the past and recall how the Protestant churches arose from papal error by fervent study of God's Word. By closely comparing Scripture with the practice of both the church and one's own life, defects can be detected and corrected. This is true reformation, which is what the Protestant Reformation was meant to accomplish from its inception. This is the means of keeping one's garments—one's character—spotless.

In many places, Jesus speaks of coming like a thief upon those who fail to watch; hence the need of constant watchfulness in order to be ready.[30] Those who have not defiled their garments, that is, their characters, are prepared at any moment. For what are they prepared? Not merely for His return at the second coming, but also for their name to come up at an unknown hour—an unknown point of the judgment hour of Revelation 14:7—*before* His return. We have no way of knowing when that takes place; hence the admonition: "behold, now is the accepted time; behold, now is the day of salvation" (2 Cor. 6:2, KJV).

While the message paints a rather dim picture of Sardis, Jesus encourages the angel of the church with the observation that "you have a few names in Sardis which have not defiled their garments." As sad a condition as the church is in, it is still His true church and not yet to be cast off.

The message to the conqueror is that he will be clothed in white garments, a spotless character. Notice that *we* are admonished not to defile our garments, and it is *we* who are to wash our robes in the blood of the Lamb (see Rev. 7:13, 14), yet it is *Jesus who gives us* the spotless garments (see Rev. 3:5; 19:8). The righteous character Jesus seeks to instill in us corresponds to a person filled with God's Spirit. The names of such will *remain* enrolled in the Lamb's scroll of life. Notice that the text does not say "once enrolled, always enrolled." By the exercise of our own free will in resisting the convictions of God's Spirit and continuing to indulge

---

[30] See, for example, Matt. 24:36–44; Luke 12:35–40; 1 Thess. 5:1–8; 2 Peter 3:10–14; Rev. 16:15.

pet idols, it is possible to remove *ourselves* from the sacred scroll.[31]
To appreciate the full significance of this, consider the first recorded
instance of God wiping something away: all the creatures that did not
board the ark with Noah—meaning He destroyed them (see Gen. 7:4, 23).
To have one's name wiped away from the scroll of life is to be assured of
everlasting destruction.

On the other hand, by continually seeking God's grace in every situa-
tion, we may keep our names enrolled. He will in no wise wipe away those
names; instead, He *will* wipe away their tears (see Rev. 7:17; 21:4). Jesus
will declare their names in the end-time judgment, acknowledging them as
His bride, for they will wear the white wedding garments of righteousness
(see 19:7–8).

The historical period for this church is the remainder of the 1,260 years
of the papal Dark Ages not already covered in the letter to the angel of
the church in Thyatira—the early years of the Protestant Reformation
(approximately the 1530s, when the Waldenses renewed their commitment to God) until the beginning of the end time on February 10, 1798,
when the papacy would receive its deadly wound (see 13:3).

Philadelphia

The letter to the city of brotherly love opens with a number of descriptions
from Isaiah: "the Holy One" (40:25), "He who is true" (65:16), and Him
"who holds the key of David" (22:22).

In Revelation 1:18, Jesus said He has the keys of death and the grave,
as He alone can reverse the curse of death. By the power of His spoken

---

[31] Those who hold to "once saved, always saved" may object that it is impossible to lose salvation
based on the following text: "I give unto them eternal life; and they shall never perish, neither shall
any man pluck them out of my hand" (John 10:28, KJV). This text merely states that one person cannot rob *another* person of salvation; it says nothing about one's own ability to *choose* to leave a saving
relationship with God. Consider the life of King Saul, upon whom came the Holy Spirit (see 1 Sam.
10:10; 11:6). Later, the Spirit withdrew (see 16:14), again came upon him (see 19:23), then withdrew
once and for all, leaving Saul to die a lost man (see 28:16; 31:4).

word, He can raise the dead from their dusty graves (see John 5:25–29). Of course, death is the wages of sin (see Rom. 6:23), and Jesus has the power to so transform the life that He can take anyone, however steeped in sin, and transform that person into His likeness, provided he or she yields all to Him. Notable examples include that most vile of all Judean kings, Manasseh, and the king of Babylon, Nebuchadnezzar (see 2 Chron. 33:11–16; Dan. 4:34–37).

The passage behind the key of David and the opening and shutting of verse 7 is Isaiah 22:15–25. In this passage, the current steward of the king's house, Shebna, is to be removed, and his office will pass to Eliakim. He will have the key of the house of David; he will open and no one shut, and vice versa. Following this judgment on Shebna, Isaiah pronounces judgment on Tyre in chapter 23 (typifying the judgment upon end-time Babylon in Revelation 18), then the entire world in chapter 24, with special emphasis on breaking God's everlasting covenant (see v. 5). The transition from Shebna to Eliakim typifies the transition to take place at the end of the judgment, i.e., from Satan as prince of this world to Jesus, whose enemies become His footstool (see Ps. 110:1).

Jesus is High Priest during the end-time day of atonement. He sets before the faithful an open door, an entry into the Holy of Holies where He is officiating. There, they have the privilege of being transformed fully into His likeness. He knows when one's character is fixed for eternity; when He affixes the seal of the living God upon the foreheads of such, they will not turn. Their case is shut or locked, as it were, and nothing will cause them to return to a life of sin.

One may object that it was not a door that led into the Holy of Holies, but a veil. That was true of the wilderness sanctuary, but as noted in the comments on Revelation 1, the sanctuary of Revelation corresponds to Solomon's temple, for which two doors did lead into the Holy of Holies (see 1 Kings 6:31).

Those who choose to remain where they are, not following Jesus into the Holy of Holies, are characterized as the synagogue of Satan. With the commencement of the end time in 1798, Jesus focused on preparing people to enter with Him into the Holy of Holies once judgment began in 1844. To that end, he raised up William Miller to preach the cleansing of the sanctuary, his first sermon being delivered in August of 1831 (Bliss, *Memoirs of William Miller*, p. 98). While Miller misunderstood the cleansing of the sanctuary to coincide with the burning of the earth by fire at Jesus' second coming, it nevertheless led to deep repentance, for without "holiness ... no man shall see the Lord" (Heb 12:14, KJV). The Millerites at that time did not fully understand the connection with the ancient Day of Atonement ritual, but they did begin to experience the repentance for which Jesus calls to make a people ready to meet Him when He does return. Like Jesus, the people who live without tasting death prior to His return will, by His grace, attain the experience of living without indulging sin (see Heb. 4:15; 9:28).[32]

Jesus will cause those who profess to serve the living God but have refused to enter the Day of Atonement experience to come and worship at the feet of those who have responded. This occurs at the close of the antitypical day of atonement, just before the second coming:

> The 144,000 were all sealed and perfectly united. On their foreheads was written, God, New Jerusalem, and a glorious star containing Jesus' new name. At our happy, holy state the wicked were enraged, and would rush violently up to lay hands on us to thrust us into prison, when we would stretch forth the hand in the name of the Lord, and they would fall helpless to the ground. Then it was that the synagogue of Satan knew that God had loved us who could wash one another's feet and salute the brethren with a holy kiss, and they worshiped at our feet.
>
> Soon our eyes were drawn to the east, for a small black cloud had appeared, about half as large as a man's hand, which we all knew was the sign of the Son of man. (White, *EW*, p. 15)

---

[32] Character perfection (not indulging sin) is not to be confused with *perfectionism*, the heresy that holds that people can attain so-called "holy flesh," a nature that cannot be tempted. Jesus Himself was tempted while in the flesh (see Heb. 2:18). We can live without indulging temptations when, like Jesus, we learn to be surrendered to our heavenly Father *continuously*.

While worshipping at the believers' feet is still future, the refusal to enter the experience of deep repentance characterizing the end-time day of atonement was typified in the days of the Millerites leading up to the Great Disappointment of October 22, 1844. As the date drew nearer, the established churches became more critical of the Millerites, disciplining them and removing them from fellowship (Schwarz, *Light Bearers*, p. 45). Those removed from the churches consequently had little power within their own ranks, yet by their faithfulness, they kept Jesus' word and did not deny His name. One of the most prominent Millerites, Charles Fitch, penned his sermon, "Come Out of Her, My People," asserting that Babylon embraced not only Roman Catholicism, but Protestant Christendom as well. "Is the Catholic Church, only, opposed to the personal reign of Christ? What shall we say of Protestant Christendom in this respect? … THEY are ANTICHRIST" (Fitch, *"Come Out of Her, My People," A Sermon*, pp. 10, 13). The refusal on the part of Protestant churches as a whole to heed Jesus' call for a soul-searching repentance, not yet experienced in sacred history, confirmed these churches as "the synagogue of Satan." They claimed to be "Jews," i.e., true believers, yet refused to walk in the light; hence darkness came upon them (see John 12:35, 36).

There is an hour of testing soon to come upon the entire world. Jesus promises to keep (protect) those who persevere. When probation closes for the world, Jesus seals those who have surrendered all to Him. Immediately thereafter, the 7 last plagues fall. Those who have been sealed with the seal of the living God do not turn from their allegiance to Him, for He has made them a pillar in His temple. According to God's pledge in Revelation 3:10, such do not suffer during the 7 last plagues, just as during the 10 plagues that befell Egypt, God made a distinction between His people and the unrepentant Egyptians during the last 7 of those plagues (see Exod. 8:21–23). On the other hand, those who have cherished any idol in their lives feel the wrath of an offended God as the plagues fall. During this time of testing, their character is revealed: rather than repent, the wicked blaspheme God, blaming Him for their pain (see Rev. 16:8–11).

Jesus reminds the faithful in Philadelphia to *remain* faithful, for He is coming quickly. Once again, He makes clear that no one can sit back and rest on yesterday's profession of faith or one's past faithful service. The believer's life of character development is always onward and upward. Those who refuse to persevere as Jesus leads them on are permitting another to take their crown.

Jesus promises to make the conqueror in the battle with sin a pillar in the temple of His God. A pillar does not go outside, for it is a support for the temple. While all of these conquerors were once sinners, they made their dwelling in heavenly places during this life (see Eph. 1:3; 2:6). Their characters are fixed for eternity. The word "temple" in Revelation 3:12 can refer to the entirety of the heavenly sanctuary, just as Solomon's temple comprised both Holy Place and "oracle" (Most Holy Place). Nevertheless, emphasis is placed upon the Holy of Holies with the mention of the New Jerusalem. Our study of Revelation 21 will show that the New Jerusalem is indeed the Holy of Holies. Those who conquer follow Jesus into the Holy of Holies. Upon these conquerors is written the name of Jesus' God, *Yahweh*, a reminder that He is the covenant-keeping God who holds our hand fast (see Isa. 42:6) as we hold fast to His covenant promise (see Isa. 56:4–6). Jesus and the New Jerusalem share this precious name, "*Yahweh* our righteousness" (Jer. 23:6; 33:16). Tied as it is to *Yahweh's* covenant, this name also points to the Sabbath (see Isa. 56:4–6), the sign of the everlasting covenant (see Exod. 31:16, 17), a point that will become clearer when we examine the link between the name of God and His seal in Revelation 7. In short, the bride will take Jesus' name during the wedding to take place in the Most Holy Place.

The church of Philadelphia was the church in existence during the time of the Millerite movement, when Charles Fitch, in the summer of 1843, identified not merely Roman Catholicism as Babylon the great, the mother of harlots in Revelation 17:5, but further identified the Protestant world as her daughters. The call to "come out of her My people" (Rev. 18:4) began to sound louder and louder as the expected date of Christ's return, October 22, 1844, drew closer. The door was open to leave the fallen churches and prepare to meet Christ.

The historical period for Philadelphia is February 10, 1798 (capture of Pope Pius VI, marking the beginning of the end time) until the end-time judgment starts (October 22, 1844).

Laodicea

The final letter to the churches is addressed to Laodicea, a name that combines two Greek words: λαος, signifying "people," and either δικαιοσυνη ("righteousness"), δικαιος ("righteous, just"), or δικαιως ("rightly, justly"). Hence, the true church during the seventh and final period of church history, Laodicea, is to be understood as composed of a people who proclaim a message concerning righteousness, which is the character requirement for those who wish to stand in the end-time judgment.

Jesus' description in 3:14 confirms this understanding of the message addressed to Laodicea. Jesus is called the Amen, a term used of "the God of *amen* ["faithfulness"]" (see Isa. 65:16). The Hebrew *amen* comes from the Hebrew verb that first appears in Genesis 15:6, in which Abram's exercise of faith is counted as righteousness by God. This suggests that the letter to Laodicea focuses on righteousness by faith.

Next, Jesus is called the faithful and true Witness; this description points to Him as in a trial setting. He has a perfect knowledge of our life record and can be expected to render a faithful account of each person's life in accord with His law and principles, in turn securing a proper verdict. Thus, the letter concerns the measurement of our character in a legal setting, i.e., the end-time judgment.

Finally, Jesus is referred to by a Greek word carrying the ideas of both "Initiator" (i.e., Creator) and "Head": Jesus is Head of all because He is Creator. To that end, Jesus is the faithful and true Witness *because* He is Creator of all.

This summary description of Jesus matches perfectly the message that he gives the Laodicean church to proclaim to the world in the end time—the 3 angels' messages of Revelation 14:6–12. In other words, here in Revelation 3:14–22, Jesus is telling those in the remnant church exactly what they themselves need to know about Him before they can ever give the message with power to others. The 3 angels' messages begin with a proclamation concerning the end-time judgment and worshipping the Creator, and they conclude with a summary description of those who accept this message: they keep God's commandments because they keep the faith of Jesus, i.e., they are righteous *because* they hold fast to Jesus' faith. When the church accepts this message in its fullness, it is duty-bound to give the message to the world, ushering in the final events preceding the second coming.

Jesus' message to Laodicea is not flattering. He pictures His people as water (see Isa. 17:12; Rev. 17:15) in His mouth. Cold water is appreciated by a weary person (see Prov. 25:25), and hot water can be used for remedial agencies (hot foot baths, compresses, and the like). However, Laodicea is neither; it is simply complacent. As a body, its members do not value or, by extension, live out and share, the judgment-hour message entrusted to them. They are comfortable in their complacency, and of course one who is comfortable does not budge. Laodicea does not recognize any problem with its condition before God; hence it has no zeal to get things right in order to stand before Jesus in the judgment.

The condition is so bad that Jesus is about to vomit them out of His mouth. Note that He does not say He *will* vomit them out, but that He is on the *verge* of so doing. Should Laodicea, as a body, repent, it will not be spewed out. There is a powerful irony here, for it has already been noted that the sharp, double-edged sword (pointing back to the Edenic sanctuary and God's Word) proceeds from His mouth. If His people lose their zeal for living out the salvific truths of the sanctuary found in His Word, Jesus will vomit them out of the same mouth!

The end-time church that emerged from the Millerite movement of the Philadelphian period has a problem: it has so much biblical truth (its "riches") that has been rescued from the error and rubbish cast upon the Word during the Dark Ages that it is prone to sit back and commend itself for *knowing* these truths. It is not any accomplishment on the part of the church to *know* these truths, for such knowledge is a gift from God. Rather, He expects His people to *proclaim* these truths by *living* them out. The contrast with Smyrna, whom He declares rich in Revelation 2:9, is stark.

This means that God's end-time remnant church suffers from the same problem as does all of humanity: pride. In fact, her pride is *worse* than that of others, precisely *because* she has so much biblical truth. By not acting upon this truth, she is a hypocrite. Hence, while Laodicea may be able to look around and (correctly) point out the errors of other religious bodies, she does not realize that she is "the one wretched, the one pitiful, poor, blind, and naked." She is the apple of God's eye, yet her condition is the worst of all on the earth. God's heart breaks, for He has seen this condition previously among the Jews of Jesus' day, who were so blind as to secure the cooperation of Rome to kill the Messiah, and the probationary period allotted them to continue as God's special people closed 3.5 years later with the stoning of Stephen (see Dan. 9:24–27; Acts 7:55–60). Jesus has no desire for the hearts of His people to be so hard that probation closes for them and they are cut off from His presence forever. Rather, His aim is to change their hearts of stone into hearts of flesh (see Ezek. 36:25–27). Those who willingly submit to and endure such transformation, Jesus pronounces fit for heaven. He seals them, and they go forth proclaiming truth, winning others whose hearts are willing to yield.

Just as Jesus' self-description in verse 14 is threefold, so the cure for His proud people is threefold. The first step is to buy gold tried in the fire. This does not mean purchasing or earning salvation. Rather, it refers to paying the ultimate price for that which is ironically free (ref. Isa. 55:1): they need to "purchase" this gold by giving their hearts—their entire selves—to Jesus. That which God tries in the fire is each person's faith. The Greek of 1 Peter 1:7 says that this trial, this proving, this purification of our faith—rather than the faith itself—is what is more precious than gold which perishes. This should be no surprise, for with God tending the refiner's fire, our faith becomes absolutely pure. Likewise, Paul refers to this purified "faith which works by love" (Gal. 5:6), love being God's character (see 1 John 4:8, 16).

The second step is to buy white garments. Any pretended righteousness on our part is seen by God to be as foul as are menstrual garments (see Isa. 64:6). God longs to clothe us with the "garments of salvation"; to cover us with the "robe of righteousness" (Isa. 61:10). If we try to cover ourselves with any manufactured righteousness, we are right back where Adam and Eve were when they sinned, forfeiting the garments of God's light and attempting to cover themselves with fig leaves (see Ps. 104:2; Gen. 3:7). We may think we have covered ourselves pretty well, but the shame of our condition is laid bare before Him.

Of course, procuring this purified character—the faith that works by love and the white garments—presupposes that one recognizes the need for them. Hence, the third and final component of Jesus' cure: eye salve so that we may see our need. The problem with blindness is not limited to one's inability to see well; those who are blind are unable to *recognize* their blindness on their own. Those who wear glasses know the process of self-deception that takes place when others begin pointing out our need for them: we get defensive, making excuses in a vain attempt to mask the blindness. If one persists in a refusal to get the needed correction, vision can deteriorate rapidly and markedly. The sooner one surrenders and undergoes an eye examination, the sooner one experiences the blessing of corrected vision.

We need to *humble* ourselves to the point that we are willing to let the truth cut so that we may experience healing. Just as Jesus humbled Himself and was subsequently exalted by the Father (see Phil. 2:5–11), so to those who humble themselves, Jesus promises He will exalt them in due time (see 1 Peter 5:6; Luke 14:10). God knows that this is contrary to everything in our carnal nature, so He assures us that He does this in love. He is longsuffering with us as He seeks to win our cooperation (see 2 Peter 3:9). In grateful appreciation for His divine patience, Jesus counsels us, "Be zealous, and repent!"

In Revelation 3:20, we encounter a door once again. God informed the Philadelphian believers that He had given them an open door through which to enter the Holy of Holies. Now, Jesus stands at another door— the door of a different temple. Paul speaks of this temple, referring to the church members collectively (see 1 Cor. 3:16, 17; 6:19, 20). In other words, Jesus stands at the door of each person's heart, seeking entrance. He invites believers to enter into His presence in the letter to Philadelphia, then He seeks entrance into their hearts in the letter to Laodicea. There is a mutual dwelling—we in Him and He in us—that must take place (see John 15:4). As we abide in the heavenly Holy of Holies by faith, He cleanses the record of our sinful lives; as He abides in our hearts by His Holy Spirit, He cleanses *us*.

Jesus says we are to hear His voice, just as Adam and Eve heard His voice in the garden after they sinned (see Gen. 3:8). When Cain grew jealous of his brother Abel, whose offering *Yahweh* accepted, *Yahweh* informed Cain that sin lay at his door, crouching as though ready to pounce upon and destroy him (see Gen. 4:7). With such imminent danger lying at our door, how beautiful it is that Jesus is there as well, ready to save us from the death our sins are surely bringing! Ironically, Laodicea's reaction seems akin to that of Cain, one of *self-justification*, a determination to remain in the same state.

The text states that Jesus is not merely at the door, sitting or assuming a casual posture, but He *stands* at the door. This points to Jesus entering into judgment: The Judge *stands* at the door (see James 5:9); God *rises* to judge (see Ps. 76:9); Michael (Jesus) *stands* when judgment is complete (see Dan. 12:1).

It should be incredibly good news that Jesus is so eager to complete His work of judgment, endeavoring to secure a positive verdict for us. To understand the bride's response to Jesus in the history of the Laodicean church, we first turn to Solomon's Song of Songs, because the imagery of Jesus speaking at the door comes from 5:2–7. The Song of Songs is about Solomon and his Egyptian bride, the Shulammite. We have already noted how the heavenly sanctuary in Revelation corresponds to Solomon's temple. Now we recognize that the relationship of Solomon and the Shulammite typifies the relationship between Jesus and His end-time remnant church, whom He delivers from spiritual Egypt (see Isa. 27:1, 12, 13; Rev. 12:14–17).

Following the commencement of the end-time judgment in 1844, has Jesus at any time shown a special eagerness to meet His bride in the Holy of Holies? To answer, we need to identify the end-time remnant church and determine a time when they responded as did Solomon's bride, making excuses for not opening the door (see Song of Sol. 5:3). We provide the necessary evidence to positively identify the end-time remnant church in our study of Revelation 10 and 12. For now, we will assert without proof that it is the Seventh-day Adventist Church. This church was formally established in 1863, and the 1888 General Conference session began October 17 in Minneapolis, during which special presentations on the subject of justification by faith were presented by E. J. Waggoner and A. T. Jones, who were given special insight as to how Jesus works out His righteousness in us. The church was informed that this message was the beginning of the long-awaited latter rain (special outpouring of the Holy Spirit that enables the end-time message of Revelation 14:6–12 to be given with the power attending the loud cry of Revelation 18:2):

> Several have written to me, inquiring if the [1888 Minneapolis] message of justification by faith is the third angel's message, and I have answered, "It is the third angel's message in verity." The prophet declares, "And after these things I saw another angel come down from heaven, having great power; and the earth was lightened with his glory." Brightness, glory, and power are to be connected with the third angel's message, and conviction will follow wherever it is preached in demonstration of the Spirit. How will any of our brethren know when this light shall come to the people of God? As yet, we certainly have not seen the light that answers to this description. God has light for his people, and all who will accept it will see the sinfulness of remaining in a

lukewarm condition; they will heed the counsel of the True Witness when he says, "Be zealous therefore, and repent. Behold, I stand at the door, and knock: if any man hear my voice, and open the door, I will come in to him, and will sup with him, and he with me." (White, *RH*, April 1, 1890)

The loud cry of the third angel has already begun in the revelation of the righteousness of Christ, the sin-pardoning Redeemer. This is the beginning of the light of the angel whose glory shall fill the whole earth. (White, *RH*, Nov 22, 1892)

Unfortunately, this special blessing was not well-received by much of the leadership at this 1888 General Conference session. In fact, some of those present, ministers whom God had appointed as watchmen on the walls of Zion, were downright hostile: "The watchmen that went about the city found me, they smote me, they wounded me; the keepers of the walls took away my veil from me" (Song of Sol. 5:7, KJV). Note the leaders' treatment of the message, and how Jesus regarded this:

I inquire of those in responsible positions in Battle Creek, What are you doing? You have turned your back, and not your face, to the Lord. There needs to be a cleansing of the heart, the feelings, the sympathies, the words, in reference to the most momentous subjects—the Lord God, eternity, truth. What is the message to be given at this time? It is the third angel's message. But that light which is to fill the whole earth with its glory has been despised by some ... who claim to believe the present truth. Be careful how you treat it. Take off the shoes off your feet; for you are on holy ground. Beware how you indulge the attributes of Satan, and pour contempt upon the manifestation of the Holy Spirit. I know not but some have even now gone too far to return and to repent. (White, *TM*, pp. 89, 90)

That men should keep alive the spirit which ran riot at Minneapolis ... is an offense to God. (White, *TM*, p. 76)

Now our meeting is drawing to a close, and not one confession has been made; there has not been a single break so as to let the Spirit of God in.

Now I was saying what was the use of our assembling here together and for our ministering brethren to come in if they are here only to shut out the Spirit of God from the people? We did hope that there would be a turning to the Lord here. Perhaps you feel that you have all you want. ...

I never was more alarmed than at the present time. (White, *1888*, p. 151)

My burden during the meeting was to present Jesus and His love before my brethren, for I saw marked evidences that many had not the spirit of Christ. My mind was kept in peace, stayed upon God, and I felt sad to see that a different spirit had come into the experience of our brother ministers, and that it was leavening the camp. There was, I knew, a remarkable blindness upon the minds of many, that they did not discern where the Spirit of God was and what constituted true Christian experience. To consider that these were the ones who had the guardianship of the flock of God was painful. The destitution of true faith, the hands hung down, because not lifted up in sincere prayer! Some felt no need of prayer. Their own judgment, they felt, was sufficient, and they had no sense that the enemy of all good was guiding their judgment. They were as soldiers going unarmed and unarmored to the battle. Can we marvel that the discourses were spiritless, that the living water of life refused to flow through obstructed channels, and that the light of heaven could not penetrate the dense fog of lukewarmness and sinfulness. (White, *1888*, pp. 216, 217)

I would speak in warning to those who have stood for years resisting light ... and cherishing the spirit of opposition. How long will you hate and despise the messengers [E. J. Waggoner and A. T. Jones] of God's righteousness? God has given them

His message. They bear the word of the Lord. There is salvation for you, but only through the merits of Jesus Christ. The grace of the Holy Spirit has been offered you again and again. Light and power from on high have been shed abundantly in the midst of you. Here was evidence, that all might discern whom the Lord recognized as His servants. But there are those who despised the men and the message they bore. They have taunted them with being fanatics, extremists, and enthusiasts. Let me prophesy unto you: Unless you speedily humble your hearts before God, and confess your sins, which are many, you will, when it is too late, see that you have been fighting against God. Through the conviction of the Holy Spirit, no longer unto reformation and pardon, you will see that these men whom you have spoken against have been as signs in the world, as witnesses for God. Then you would give the whole world if you could redeem the past, and be just such zealous men, moved by the Spirit of God to lift your voice in solemn warning to the world; and, like them, to be in principle firm as a rock. Your turning things upside down is known of the Lord. Go on a little longer as you have gone, in rejection of the light from heaven, and you are lost. "The man that shall be unclean, and shall not purify himself, that soul shall be cut off from among the congregation."

I have no smooth message to bear to those who have been so long as false guideposts, pointing the wrong way. If you reject Christ's delegated messengers, you reject Christ. Neglect this great salvation, kept before you for years, despise this glorious offer of justification through the blood of Christ and sanctification through the cleansing power of the Holy Spirit, and there remaineth no more sacrifice for sins, but a certain fearful looking for of judgment and fiery indignation. I entreat you now to humble yourselves and cease your stubborn resistance of light and evidence. (White, *TM*, pp. 96–98)

All assembled in that meeting had an opportunity to place themselves on the side of truth by receiving the Holy Spirit, which was sent by God in such a rich current of love and mercy. But in the rooms occupied by some of our people was heard ridicule, criticism, jeering, laughter. The manifestations of the Holy Spirit were attributed to fanaticism. Who searched the Holy Scriptures, as did the noble Bereans, to see if the things they heard were so? Who prayed for divine guidance? The scenes which took place at this meeting made the God of heaven ashamed to call those who took part in them, his brethren. All this the heavenly Watcher noticed, and it is written in the book of God's remembrance. (White, *1888*, p. 1565)

I stated that the course that had been pursued at Minneapolis was cruelty to the Spirit of God; and those who went all through that meeting and left with the same spirit with which they came to the meeting, and were carrying on the same line of work they did at that meeting and since they had come from it, would—unless they were changed in spirit and confessed their mistakes—go into greater deceptions. They would stumble and know not at what they were stumbling. I begged them to stop just where they were. But the position of Elder Butler and Elder Smith influenced them to make no change but stand where they did. No confession was made. The blessed meeting closed. Many were strengthened, but doubt and darkness enveloped some closer than before. The dew and showers of grace from heaven which softened many hearts did not wet their souls. (White, *1888*, p. 360)

I know that at that time the Spirit of God was insulted. (White, *1888*, p. 1043)

If the hearts of God's people were filled with love for Christ, if every church member were thoroughly imbued with the spirit of self-sacrifice, if all manifested thorough earnestness, there would be no lack of funds for home or foreign missions. Our resources would be multiplied; a thousand doors of usefulness would be opened, and we should be invited to enter. Had the purpose of God been carried out by His people in giving to the world the message of mercy, Christ would, ere this, have come to the earth, and the saints would have received their welcome into the city of God. (White, *6T*, p. 450)

This small sampling of quotations relative to the message presented in 1888 and its defiant rejection by a number of the ministerial brethren shows how Jesus was slighted when He so longed to pour out the Holy Spirit on the leaders present. Note how the foregoing quotations apply the Laodicean message to the events at the 1888 General Conference: the quotation from Revelation 3:19–20, the reference to "lukewarmness," "remarkable blindness," and the statement "some felt no need of prayer. Their own judgment, they felt, was sufficient." Further, note allusions to Song of Songs 5:2–7, such as the "dew and showers of grace from heaven" (v. 2), "let the Spirit of God in" (ibid.), "shut out the Spirit of God from the people" (v. 3), and "the Spirit of God was insulted" (verse 6).[33]

Is it any wonder that Jesus addresses the angels of each church, and that it is the angel of the church of Laodicea—those with "guardianship of the flock"—its leadership—that is addressed with an especially strong rebuke? The leaders' stubborn refusal to accept truth "was leavening the camp," thus the church at large would not see the beauty of the end-time message, and hence the rest of the world would be deprived of the life-giving message of the righteousness of Christ.[34]

---

[33] To more clearly see the connection with the Holy Spirit in Song of Songs 5:2–7, note the words, "My Beloved withdrew His hand from the hole" (verse 4). Scripture often refers to the Holy Spirit with "hand" (see especially Ezek. 1:1, 3; 3:14; 8:1, 3; 37:1; 40:1). Prophetic messages inspired by the Holy Spirit are referred to by a formula such as "by the hand of Haggai the prophet" (Hag. 1:1, 3; 2:1). The Holy Spirit is in God's hand (compare Job 27:3 and Dan. 5:23). The hand in Daniel 5 is the Holy Spirit (see *THE STAND*, remarks on Daniel 5). Scripture records the reception of the Holy Spirit following the laying on of hands (e.g., Acts 8:17; 13:3, 4; 19:6).

[34] The interested reader can read in great detail the happenings at the 1888 General Conference and the years following by consulting *The Ellen G. White 1888 Materials*, as well as Ron Duffield's *The Return of the Latter Rain*.

Jesus' promise to dine with those who open the door of their hearts to Him hints that judgment is in view. As people's names come up for review in the judgment in the Holy of Holies, and their records are found to be of faithful submission while Jesus led them through the process of character purification, the marriage takes place. Following the judgment, Jesus returns to take His faithful church bride to heaven, where believers enjoy the "wedding supper of the Lamb" (Rev. 19:9, which uses the same Greek root as "dine" in 3:20), fulfilling His promise to dine with the conquerors. Again, the unrepentant wicked who are slain at Jesus' return are the fare at the "great feast of God" (19:17, which uses the same Greek root as "dine" in 3:20) when the birds consume their corpses—a miserable judgment.

Jesus' promise to Laodicea is staggering: those who are willing may sit *with* Him on *His* throne as His bride! We may take comfort that His call to conquer is something He too had to experience when He came to earth, cloaking His divinity with humanity, and He succeeded by the same grace of God that He offers us (see Heb. 2:17, 18; 4:15, 16; 5:7–9). "He raiseth up the poor out of the dust, and lifteth up the beggar from the dunghill, to set them among princes, and to make them inherit the throne of glory" (1 Sam. 2:8, KJV). He calls us to be kings, just as he is King (see Rev. 20:4, 6). Since judgment takes place on the throne (see 1 Kings 7:7), and David's sons, including Solomon, judged (see 2 Sam. 15:2; 2 Chron. 1:10, 11; 1 Kings 3:28; compare 1 Sam. 8:5, 6, 20), it is plain that Jesus grants the faithful the privilege of *judging* with Him following the second coming. Paul confirms this, stating that we will judge both the world and fallen angels (see 1 Cor. 6:2, 3).

The historical period for Laodicea is October 22, 1844 until the second coming. One might say that the seventh church represents a close inspection of the sixth church in its latter stages. Similarly, the sixth seal, the sixth trumpet, and the sixth plague take us to the second coming, while the seventh seal, seventh trumpet, and seventh plague focus especially on the work of judgment just prior to the second coming.

PART 2: THE KEY POINTS

REVELATION 1:9–3:22: JESUS

The trumpet-like voice is that of Jesus. He appears to John dressed in high priestly, day-of-atonement garb. Jesus "resurrects" John when he falls at His feet as though dead. He addresses the 7 churches, highlighting His own character and identifying issues (commendable or faulty) of each church. Jesus especially desires to reveal His righteousness to the final church, Laodicea, that the church may in turn reveal His righteousness to the world, hastening His second coming.

REVELATION 3:20: JESUS STANDS FOR HIS BRIDE

Jesus' first stance in Revelation occurs in the message to the angel of the church in Laodicea. After pointing out the church's desperate need in a scathing rebuke to the leadership, Jesus notes that He is standing at the door, knocking, inviting His bride-to-be to become wedded to Himself in the judgment, perfectly like Him in character. The wedding chamber behind this door will appear in Revelation 4 and 5.

REVELATION 1:9–3:22: KEY THEMES

The "Lord's day" is the Sabbath, not Sunday. Jesus' trumpet-like voice points back to the 10 Commandments at Sinai, signaling preparation for the end-time day of atonement. The Day of Atonement is a day of deliverance when God fulfills His everlasting covenant with mankind. The 7 churches are represented as 7 menorahs with a total of 49 lamps, indicating that the close of the seventh church period ushers in the church's long-awaited jubilee deliverance, when Jesus comes for His bride.

The 7 churches of John's day symbolize God's true church throughout 7 periods of church history. Major themes are the heavenly sanctuary (where Jesus' wedding takes place), Sabbath (Jesus' marital pledge), everlasting covenant (Jesus' marriage itself), and idolatry (unfaithfulness to the marriage vow). In the letter to the seventh church, Laodicea, the twin subjects of justification by faith and the righteousness of Christ are supreme, as they are the key subjects to prepare people to stand in the judgment.

REVELATION 1:9–3:22: THE WEDDING THEME

Jesus is the Son of man, the central figure in the end-time judgment— His wedding with His people. He voluntarily became one flesh (see John 1:14) with His people. Since He experienced all the same struggles with flesh that we do, He sympathizes with us (see Heb. 2:17–18), and is alone qualified to judge His people, and enter into everlasting marital covenant with them.

The promises Jesus makes to the conquerors highlight the wedding theme. They will have access to the tree of life in the Garden of Eden, where marriage was first instituted as an everlasting covenant. Resurrection awaits those who have partaken of the divine nature and become one flesh with Jesus (cf. Gen. 2:24). The hidden manna of the Sabbath and the white stone of heart circumcision point to the everlasting covenant, while the new name refers to the new character God gives when He writes the new covenant, His law, in the hearts of His people. These are all covenant pledges—His promise to marry His people. Jesus warns against fornicating with Jezebel, for He will cast her and her lovers into a bed of great tribulation. Jesus will declare the names of the faithful in the end-time judgment, acknowledging them as His bride, for they will wear the white wedding garments of righteousness (see 19:7–8). He invites us through the open door into the temple (the Most Place, the wedding chamber), where the bride takes His name. Jesus promises to "sup" with the conquerors, referring to the wedding supper of the Lamb, after which they will sit on His throne as His bride.

REVELATION 2 AND 3: DECISION QUESTION

Jesus stands at the door, inviting us to stand with Him during the judgment hour, His wedding. Do you desire a spotless character that will stand in the judgment? No outward observances can take the place of simple faith and entire renunciation of self. However, no one can empty oneself of self. We can only consent for Christ to accomplish the work. If He has shown you your great need of His character and enabling grace, will you open the door wide and invite Him in to take complete control of your life? Are you willing to procure a faith that works by love by choosing to let the Holy Spirit humble you?

Just now, will you let the language of your soul be, "Lord, take my heart; for I cannot give it. It is Thy property. Keep it pure, for I cannot keep it for Thee. Save me in spite of myself, my weak, unchristlike self. Mold me, fashion me, raise me into a pure and holy atmosphere, where the rich current of Thy love can flow through my soul" (White, *COL*, p. 159)?

3:
BRIDE PREPARED TO STAND BEFORE JESUS' THRONE

REVELATION 4–8:1: PRE-ADVENT JUDGMENT: THRONE, SCROLL, SAINTS STAND

The Open Door

4 ¹Afterward I looked, and behold, a door open in heaven, and the first voice (which I had heard like a trumpet) was speaking with me, saying, "Come up here, and I will show you things which must take place afterward."

The Throne

²Immediately I came to be in the Spirit, and behold, a throne was situated in heaven. Upon the throne was One seated, ³like a jasper and sardius stone in appearance; likewise, an arch of light was encircling the throne—an appearance of emeralds.

⁴Encircling the throne were 24 thrones; upon the thrones the 24 elders were sitting, clothed in white garments and upon their heads golden crowns. ⁵Emanating from the throne were lightning flashes, voices, and thunderclaps; 7 fiery lamps, which are the 7 spirits of God, were burning before his throne. ⁶Before the throne was something like a sea of glass—like crystal.

In the immediate vicinity of the throne, in a circle about the throne, were 4 living creatures full of eyes front and back: ⁷the first living creature was like a lion; the second living creature was like a calf; the third living creature had a man's face; the fourth living creature was like a flying eagle. [8]And the 4 living creatures, each having 6 wings extended upward around [the throne][35] and full of eyes inside, have no cessation, day nor night, saying, "Holy, holy, holy is *Yahweh*, God of hosts, He who was, He who is, and He who is coming."

[9]When the living creatures should give glory, honor, and thanks unto the One seated upon the throne—to Him who lives forever and ever—[10]the 24 elders will fall down before the One seated upon the throne and prostrate themselves in worship of Him who lives forever and ever, and lay their crowns before the throne, saying, [11]"Worthy are you our Lord and God, the Holy One, to receive glory, honor, and power, for You created all things; by Your will they existed and were created."

The Scroll

5 [1]Then I saw upon the right hand[36] of the One seated upon the throne a scroll written within and without, sealed with 7 seals. [2]Next, I saw a strong angel proclaiming in a loud voice, "Who is worthy to open the scroll and loose its seals?" [3]Yet no one in heaven above, nor upon the earth, nor under the earth, was able to open the scroll, nor to look into it.

The Lion and Lamb

[4]So I began weeping profusely, for no one worthy was found to open the scroll, nor to examine it. [5]Then one of the elders said to me, "Stop weeping!

---

[35] Greek ανα can be translated "each" (when following numerals) or "upward." Given the plain connection between this passage and Isaiah's vision of "*Adonai* sitting upon a throne, high and elevated" (Isa. 6:1), the evidence suggests "upward" is the correct translation. The Greek adverb κυκλοθεν ("around") matches the Greek preposition translated "in a circle" in verse 6. Hence, the wings are open tip-to-tip, completing the circle, as it were, in which the 4 living creatures stand about the throne.

[36] This expression signifies "in the open right hand." "There in His open hand lay the book" (White, *12MR*, p. 296).

Behold, the Lion from the tribe of Judah, the Root of David, has conquered. *He* is the one to open the scroll and its 7 seals." [6]In the space intervening the throne and 4 living creatures, and the elders,[37] I saw a Lamb **standing**—as though slaughtered—having 7 horns and 7 eyes, which are the 7 spirits of God sent into all the earth. [7]He came and took it from the right hand of the One seated upon the throne.

The New Song

[8]When He took the scroll, the 4 living creatures and the 24 elders fell down before the Lamb, having each a harp and golden bowls full of incense, which are the prayers of the holy people. [9]They were singing a new song:

> [Elders & living creatures]: "Worthy are You to take the scroll, and to open its seals, for You were slaughtered"
>
> [The holy people]: "And You redeemed us to God by Your blood out of every tribe, tongue, people, and nation,"
>
> [Elders & living creatures]: [10]"And made them kings and priests unto our God, and they will reign upon the earth."

[11]I looked, then heard what was like the voice of many angels in a circle about the throne, the living creatures, and the elders—their number was myriads of myriads, thousands upon thousands—[12]saying in a loud voice, "Worthy is the slaughtered Lamb to receive power, riches, wisdom, strength, honor, glory, and praise!" [13]Then every creature which is in heaven, upon the earth, under the earth, upon the sea, and all things therein I heard saying, "Unto the One seated upon the throne and unto

---

[37] Literally, "in the midst of the throne and living creatures, and in the midst of the elders." This common Hebrew idiom very precisely locates the Lamb in relation to the throne, living creatures, and elders. This construction appears in Genesis 1:7: the firmament "divided between the waters which were under the firmament and between the waters which were over the firmament." Hence, the Lamb stands before the throne on an imaginary ring, within which are the 4 living creatures encircling the throne, while the 24 elders are seated farther away outside the ring.

the Lamb be praise, honor, glory, and dominion forever and ever. Amen!" [14]As the 4 living creatures were saying the "Amen," the elders fell down and prostrated themselves in worship.

Seals 1–6

6[1]I saw that[38] the Lamb opened 1 of the 7 seals, and I heard [number] 1 of the 4 living creatures saying like a voice of thunder, "Come!" And [to me he said,] "Look!"[39] [2]Behold, a white horse: he who was seated thereon was holding a bow, and to him was given a crown. He went forth a conqueror, with the aim of conquering.

[3]When He opened the second seal, I heard the second living creature saying, "Come!" [4]And there went forth another horse, fiery red [in appearance]: to him who was seated thereon it was granted to take peace from the earth, that they might slaughter each other; a great dagger was given him.

[5]When He opened the third seal, I heard the third living creature saying, "Come!" and [to me he said,] "Look!" Behold, a black horse: he who was seated thereon was holding a balance scale in his hand. [6]Then I heard a voice from among the 4 living creatures saying, "A choinix of wheat for a denarius, and 3 choinixes of barley for a denarius—but the olive oil and the wine you shall not price unrighteously."[40]

---

[38] BYZ reads οτι ("that"); NTG and TR read οτε ("when").

[39] BYZ reads, "Come and see," NTG reads, "Come," and TR reads, "Come and look." This same difference in reading also occurs with the opening of the third and fourth seals. However, with the opening of the second seal, BYZ and NTG agree with "Come," while TR reads, "Come and look." The majority of manuscripts (BYZ) are clear that the second living creature gives the command to the second horse, not to John, to come forth. This suggests that the first, third, and fourth living creatures likewise command the horses to come, while John is directed to look. Indeed, this is so, for in the first, third, and fourth seals, John does indeed "behold," while in the second seal, no such response is indicated.

[40] Literally, "you shall not do unrighteously," meaning "you shall not price exorbitantly," as with famine prices for wheat and barley. Revelation focuses on the formation of a righteous character, so the translation reads, "you shall not price unrighteously."

[7]When He opened the fourth seal, I heard the fourth living creature saying, "Come!" and [to me he said,] "Look!" [8]Behold, a grass-green horse:[41] he who was seated upon it had the name Death, and the Grave was following him. He was given authority over the fourth part of the earth to kill by sword, by famine, by deadly disease,[42] and with the wild beasts of the earth.

[9]When He opened the fifth seal, I saw underneath the altar the lives of those who had been slaughtered for the Word of God, and for the testimony of the Lamb which they held. [10]They cried out in a great voice, saying, "How long, *Adonai*, Holy and True, do You not judge and vindicate our blood [shed] by those dwelling upon the earth?" [11]Then was given to each of them a white robe, and it was told them that they were to cease for a time longer,[43] until should be fulfilled [the number of][44] both their fellow servants and their brethren, i.e., those who were to be killed as also they [were killed].

[12]I saw when He opened the sixth seal: there was a great earthquake, the sun became black as hairy sackcloth, the full moon became like blood [13]and the stars of heaven fell unto the earth like a fig tree which has cast its unripe figs when shaken by a great wind. [14]Then the heaven disappeared[45]

---

[41] Traditionally, "pale horse." However, a survey of the Greek χλωρός throughout the LXX and New Testament shows that it *always* refers to healthy, green ("chlorophyll-colored") vegetation. The immediate connection with Death and the Grave might suggest a sickly, pale color, but it seems that a vibrant "grass-green" is used as an *intentional* contrast with Death. The interested reader may satisfy oneself by reviewing this exhaustive list for χλωρός: Gen. 1:30; 2:5; 30:37; Exod. 10:15; Num. 22:4; Deut. 29:23; 2 Kings 19:26; Job 39:8; Prov. 27:25; Isa. 15:6; 19:7; 27:11; Ezek. 17:24; 20:47; Mark 6:39; Rev. 6:8; 8:7; 9:4.

[42] Ezekiel 5:17 refers to the same four agents of death. The LXX uses "death" to translate the Hebrew word for "pestilence."

[43] BYZ reads, "time"; TR and NTG read, "short time." It is tempting to justify the "short time" reading, as it might appear to match with the "short time" of Revelation 20:3. However, the time for the martyrs of the fifth seal is the pre-advent, investigative judgment prior to their resurrection, which matches the *lengthy* 1,000-year investigative judgment of the wicked prior to their resurrection.

[44] The phrase "the number of" has been supplied to make clear that it is not "the time" (singular) that is fulfilled, but rather the martyrs (plural), since the Greek for "fulfilled" is plural.

[45] Isaiah 34:4 indicates that "all the host of the heavens will dissolve." Some Greek Old Testaments do not include this reference to the dissolution of the heavens, but those that do so employ a

like a scroll being rolled up; every mountain and island were moved out of their places. **15**So the kings of the earth, the men of high office, the principal military figures, the rich, the strong—everybody, slave and free—hid themselves in the caves and among the rocks of the mountains, **16**saying to the mountains and to the rocks, "Fall upon us, and hide us from the face of the One seated upon the throne, and from the Lamb's retribution,[46] **17**for the great day of His retribution[47] has come, and who is able to stand?"

The Seal of the Living God

7 **1**After this, I saw 4 angels standing at the 4 corners of the earth, holding fast the 4 winds of the earth, that wind should not blow upon the earth, nor upon the sea, nor against any tree. **2**Then I saw another angel coming up from where the sun rises, having the seal of the living God; he cried out in a loud voice to the 4 angels to whom it was granted to corrupt[48] the earth and the sea, saying, **3**"You are not to corrupt the earth, neither the sea, nor the trees, until we seal the servants of our God upon their foreheads."

4Then I heard the number of those who were sealed: 144,000 sealed from every tribe of the sons of Israel. **5**From the tribe of Judah, 12,000 sealed; from the tribe of Reuben, 12,000; from the tribe of Gad, 12,000; **6**from the tribe of Asher, 12,000; from the tribe of Naphtali, 12,000; from the tribe of Manasseh, 12,000; **7**from the tribe of Simeon, 12,000; from the tribe of Levi, 12,000; from the tribe of Issachar, 12,000; **8**from the tribe of Zebulun, 12,000; from the tribe of Joseph, 12,000; from the tribe of Benjamin, 12,000 sealed.

---

different Greek word than that used in Revelation 6:14. The word in Revelation 6:14 seems to refer to "being set aside" or "parting ways," attested elsewhere only in Ezekiel 43:21 and Acts 15:39. The present translation goes with "disappeared" (as does NJB); ESV, RSV, and NRSV read, "vanished."

[46] Greek οργη, commonly translated "wrath." Οργη focuses on death as the outcome of God's judgment on sin (see John 3:36).

[47] See footnote 46.

[48] Greek αδικεω = "make unrighteous," "corrupt," "damage," or "injure." "Corrupt" was chosen to blend the idea of injury with the overall theme of character perfection/corruption in Revelation.

[9]Afterward I looked, and behold, a vast multitude which no one was able to number, from every nation, all tribes, peoples, and tongues, standing before the throne and before the Lamb, clothed in white robes and palm branches in their hands, [10]crying out in a great voice, saying, "Salvation is due to our God who sits upon the throne, and to the Lamb."

[11]All the angels standing in a circle about the throne, the elders, and the 4 living creatures, fell before the throne upon their faces and prostrated themselves in worship of God, [12]saying, "Amen! Praise, glory, wisdom, thanksgiving, honor, power, and strength is due to our God forever and ever. Amen!"

[13]Then one of the elders addressed me, saying, "These who are clothed in the white robes—who are they, and where do they come from?" [14]I said to him, "My lord, *you* know." Then he said to me, "These are the ones who come out from the great tribulation; they washed their robes and whitened them with the blood of the Lamb. [15]This is why they are before the throne of God, serving Him day and night in His temple, and He who sits upon the throne will spread His tent over them. [16]They will hunger no more, nor thirst any more, neither is it possible the sun['s rays] will fall on them, nor any searing heat, [17]for the Lamb which is in the midst of the throne shepherds them, leading them to springs of living water. God will wipe away every tear from their eyes."

The Seventh Seal

8 [1]When He opened the seventh seal, there was silence in heaven for about half an hour.

COMMENTARY

The chapter opens with reference to 2 items previously mentioned in Revelation. The door open in heaven takes one back to the open door in the history of Philadelphia, the true church just *prior* to the end-time judgment (see 3:8). The first voice like a trumpet is that of the Son of man (see 1:10), pointing back to the giving of the 10 Commandments at Sinai (see Exod. 19:13–19; 20:18). The 10 Commandments are the basis of the end-time judgment (see Eccl. 12:13, 14), and the Son of man is the central figure therein (see Dan. 7:10, 13). Further, 9 days prior to the Day of Atonement, trumpets heralded its imminence, serving as a call for everyone to get ready (see Lev. 23:24–27).

In Revelation 1:19, John was told to write out the things he sees, "both those which are [before the end-time judgment], as well as those which must take place afterward" (i.e., after the end-time judgment commences). Revelation 4:1 picks up on this language of "things which must take place afterward," indicating that what follows concerns the end-time judgment. This makes perfect sense, as the reference to the open door refers us back to Philadelphia, the church that corresponded to the Millerite movement, ushering in the end-time judgment.

The Open Door

At this point, we inquire why John sees a *door*, and why it is said to be open "in heaven." Recall that John has already seen Jesus in the Holy Place of the heavenly sanctuary in chapter 1, and Jesus has continued speaking with John with no break since then. In other words, John's initial vision has not ended, so he has remained in the heavenly sanctuary continuously. Hence, in the Holy Place of the heavenly sanctuary, John is able to see a door "open in heaven," behind which is a "throne situated in heaven." Recalling that Solomon's temple was patterned after the heavenly sanctuary, we expect the heavenly sanctuary, as well as the Holy of Holies (second apartment), to have doors (see 1 Kings 6:31–34; 7:50).

With that said, why is the door "open in heaven?" Since John is already in the heavenly sanctuary, adding the descriptive "in heaven" might seem redundant. However, this description provides the key by which we can properly discriminate between the door to the temple as a whole and the door to the Most Holy Place. According to 1 Kings 6:2, Solomon's temple measured 60 cubits long, 20 cubits wide, and 30 cubits high. However, the Holy of Holies (the "oracle," KJV; in modern English, we might say "place of pronouncement") measured 20 cubits by 20 cubits by 20 cubits, a perfect cube. Hence, its length was a third the total length of the temple, just as with the wilderness sanctuary, and its width was the same as for the temple as a whole. However, the height was only 20 cubits, not 30 cubits, implying that the Most Holy Place was elevated 10 cubits, or about 15 feet, relative to the Holy Place. This is in harmony with Solomon's throne of judgment, which was ascended by 6 steps (see 1 Kings 7:7; 10:19, 20).

Together, the open door in heaven and the trumpet-like voice introduce the pre-advent judgment—the wedding is now to begin.

The Throne

Next, John sees a throne, also said to be "situated in heaven." This is because it is within the Holy of Holies, which was higher than the Holy Place by a third of the height of the temple.[49] Lest one object that Scripture does not *explicitly* say that the Most Holy Place of Solomon's temple was accessed by steps, note the abundance of testimony concerning the *height* of God's throne in His sanctuary:

> Isa. 6:1: I saw *Adonai* sitting upon a throne, high and elevated, and the ends of His robe filled the temple.

> Ezek. 1:26: Above the firmament … in appearance like a sapphire stone, was the likeness of a throne. Upon the likeness of the throne was, in appearance, the likeness of a man upon it, high above.

> Ps. 99:2: *Yahweh* is great in Zion; He is high above all the peoples.

> Ps. 103:19: *Yahweh* has established His throne in heaven.

---

[49] The author is indebted to Treiyer (*The Final Crisis in Revelation 4–5*, p. 21) for this insight regarding the direction to "come up here."

Isa. 66:1: Heaven is My throne, the earth is My footstool.

Ps. 11:4: *Yahweh* is in the temple of His sanctuary; *Yahweh*—in heaven is His throne.

Jer. 17:12 (KJV): A glorious high throne from the beginning is the place of our sanctuary.

He who is seated upon the throne is described as a blend of jasper and sardius in appearance. This points back to the high priest's breastplate of judgment, in which are 12 gemstones, the last of which is a jasper, the first a sardius (see Exod. 28:17–20). Thus, these 2 extremities are a concise reference to *all* the gems of the breastplate. Since the names of the 12 tribes are sealed on these 12 gems (see Exod. 28:21), the gem-like appearance of the One seated upon the throne sets the stage for the sealing of the 12 tribes of Israel in Revelation 7:1–8. Further, since the 12 gems are on the breastplate of *judgment*, we are to expect that the sealing of God's people occurs at the culmination of the end-time *judgment*.

Hence, while the One on the throne is certainly the King, the details of Revelation 4:1–3 picture Him as High Priest and Judge. This is entirely natural, for God calls His people to be a kingdom of priests (see Exod. 19:6), and our discussion of Laodicea showed that biblical kings exercise judgment.

The picture of God as High Priest becomes clearer with the mention of the "arch of light" about the throne. The Greek word ιρις ("iris") refers to a circle of light (e.g., consider the iris of one's eye), suggesting something like a halo surrounding the throne, much like the petals of an iris plant extend upward, then fold down, forming an umbrella shape. In fact, this suggests the rainbow, as nearly every translation so renders it in English. While the Greek τοξον ("rainbow") is not used here, what John sees in Revelation 4 clearly matches Ezekiel's vision, in which the appearance of the brightness about the throne is said to be like the appearance of the rainbow (see Ezek. 1:26–28).

Curiously enough, the Greek word for "brightness" in Ezekiel 1:28 differs from ιρις ("iris") as well, though they both refer to light. John's substitution of ιρις leads to the discovery that ιρις is used only once in the Septuagint, namely, Exodus 30:24. The iris has an aromatic root, the orris-root (VGNT, entry on ιρις). It is the last of 4 spices (along with olive oil) used in compounding the special anointing oil, used *only* to anoint and consecrate the tent of meeting (i.e., the sanctuary), the ark of the testimony, the 3 furnishings of the holy place, the courtyard furnishings, the high priest, and his priestly sons. Anyone compounding it for common use was to be cut off from God's people (see vs. 23–33).

Why might the anointing oil be alluded to in Revelation 4? Since the iris-like rainbow surrounds the throne and the One seated upon it, this suggests that both have already been inaugurated for their sanctuary role. What exactly is this role? The iris-like rainbow answers the question. The rainbow is first mentioned as the symbol of God's everlasting covenant with mankind (specifically Noah) following His judgment via the flood upon a wicked world (see Gen. 9:16, 17). This everlasting covenant is later confirmed with Abram (see chs. 15 and 17). Scripture makes clear that the covenant with both men was one of righteousness by faith (see 15:6; Heb. 11:7–9, 17). Hence, the One seated upon the throne oversees the working out of the everlasting covenant in His people. It is God who reproduces His holy character in His people, setting them apart as His faithful representatives.

One might reasonably wonder if the One seated on the throne is Father or Son. It is the Ancient of Days who sits to *convene* the judgment, after which the Son of man is brought before Him (see Dan. 7:9, 10, 13). This same sequence is observed in Revelation: The King is seated (see Rev. 4:2), then the Lamb stands before the One seated upon the throne (see 5:6, 7). Since Revelation unseals the book of Daniel (see Dan. 12:4, 9; Rev. 22:10), we conclude that the One seated upon the throne is the Ancient of Days (the Father) and the Lamb is Jesus.

In our study of Revelation 5, we will make a comparison with 1 Chronicles 23–29, in which Solomon was made king a *second* time, being anointed as God's earthly representative or agent, while Zadok was anointed as high priest. With this second anointing, Solomon began to reign in his father's stead. Likewise, in Revelation 5, Jesus is anointed a second time (having been anointed previously at His ascension), assuming the offices of King and High Priest in his Father's stead during the end-time day of atonement. However, why would Jesus be anointed a second time? Up until October 22, 1844, Jesus had been *sitting* with the Father as King on His throne (see Rev. 3:21). During this time, he was High Priest, awaiting the time when He would begin to receive the kingdom (see Ps. 110:1, 4–6). Jesus does not begin to receive His kingdom until the end-time day of atonement opens (see Rev. 11:17). At that time, His high-priestly role takes on the role of Judge, in addition to Intercessor. During the judgment hour (from October 22, 1844 onward), Jesus *stands*, interceding before the Father's throne.[50]

Some may object, for according to Exodus 40:1–15, the high priest was inaugurated following the inauguration of the furnishings of the sanctuary. Among the various furnishings anointed were the altar of burnt offering, pointing to Jesus' atoning death, and the ark of the testimony, wherein the law of God is kept, which is the basis of the end-time judgment. The altar of burnt offering, typifying Jesus' atoning death on Calvary, was inaugurated *prior* to any sacrifice offered upon it. Since Jesus died in the spring of AD 31, it follows that the inauguration of the sanctuary furnishings occurred at least some 65 years *prior* to John's vision during the closing years of the first century. In fact, Jesus was anointed *for His death* on the first day of the week of His crucifixion (see John 12:1–3, 7). Following His ascension, He received His firth anointing as High Priest, coincident with the outpouring of the Holy Spirit (see Acts 2:1–4, 30, 33; Ps. 24:3, 7–10).

These observations lead some to conclude that Revelation 4 and 5 picture Jesus' inauguration as High Priest following His ascension, apparently confirmed by the mention of the slaughtered Lamb in Revelation 5:6. However, when we recognize that the Old Testament types suggest not one, but two, inaugurations for Jesus, it is not essential that Revelation 4 and 5

---

[50] The author is indebted to Treiyer (*The Final Crisis in Revelation 4–5*, pp. 28, 29) for this insight regarding Jesus sitting during His Holy Place ministry (prior to October 22, 1844) and standing during His Most Holy Place ministry (after October 22, 1844).

take place immediately after the ascension. We may let the remainder of Revelation 4 and 5 inform us of the appropriate timeframe.

The iris surrounding the throne is described as having the "appearance of emeralds." This again points to the high priest. The third stone of the first row of the breastplate was an emerald (see Exod. 28:17). Further, the Septuagint designates the stones upon the shoulders of the high priest (those engraved with the names of the sons of Israel) as emeralds (see Exod. 28:9, LXX).

Making a final observation, God's throne is for establishing righteousness via *judgment*:

> Ps. 9:4 (KJV): Thou satest in the throne judging right.
>
> Ps. 9:7 (KJV): [*Yahweh*] hath prepared his throne for judgment.
>
> Ps. 89:14 (KJV): Justice [better, "righteousness"] and judgment *are* the habitation of thy throne.
>
> Ps. 97:2 (KJV): Righteousness and judgment *are* the habitation of his throne.
>
> Ps. 122:5 (KJV): There are set thrones of judgment, the thrones of the house of David.
>
> 1 Kings 7:7 (KJV): Then [Solomon] made a porch for the throne where he might judge, *even* the porch of judgment.
>
> 1 Kings 10:9 (KJV): [*Yahweh*] thy God ... set thee on the throne of Israel: because [*Yahweh*] loved Israel for ever, therefore made he [Solomon] king, to do judgment and justice.
>
> 2 Chron. 9:8 (KJV): [*Yahweh*] ... set thee on his throne, *to be* king God for [*Yahweh*] thy God: because thy God loved Israel, to establish them for ever, therefore made he [Solomon] king over them, to do judgment and justice.
>
> Isa. 9:7 (KJV): Upon the throne of David, and upon his kingdom, to order it, and to establish it with judgment and with justice from henceforth even for ever.

Isa. 16:5 (KJV): In mercy shall the throne be established: and he shall sit upon it in truth in the tabernacle of David, judging, and seeking judgment, and hasting righteousness.

The text now introduces a new group: the 24 elders. Noting that 24 is the sum of 12 and 12, the temptation for some is to posit that the 24 elders are a blend of the 12 sons of Israel and the 12 apostles of Jesus. Such a fanciful view is not tenable, for the text nowhere suggests breaking down 24 into 12 plus 12. Further, who would we identify as the 12 apostles? Obviously, Judas would be excluded. True, Matthias was selected to take his place (see Acts 1:26), but Paul identifies himself as an apostle in all but four of his letters. Further, the New Testament mentions other apostles, such as Andronicus and Junias (see Rom. 16:7).

The correct approach is to see the 24 elders in relation to the sanctuary setting already introduced in Revelation 4. The 24 elders sit on thrones, indicating that they are royal judges and priests (see Ps. 122:5; Rev. 20:4, 6). The descendants of Aaron (16 sons of Eleazar and 8 sons of Ithamar) were set as rulers of God over the sanctuary, hence judges (see 1 Chron. 24:1–19). One must recognize, though, that these 24 rulers did not sit on thrones, and they worked in *separate* shifts throughout the year (see Luke 1:8).

If they are not 12 apostles and 12 tribes or 24 rulers over the sanctuary, then who are these 24 elders/judges? They wear white robes, which Revelation assigns to victors over sin (see Rev. 6:11; 7:14; 19:8), as well as angels (see Rev. 15:6). They also wear golden crowns. The particular crown worn is the *stephanos*, often associated with victory in competitive sports (see 1 Cor. 9:25). Hence, some conclude that the crowns worn by the 24 elders are victors' crowns, i.e., they have been victors in the battle with sin—people redeemed from this world. This has a degree of plausibility, since Jesus did take some people to heaven with Him at His ascension (see Matt. 27:52, 53; Eph. 4:8; Ps. 68:18). However, the fact is that Revelation draws all of its imagery from the Old Testament, and in the Septuagint, the *stephanos* was not worn by victorious athletes, but by kings and priests (see 2 Sam. 12:30; Esther 8:15; Zech. 6:11).

At this point, we know for certain that the 24 elders are royal judges and priests. Are they people or angels? In fact, the context of Revelation makes it very plain who the 24 elders are, and the answer is fairly straightforward, yet surprising to many.[51] One of the elders asks John the identity of those who wear white robes. When John demurs, the elder informs him that they are those who have come out of the great tribulation (see Rev. 7:13, 14). Thus, the elder is not a redeemed person, otherwise he would be among the very redeemed he is discussing. We conclude that he is an angel, just as one of the angels standing by (see Dan. 7:10, 16) explains to Daniel the vision of chapter 7. The following quotations explicitly identify the elders of Revelation as angels; the last confirms that angels wear crowns during the pre-advent judgment:

> [John's] soul was wrought up to such a point of agony and suspense that one of the strong angels had compassion on him, and laying his hand on him assuringly, said, "Weep not: behold, the Lion of the tribe of Juda, the Root of David, hath prevailed to open the book, and to loose the seven seals thereof." (White, *12MR*, pp. 297)

> [Note that "one of the elders" (Rev. 5:5) is identified as "one of the strong angels" (compare v. 2)]

> Angels offer the smoke of the fragrant incense for the praying saints. (White, *CG*, p. 519)

> [This refers to Revelation 5:8, in which the 4 living creatures and 24 elders offer up the incense.]

> Then Jesus ceases His intercession in the sanctuary above. He lifts His hands and with a loud voice says, "It is done;" and all the angelic host lay off their crowns as He makes the solemn announcement: "He that is unjust, let him be unjust still: and he

---

[51] The author is once again indebted to Treiyer (*The Final Crisis in Revelation 4–5*, pp. 45, 46) for putting together the evidence to correctly identify the 24 elders.

which is filthy, let him be filthy still: and he that is righteous, let
him be righteous still: and he that is holy, let him be holy still."
(White, *GC*, p. 613)

Before continuing, let us establish clearly what point in time is in
view here. It is plain that Revelation 4 and 5 draw most strongly from
Daniel 7:9–14 (e.g., the One seated upon the throne, the Lamb before
Him in Revelation 5, the 24 elders seated upon their thrones; note also the
angelic interpreter in Revelation 7:13–14, as in Daniel 7:16). Further, the
lone scroll of Revelation 5, as well as the numerous scrolls at the *conclusion* of judgment in Revelation 20:12, answer well to the scrolls opened in
Daniel 7:10. While some insist that no scrolls are opened in Revelation 5
(which Daniel 7:10 explicitly links to the commencement of judgment),
observe that the scroll of chapter 5 begins to be unsealed in 6, which is part
of the same vision as are 4 and 5. Recall that John saw an open door in 4:1,
this open door having been introduced in the timeframe of Philadelphia,
the church that *precedes* Laodicea, the church during the end-time judgment. Hence, Revelation 4 takes place sometime during Philadelphia,
chapter 5 marks the beginning of the pre-advent judgment (October 22,
1844), and the opening of the seals in 6 and 7 continues on to the close of
the pre-advent judgment.

The lightning flashes, voices, and thunderclaps point back to Sinai
(see Exod. 19:16, 19; 20:18), where God brought back to Israel's collective
remembrance His 10 Commandment law, long forgotten during the years
of Egyptian slavery. Notice the absence of earthquake and hail in connection with the lightning, voices, and thunder (compare Rev. 8:5; 11:19;
16:18, 21). Since God's law is the basis of the end-time judgment (see Eccl.
12:13, 14), and the earthquake and hail are part of the seventh and final
plague at the conclusion of the pre-advent judgment, it follows that the
lightning, voices, and thunder of Revelation 4:5 mark the *commencement*
of the pre-advent judgment.

The 7 Spirits of God are identified as 7 fiery lamps—in other words,
a menorah—in the Holy Place. Though identified as 7 Spirits, the fact

that these 7 lamps are all part of a single menorah confirms our earlier assertion that the 7 Spirits of God are really 1 Holy Spirit working with the church throughout 7 periods of church history. Recall that Solomon's temple had 10 menorahs in the Holy Place; we have encountered 8 menorahs thus far in Revelation (7 menorahs in chapter 1, 1 in chapter 4). We will encounter the remaining 2 menorahs in chapter 11.

The 7 fiery lamps point back to Genesis 15:17, wherein God employs a fiery lamp/torch (the Septuagint reads "fiery lamps/torches") when cutting His covenant with Abram. Of course, it is through the indwelling of the Holy Spirit that His new or everlasting covenant is fulfilled. The Bible clearly states that God's covenant is the re-writing of His law upon our inmost beings and minds (see Jer. 31:31–34; Heb. 8:10). God's law and covenant are really different sides of the same coin, for He states that His 10 Commandment law *is* His covenant (see Exod. 34:28; Deut. 4:13; 1 Kings 8:9, 21).[52] Fulfilling this everlasting covenant, writing His law on the hearts of His people, is the grand theme of Revelation.

To understand the crystal-like sea of glass before the throne, consider the following:

> Ezek. 1:22, 26: Over the heads of the living creature[s] was the likeness of the firmament, like the gleam of awe-inspiring crystal, stretching upward over their heads. ... Above the firmament ... was the likeness of a throne.

> Exod. 24:10: Under [the God of Israel's] feet was something like a work of sapphire pavement, clear as heaven itself.

> Rev. 21:21: The public square of the city was pure gold, like transparent glass.

> Rev. 22:1: A pure river of living water, sparkling like crystal, proceeding from the throne.

---

[52] Certainly, the old covenant occurred at Sinai as well, but the fault was not with God's words, i.e., the 10 Commandments, but with "them" (masculine plural in the Greek), referring to the *people of Israel*. They entered into the old covenant experience by pledging to do all that God required *while relying solely upon their own strength*, not His (see Jer. 31:32; Heb. 8:8; Exod. 24:3).

The description of Ezekiel's vision pictures the firmament separating God's throne above and the 4 living creatures beneath. Ezekiel has to look up to see it, hence his description of the throne above the firmament (identified with "heaven" in Genesis 1:8). By contrast, John has been called to "come up here" (Rev. 4:1) into "heaven," where he sees the 4 living creatures about the throne in the Holy of Holies. From his vantage point, the crystal-like volume is *beneath* the throne, like a sea of glass. These descriptions are in no way contradictory. In Genesis 1:6–8, God put a firmament between the waters and called it "heaven." Those of us on earth look up and see the sky (firmament or heavens), while birds (or people in airplanes) in the sky see water below. Ezekiel and John's visions agree perfectly, placing God's throne in heaven.

The stone that struck the image in Nebuchadnezzar's first dream, representative of Christ's kingdom at the second coming, corresponds to the sapphire pavement in Exodus 24:10 (see *THE STAND*, remarks on Daniel 2). Upon this sapphire stone were carved the 10 Commandments. This sapphire stone is described as "clear as heaven itself," no doubt because it came from the base of God's heavenly throne.

The inside of Solomon's temple, including the floor, was overlaid with gold (see 1 Kings 6:20–28). According to Revelation 21:21, the area before the city (to be equated with the Holy of Holies in our study of Revelation 21) is "pure gold, like transparent glass." Hence, not only are the sanctuary gemstones (like the just-mentioned sapphire) "clear as heaven," but the sanctuary gold also transmits light like transparent glass. In fact, the water of life that flows from the throne at the end of the book of Revelation is also described as "sparkling like crystal."

What do we learn from this crystal description of the gemstones, gold, and water? To understand, let us consider what happened when Moses saw the disobedient children of Israel dancing before the golden calf (see Exod. 32) just after God uttered the 10 Commandments at Mount Sinai: he broke the 10 Commandments (sapphire gemstone) at the base of the mountain (at the top of which rested God's throne), burned the golden calf with fire, crushed it into powder, scattered it on the water, and made the Israelites drink it. In this story, we have all the same elements as in the heavenly sanctuary. The Israelites were to drink this water as part of the remedy for their disobedience. God invites His people now to drink from the crystal-clear waters of life while probation lingers, that we may enjoy it for all eternity (see Rev. 21:6; 22:17).

We are now introduced to 4 living creatures in a circle about the throne. Since they have the same 4 faces mentioned in Ezekiel 1:10, and they are full of eyes as in 1:18 and 10:12, we conclude they are the same 4 living creatures (cherubs) of Ezekiel's visions. Their many eyes indicate that they are full of the Holy Spirit (compare with the 7 eyes of the Lamb, identified as the 7 Spirits of God in Revelation 5:6). Indeed, the living creatures move in accordance with the Spirit (see Ezek. 1:12, 20, 21).

These 4 living creatures are identical with the seraphim ("burning ones") in Isaiah's vision, for they too have 6 wings and cry, "Holy, holy, holy is *Yahweh*, God of hosts" (compare Isa. 6:2, 3). In Ezekiel's vision, they are underneath the throne, serving as a wheeled transport (God rides upon the cherub; see Ps. 18:10); in Isaiah's vision, they are stationed above the throne, hovering on each side (see Isa. 6:2).[53] Here in John's vision, they encircle the throne (God sits between the cherubs; see Ps. 99:1). The fourth is "like a flying eagle," no doubt because of its eagle face, and as a cherub, it hovers over God on His throne.

We have noted a number of similarities between Revelation and the record of Solomon's life, and here is no exception. In 1 Kings 7:7, Solomon builds a portico of judgment where he places his throne for judgment. This portico is part of his palace, distinct from the temple. This permitted Solomon to represent God as king and judge, since he could not enter the Holy of Holies like the high priest could. This also serves as an indicator that God is not limited to sitting upon His throne in the Holy of Holies. When He deems fit, He employs a portable throne, as in Ezekiel 1

---

[53] "[Isaiah] was permitted to gaze within, upon the holy of holies, where even the prophet's feet might not enter. There rose up before him a vision of Jehovah sitting upon a throne high and lifted up, while the train of His glory filled the temple. On each side of the throne hovered the seraphim, their faces veiled in adoration, as they ministered before their Maker and united in the solemn invocation, 'Holy, holy, holy, is the Lord of hosts: the whole earth is full of His glory'" (White, *PK*, p. 307).

and Psalm 18:10. Like the throne in the Holy of Holies, Solomon's was elevated, being ascended by 6 steps.

What has Solomon's throne of judgment to do with the animal-like descriptions of the angelic beings in Revelation 4:7? Beside each armrest of the throne of judgment stood a lion, with an additional 2 lions on each step (see 1 Kings 10:19, 20). The fact that they are *standing*, not sitting or lying down, confirms that the throne is   for *judgment*. The concept of *standing* is prominent in the book of Daniel (the companion to the present work, *THE STAND: Jesus in the Book of Daniel*, persuasively brings out the connection between standing and judgment).

There is further evidence linking the lion to judgment. As God announces judgment upon the nations, He is described as "roaring" from the heavenly sanctuary and as a lion leaving its lair. In Joel 1:6, God describes the nation He sends in judgment against His people as a lion. In Amos 3:14, He states that He will *visit* the rebellious deeds of Israel upon him.[54] He describes this judgment as a lion roaring in the forest, reminding them that they are to fear when the lion roars. His people will be rescued, yet as pieces of a maimed animal out of the mouth of the lion (see Amos 3:4, 8, 12). When the end-time judgment commences, Jesus roars like a lion, for He is the Lion from the tribe of Judah, the Lawgiver (see Rev. 10:3; 5:5; Gen. 49:9, 10).

Concerning the second living creature, the calf, let us return to the throne of judgment in 1 Kings 10:19. The Hebrew text in use today is pointed with vowels indicating that the throne has a round top. At the time of the Septuagint translation, the Hebrew text was written with only consonants, with no vowel pointings provided. The translators read the text understanding different vowels, thus the Septuagint indicates that there is a calf's head behind the throne.[55] While this does not definitively establish the calf in connection with the throne of judgment, it certainly

---

[54] In the Bible, God visits *judgment* upon people (see Exod. 32:24; Jer. 6:15; 14:10; 23:2; 50:31).

[55] The RSV translates "calf's head," and the ESV notes the alternative reading of "calf's head."

suggests that we search further in Scripture to see what other evidence may exist to connect the calf with judgment.

We meet with the calf also in the annual Day of Atonement. In order to come into the sanctuary, Aaron was to have a young bull ("calf" in Greek) whose blood was for himself (see Lev. 16:3, 6, 11). All earthly priests were sinful and needed atonement for themselves before they could represent the true High Priest, Jesus. Of course, Jesus does not need any atonement for His own sinless life, yet we can understand this calf as representing His own self-sacrifice at Calvary, for He voluntarily came from heaven to be our substitute and surety. Hence, the calf links Jesus' atoning self-sacrifice to the *application* of that blood right now during the judgment, the end-time day of atonement.

Finally, we read in 1 Kings 7:27–39 about the 10 bases and lavers prepared for Solomon's temple. The 10 bronze bases were adorned with lions, oxen, and cherubs, and each of these bases was portable, having 4 wheels. These lavers match well with God's portable throne, for it is supported by 4 cherubs (with faces of cherubs, lions, oxen, and eagles), each of whom has a wheel beside it (see Ezek. 1:15).

As for the living creature with a man's face, we discover in the Holy of Holies of Ezekiel's temple an alternating pattern of cherubs and palm trees. The cherubs have the face of a man toward one palm tree, the face of a young lion toward the other palm tree (see Ezek. 41:18, 19). This union of lion (representing Jesus as Judge) and man (Jesus took our nature and became sin for us; see 2 Cor. 5:21) finds perfect fulfillment in Jesus as the divine Mediator.

As for the eagle, Revelation itself provides the explanation. To protect His faithful people from the wrath of the serpent (Satan) during the 1,260 years of papal persecution, God transports His people into the wilderness with 2 wings of an eagle (see Rev. 12:14). This draws upon Exodus 19:4, in which *Yahweh* tells Moses that He bore His people on eagle's wings out of Egypt and brought them to Himself at Sinai, where He declared the law of liberty (see James 1:25; 2:12). Thus, the eagle represents God's deliverance—ultimately from sin via His everlasting covenant.

The 4 living creatures present a brief outline of the plan of salvation: the lion points us to God's judgment (the final phase of atonement); the calf points us to Jesus' self-sacrifice (the first phase of atonement); the living creature with a man's face points to Jesus as the divine Mediator on behalf of fallen humanity; the flying eagle points to the goal of God's perfect atonement: deliverance from sin and restoration unto Himself. Table 2 summarizes the significance of each of the 4 living creatures:

Table 2: Relation of the 4 Living Creatures to God's Work of Atonement

CREATURE	SCRIPTURE	SYNOPSIS	RELATION TO ATONEMENT
Lion	1 Kings 7:7; 10:19	Lions standing at each armrest of Solomon's throne of judgment.	Atoning judgment: Jesus is Judge.
	Amos 1:2; Rev. 5:5; 10:3; Gen. 49:9, 10	Judgment commences: Jesus roars from Zion as Lion of tribe of Judah, the Lawgiver.	
Calf	2 Cor. 5:21; Lev. 16:3	Jesus became sin for us. Calf's blood for high priest on Day of Atonement.	Atoning sacrifice: Jesus is substitute and surety.
	1 Kings 10:19	Calf's head (LXX) behind Solomon's judgment throne.	
	1 Kings 7:27–39; Ezek. 1:15	Laver bases match details of God's portable throne of judgment.	
Face of man	Ezek. 41:18, 19	Holy of Holies in Ezekiel's temple: cherubs with face of man and young lion.	Jesus is Judge (lion) and man—the divine Mediator.
Eagle in flight	Exod. 19:4	Eagles' wings delivered Israel from Egypt and brought them to God.	Atonement results in deliverance, restoration to God.
	Rev. 12:14	God delivered Waldenses from papal persecution during 1,260 years.	

Why do these 4 seraphim have 6 wings apiece? Their total number of wings is a perfect complement to their angelic counterparts, the 24 elders.

The seraphim outline the phases of God's atonement in our lives, while the 24 elders sit in judgment to confirm this work.

Some people reason that since mankind is sinful and was created on the sixth day, the number 6 signifies imperfection. Such reasoning misses the painfully obvious fact that humanity was created perfect on the sixth day of creation week, after which God declared His creation "very good" (Gen. 1:31).

In fact, 6 is a number of *perfection*. Let there be no misunderstanding: 7 is the number of perfection of things *divine*, as, for example, God and His seventh-day Sabbath; 6 is the number of perfection of things *created*. If it sounds weird to make a distinction between types of perfection, consider the words of Jesus in His sermon on the mount: "Therefore you will be perfect, just as your Father who is in the heavens is perfect" (Matt. 5:48). Consider the following explanation of this text:

> Man is to be perfect in his sphere, even as God is perfect in His sphere. How can such a lofty standard be reached? The required perfection is based on the perfection of Christ, "who of God is made unto us wisdom, and righteousness, and sanctification, and redemption." He gave the command requiring perfection, He who was by birth a human being, though allied to divinity. He has passed over the road we are to tread, and He says, "Without Me ye can do nothing." But with Him we can do everything. Thus a perfect character can be obtained. God never issues a command without furnishing the grace sufficient for its fulfillment. Ample provision has been made that man shall be a partaker of the divine nature. (White, *ST*, July 26, 1899)

The idea that 6 is a number of perfection for created beings runs contrary to nearly every scholar today, regardless of religious affiliation. This idea comes to the fore in discussions of the number 666, with many today positing that 666 represents "triple imperfection," a vague notion with no scriptural support. On the other hand, 6 as a number of perfection is by no means a view original with the present author. In fact, ancient pagan mathematicians as far back as Pythagoras (died circa 495 BC) held that 6 was the number of perfection. So also did early church notables Origen and Methodius, the eminent Catholic Church father Augustine, and the so-called Venerable Bede, whose comment on Revelation 13:18 reads, "Who is ignorant, that the number six, in accordance with which the world was created, signifies the perfection of work?" The great Protestant Reformer Martin Luther (commenting on Psalm 85:10) also states 6 to be the number of perfection (de Kock, *The Truth About 666 and the Story of the Great Apostasy*, vol. 3, pp. 140, 212–214). The Geneva Bible study notes (available on any freely downloadable Bible software) for Revelation 13:18 refer to the number 6 as "a number perfect."

Even nature itself attests to the perfection of the number 6. Perhaps the best example is found in the honeybee's perfectly engineered honeycombs, composed of hexagons. The six-sided hexagon provides the best area-to-perimeter ratio when tiling shapes, as well as structural soundness (e.g., one can tile squares, but the structural soundness is far inferior).

We have already noted that being full of eyes signifies that the living creatures are full of the Holy Spirit. Commensurate with this, they take note of every event in the lives of candidates for heaven, nothing escaping their notice (see 2 Chron. 16:9; Zech. 4:10). In praising *"Yahweh*, God of hosts," they invoke His covenant name, suggesting that their job, under the direction of the Most High, is to fulfill the everlasting covenant—to perfect Christian character—in the lives of those who will one day enter the heavenly city. Their activity will be most marked in the closing days of earth's history, for Isaiah 6:3 records their song as "Holy, holy, holy is *Yahweh* of hosts—the whole earth is full of His glory." The fulfillment of these words occurs when the final message of mercy is lived out by God's holy people—i.e., the everlasting covenant is fulfilled in their lives—just prior to Jesus' return (see Rev. 18:1).

These 4 living creatures "have no cessation" in their song of praise. Cessation is the root idea in the Hebrew word "Sabbath," and the Greek word employed here is a variant of the word the Septuagint uses in

Genesis 2:3 when God "ceased" or "rested" after instituting the Sabbath. We have noted before that not only are the 10 Commandments the covenant (see Exod. 34:28; Deut. 4:13; 1 Kings 8:9, 21), but as the crowning mark of the law, the Sabbath commandment is the only commandment given the same designation of "everlasting covenant" (see Exod. 31:16, 17). Thus, these seraphim, who depict the outworking of the everlasting covenant among God's people during the end-time judgment, speak "unceasingly" about the God of the everlasting covenant—the Lord of the Sabbath. As the remainder of Revelation will make clear, sacred Sabbath observance will be the badge of the faithful remnant in the last days.

The acclamation that closes Revelation 4 acknowledges God as *Creator*. Notice how perfectly such praise dovetails with the foregoing discussion of cessation and the Sabbath:

> Exod. 20:8–11: Remember the Sabbath day, to keep it holy. Six days you will labor and do all of your work, but the seventh day is the Sabbath of *Yahweh* your God. You will not do any work— you, your son, your daughter, your servant, your maidservant, your livestock, nor your sojourner who is within your gates. For 6 days, *Yahweh* made the heavens, the earth, the sea, and every- thing which is in them, but He rested upon the seventh day. Therefore *Yahweh* blessed the Sabbath day, and made it holy.

God is worthy of our worship as our *Creator*. When we keep holy His weekly Sabbath, we honor Him as our Creator. The Sabbath command- ment as recorded in Deuteronomy 5:12–15 adds the additional reason that He is worthy of worship because He is our Redeemer; in saving us from sin, he is our *re-Creator*. This ties the Sabbath to the introduction to the entire Decalogue, which cites redemption as the basis of observing God's law: "I am *Yahweh* your God who brought you out from the land of Egypt, from the house of enslavement" (Exod. 20:2; Deut. 5:6). The 10 Com- mandments generally, and the Sabbath particularly, are to be kept because of redemption from slavery to sin. The 10 Commandments generally, and the Sabbath particularly, are the everlasting covenant. Thus, in working out this covenant in one's life, God is working out *deliverance from sin*, resulting in a life that continuously chooses to keep all 10 Commandments, including that most controverted of all—the seventh-day Sabbath.

The Scroll

The scene in the throne room continues with the addition of a scroll sealed with 7 seals. The reader is to anticipate that Jesus is the one to unseal it, as He has the keys of death and the grave (see Rev. 1:18), as well as the key of David (see 3:7), opening that which no one will shut. What might the scroll contain? Consider the following:

1. Since Jesus has the keys of death and the grave, there is a hint that the scroll contains the names of those who have died. Reference to Isaiah 22:15–25 showed that the key of David imagery pointed to the transition from Satan as prince of this world to Jesus at the conclusion of the judgment. Thus, there is a hint that the scroll provides the information necessary to distinguish the dead as either followers of Jesus or Satan. In support of this, the structure of Revelation links the sealed scroll of Revelation 5 with the scrolls that are opened along with the scroll of life in the judgment of the wicked in Revelation 20:12. Hence, the scroll can be seen to contain all of life's choices that reveal whether one is ultimately saved or lost.[56] As the scrolls of Revelation 20:12 are opened just before executive judgment is poured out on the wicked, so the scroll in Revelation 5 is opened just before the end-time investigative judgment commences.

---

[56] "Thus the Jewish leaders made their choice. Their decision was registered in the book which John saw in the hand of Him that sat upon the throne, the book which no man could open. In all its vindictiveness this decision will appear before them in the day when this book is unsealed by the Lion of the tribe of Judah" (White, *COL*, p. 294).

2.   It is written "within and without," i.e., on both sides. The
     ark in which the 10 Commandments were housed was over-
     laid with gold "within and without" (Exod. 25:11). Further,
     the tables of the testimony were written on both sides with
     the finger of God (see 32:15). The scroll of Revelation 5 is
     sealed, just as the 10 Commandments are sealed with the
     seventh-day Sabbath of the fourth commandment. Rev-
     elation centers around the Day of Atonement—the judg-
     ment—the basis of which is the 10 Commandments (see
     Eccl. 12:13, 14).

3.   In connection with the foregoing, the 10 Commandments
     are referred to as a flying scroll written on both sides (see
     Zech. 5:1–3). The dimensions given by Zechariah corre-
     spond to the dimensions of the porch of Solomon's temple
     (see 1 Kings 6:3). Comparison with Solomon's coronation
     in 1 Chronicles 23–29, specifically 28:11–19, reveals that
     Solomon was given the plans for building the house of God.
     As Table 3 makes clear, Solomon's coronation typifies in
     many details the activity in Revelation 4 and 5, so we infer
     that the scroll has to do with building up God's house, His
     temple, the focal point of the end-time judgment.

4.   The book of Daniel was commanded to be sealed until the
     end time (see Dan. 12:4), so there is a hint that the scroll
     represents the book of Daniel.[57] Of course, Daniel focuses

---

[57] "In the Revelation, the Lion of the tribe of Judah [allusion to Rev. 5:5] has opened to the stu-
dents of prophecy the book of Daniel, and thus is Daniel standing in his place" (White, *1MR*, p. 47).

    "Daniel has been standing in his lot since the seal was removed and the light of truth has been
shining upon his visions. He stands in his lot, bearing the testimony which was to be understood at the
end of the days" (White, *1SAT*, p. 226).

    "It was the Lion of the tribe of Judah who unsealed the book and gave to John the revelation of
what should be in these last days. Daniel stood in his lot to bear his testimony, which was sealed until
the time of the end …

    "The book of Daniel is unsealed in the revelation to John, and carries us forward to the last
scenes of this earth's history" (White, *18MR*, p. 15).

on standing in the judgment, chapters 8–12 focusing especially on Jesus' work in the heavenly Holy of Holies during the end-time judgment.

5. At the coronation of 7-year old Joash, he was given the crown and testimony, i.e., a copy of the Torah, as all kings were commanded to write out upon inauguration and study all the days of their lives (see Deut. 17:18–20). After receiving these, he was made king and anointed (see 2 Kings 11:12). Comparison with Revelation 11:15–19 shows that Jesus is called both Anointed and King (i.e., anointed as king) at the *beginning of the end-time judgment.* Some see Revelation 5 as describing Jesus' anointing following His ascension in AD 31, but let it not be forgotten that He was then installed as *High Priest* to begin His work in the Holy Place, and then sat down to await the time when he would eventually receive His kingdom (see Ps. 110:1). In Revelation 5, Jesus is received as *King,* awaiting the time when the number of His subjects—His bride—is entirely made up, i.e., the end-of-the-judgment wedding. He does not sit, but stands, as does the high priest in the Holy of Holies on the Day of Atonement (see Lev. 16:15,16).

No one was found worthy to look into (i.e., perceive and understand) its contents. Those in heaven are angelic beings who have not fallen by sin. Those *upon* the earth are people *alive*, and those *under* the earth have *died*. In other words, no created being anywhere is able to open or examine this scroll. Thus, only one who is divine—Jesus—can do so. To this end, we have another proof that Jesus is fully God, contra groups such as Jehovah's Witnesses who maintain Jesus is a lesser, created god. If any created being attempted to look into the scroll, it would be a presumptuous act of self-worship, and hence, idolatry (compare Exod. 20:4–6). The book of Revelation rails against idolatry, so it is important to note this allusion. Of further interest is that an allusion to Sabbath worship—the positive counterpart to idolatry (see Lev. 26:1, 2)—appears at the close of Revelation 5 (see verse 13).

The Lion and Lamb

Why does John begin weeping when no one worthy is found to open the scroll? He recognizes that unless someone *is* found, the plan of salvation is frustrated and all hope is lost. As noted earlier, the 24 elders are angels who sit in judgment, so how appropriate, then, that one of them assures John that the Lion from the tribe of Judah will open the scroll and its seals. Of course, our study of Revelation 4 has informed us that the Lion is none other than God as Judge.

John turns and sees, not the Lion, but a Lamb. Why does the Judge appear as a Lamb standing before the throne? He stands, looking anything but a conqueror, for it appears as though He is in the very act of pouring out His blood. The imagery points back to Isaiah's prophecy: "He was sorely tried, and He was afflicted, yet He would not open His mouth. Like a lamb being led to the slaughter, as a ewe before her shearers is mute, so He would not open His mouth" (Isa. 53:7). Some maintain that this pictures Jesus at the ascension, when His sacrifice was fresh on everyone's mind, but this would be rather curious, since He *sat down* at that time (Psalm 110:1). However, when we consider events in light of the sanctuary service, a much different solution presents itself: as High Priest, Jesus would *stand* before the throne of God on the Day of Atonement, pleading His own shed blood 7 times (see Lev. 16:14, 15). Therefore, here in Revelation 5, the slaughtered Lamb *stands* before the throne, vividly presenting His shed blood. In 6:1–8:1, the 7 seals are opened, culminating in the sealing of God's people. Jesus' blood finally achieves *full* efficacy in their lives, enabling *them* to stand, no longer indulging sin, and thus fully protected when the 7 last plagues fall upon a guilty world.

In verse 6, "Christ is our Mediator and officiating High Priest in the presence of the Father. He was shown to John as a Lamb that had been slain, as in the very act of pouring out His blood in the sinner's behalf" (White, *4T*, p. 395). At the commencement of the end time in 1798, one of the heads of the beast of Revelation 13:3 looked as though *it* had been slaughtered unto death—language *identical* to that describing the Lamb in Revelation 5:6. With the papacy nearly fatally wounded at the finish of its 1,260 years as a false high priest, Jesus could safely wind down His ministration in the Holy Place and move to the Holy of Holies 46 years later to begin the end-time judgment.

We can also connect the Lamb's stance in verse 6 with the start of the judgment hour from another point of view: Jesus stands 7 times in Revelation, always in connection with judgment. We already saw Him standing during the time period of Laodicea, the church of the judgment hour, in Revelation 3:20, knocking to secure entrance to the hearts of believers. Jesus' 7 stances in Revelation form a chiasm, and the chiastic match to verse 6 is Revelation 14:1, in which Jesus as the Lamb stands on Mount Zion with the 144,000, who are *sealed* at the *conclusion* of the pre-advent judgment. We conclude that here in verse 6, Jesus is standing just prior to the opening of the *seals*, at the *beginning* of the pre-advent judgment. If we cooperate with Jesus' work in us during the end-time judgment, we can be among those who stand with Him upon Mount Zion, sealed and victorious over sin by virtue of His perfect atoning sacrifice applied to our lives during the judgment.

The Lamb has 7 horns, showing He has all strength to judge and save (see 1 Sam. 2:10; Ps. 18:2), as well as 7 eyes, showing He has all understanding (see Eph. 1:18; Dan. 4:34; Jer. 5:21). These eyes are the 7 Spirits of God, identified as "the eyes of *Yahweh*, going throughout the entire earth" (Zech. 4:10). "Not by might, nor by power, but by my Spirit" (v. 6) has the Lamb conquered. The divine strength represented by the Lamb's 7 horns is identical with the fullness of the Spirit of God that He possesses (see John 3:34). It is this strength He longs to give each one of us, and those who stand when His work of atonement/judgment is complete will likewise stand in *His* strength, full of the Holy Spirit.

The New Song

Once the Lamb takes the scroll from the Father, the 4 living creatures and 24 elders fall down as a group. They have harps, associated with the indwelling of God's Spirit (see Rev. 14:1–3; 1 Sam. 10:5, 6; 16:23). Further, they have golden bowls full of the prayers of the holy people. This is another indicator that Revelation 4 and 5 refer to the end-time judgment, for as our study of Revelation 6:9–11 will show, the holy people cry out during the Dark Ages (the 1,260 years—AD 538–1798) "How long, *Adonai*, Holy and True, do You not judge and vindicate our blood?" And it is during the sixth seal in verses 12–17 that Jesus is able to fully vindicate them. The prayers cannot be answered immediately at the close of the 1,260 years, but their fulfillment must be delayed a "time longer."

Exactly "how long, *Adonai*," must they wait? This question hearkens back to the identical question in Daniel 8:13, to which the answer comes, "Until 2,300 evening-mornings [elapse]—then the sanctuary will be restored to its righteous condition" (v. 14). The 2,300 days ended October 22, 1844, when the end-time judgment commenced.

However, a full answer to the martyrs' plea was not granted at the *beginning* of the end-time judgment; rather, according to Revelation 6:11, vindication will come once the full number of martyrs is reached. There will continue to be martyrs until the servants of the living God are sealed with the seal in their foreheads (see 7:1–8), i.e., until probation closes. At that time, God fully vindicates and avenges His people, pouring wrath upon the wicked from 7 golden bowls (see 15:7). God's judgment is perfect. Angels hold golden bowls containing the pleas of His martyrs (see 5:8) at the beginning of the pre-advent judgment; angels pour judgment upon the wicked at the close of the pre-advent judgment from these same golden bowls.

In verse 9, we learn that "they were singing a new song." To whom does "they" refer? The *Textus Receptus* (the Greek text behind the KJV) has the *redeemed* singing throughout, while the critical text (the Greek text underlying most modern translations) has the 4 living creatures and 24 elders singing *about* the redeemed throughout. In the Byzantine (Majority) text, the voices of the holy people *join antiphonally with* the 4 living creatures and 24 elders. The 4 living creatures and 24 elders lead out in praising the Lamb for His atoning sacrifice, then the prayers of the holy people join in, acknowledging their redemption, then the 4 living creatures and 24 elders (who hold the prayers of the redeemed, see verse 8) join back in seamlessly, acknowledging that the redeemed are made priests and kings who will reign on the earth (see 20:4–6).

Lest anyone object that the angels of heaven cannot sing jointly with the redeemed who are still on earth, observe that Revelation 14:1–3 pictures the 144,000, who are still on earth as the final battle of Revelation 13 rages around them, as though already in heaven, singing a "new song." Like the 4 living creatures and 24 elders of 5:8, the 144,000 also have harps and sing a new song. Further, they are identified as redeemed, just as in verse 9. This joint singing of angels and redeemed in verses 9 and 10 shows that Jesus' work in the end-time judgment brings the lives of the redeemed into perfect harmony with heaven.

In verse 9, the holy people sing about being redeemed out of "every tribe, tongue, people, and nation." These terms appear in this order in the genealogies of Ham,[58] from whom came Babylon, and Shem, from whom came the nation of Israel (see Gen. 10:20, 31). In other words, the redeemed come not just from Israel, but *all* peoples. Further, when directed to leave Haran, Abram was told to leave his land, relatives, and father's house (see 12:1). Hence, the new song of Revelation 5:9 indicates that God's true people have been delivered from all earthly ties, and their allegiance is solely to *Yahweh*. Indeed, Jesus accomplishes a *complete* surrender in the hearts of true believers in the end-time judgment, confirmed by the song of deliverance sung in Revelation 14:3 and 15:3–4.

---

[58] Actually, the third term "people" is replaced by "their lands," but these terms are synonymous (see Deut. 32:43; Mal. 3:12).

Just before John describes the rest of the heavenly host singing, he observes that the number of angels about the throne is "myriads of myriads, thousands upon thousands." This description matches the opening of the end-time judgment in Daniel 7:10.

At this point, it is helpful to compare Solomon's second coronation with Revelation 5. See Table 3:

Table 3: Comparison of Solomon's Second Coronation and Revelation 5

SOLOMON'S SECOND CORONATION	REVELATION 5: JESUS' SECOND CORONATION
1 Chron. 28:2: David had planned to build house of rest for the ark of the covenant of *Yahweh*.	Rev. 5:1–7: The scroll contains plans for God's house, wherein is the ark of the covenant.
1 Chron. 28:9: God examines all hearts.	Rev. 5:6: Lamb has 7 eyes → searches hearts (see Zech. 4:10).
1 Chron. 28:11, 12: David gives son Solomon plans written under inspiration of Spirit.	Rev. 5:1, 6: Father gives Lamb scroll. Lamb has 7 spirits of God.
1 Chron. 29:20: All prostrate themselves before *Yahweh* and king.	Rev. 5:8, 13: All creatures prostrate themselves before One on throne (Father) and Lamb.
1 Chron. 29:22: Solomon made king second time.	Rev. 5:7–13: Lamb takes scroll. (2 King 11:12: Joash receives Testimony → made king, anointed)
1 Chron. 29:22: Solomon *anointed* king, Zadok *anointed* high priest.	Rev. 11:15, 17, 18: Jesus *anointed* when He receives kingdom and begins to judge.
1 Chron. 29:23: Solomon sits on throne as king *in place of father who is still alive*.	Rev. 5:8, 13: Jesus' reign begins while Father is still on throne (see Rev. 11:15, 17).
1 Chron. 29:24: Rulers, strong men, and David's sons give hand in support of Solomon.	Rev. 5:11, 12: Angels, living creatures, and 24 elders say Lamb is worthy.
1 Chron. 29:25: *Yahweh* exalts Solomon before eyes of all Israel.	Rev. 5:13: All creatures ascribe praise to the Lamb.

Every *creature*, whether in heaven, earth, under the earth, or upon the sea, gives praise to the Lamb. This language draws on the second commandment, which forbids the worship of created images (see Exod. 20:4–6). Hence, Jesus is divine; He is not *created* in God's image, but as His Son is a perfect reflection of His glory, the exact likeness of His being, for He *is* God (see Heb. 1:1–3; John 1:1–3).

Revelation 4 ended with the heavenly beings ascribing worship to God as Creator, an allusion to the fourth commandment enjoining Sabbath worship (see Exod. 20:8–11). Chapter 5 closes with creatures worshipping the slaughtered Lamb, just as the Sabbath Commandment commands worship of the Deliverer (see Deut. 5:12–15). Hence, Revelation simultaneously upholds the second commandment forbidding worship of created images, as well as the fourth commandment enjoining worship of God as Deliverer.

Seals 1–6

As the Lamb opens the first seal, the first living creature issues the command to "Come!" In response, a white horse comes. It is only fitting that of the 4 living creatures, it is the lion who summons this horse, for this horseman is termed a conqueror and given a crown. Jesus, the Lion of the tribe of Judah, has conquered (see Rev. 5:5) and been given the royal scroll.

It is evident that the crown granted confirms the early church's victory in the battle with sin (see Rev. 2:10; 3:11). Not only was the early church a conqueror, but it went forth to conquer, i.e., sharing with others the message of repentance and victory over every idol through the indwelling grace of Jesus (see Matt. 3:2; Phil. 4:13).

Scripture tells us that "the weapons of our warfare are not fleshly, but mighty through God to the dismantling of strongholds" of sin in our lives (2 Cor. 10:4). Again, it is "not by might, nor by strength, but by My Spirit" (Zech. 4:6). With that said, why does the first horseman have a bow? In both Hebrew and Greek, the word translated "bow" can signify what is used to shoot arrows, but it is *also* used for the bow in the cloud, i.e., the rainbow. The latter is in view here, for this horseman has only a bow, no arrows. It is the bow of promise, the sign of God's everlasting covenant as given to Noah (see Gen. 9:13, 16). Further, God tells us not to put our trust in horses and chariots (see Isa. 31:1), so the pure white horse points to the heavenly forces that God sent to fight on behalf of the early church, and which He will send us as well if we choose to cooperate with Him (see 2 Kings 2:12; 6:15–17).

This horseman, representing the church in its youth, was mighty because of its connection with God. With its gospel uncorrupted by Greek philosophy and worldly compromise, it went forth holding aloft the bow of promise, conquering sin and winning souls for Jesus.

Upon opening the second seal, the second living creature, the calf, commands a fiery red horse to come forth. Most versions translate "red," which might suggest bloodshed or martyrdom. In the context of the second seal, the dagger does in one sense represent persecution, and one might even suggest that "fiery" represents the "fires of persecution," hence bloodshed. However, what lay back of the persecution?

It is important to recognize that the once-pure gospel message was being consumed with the stubble of human speculation and false philosophy mixed with truth. Early on in church history, the effects of Greek, Platonic philosophy began corrupting the biblical message. Platonic thinking influenced first-century Philo, who in turn influenced Clement and Origen. Origen propounded the allegorical interpretation of Scripture, which shies away from the plain reading of Scripture in favor of a deeper, "spiritual" meaning. Among the specious errors resulting from this method of studying Scripture are the following:

1. Origen denied biblical statements concerning creation week and the fall.

2. Commenting on the Gospel of John, Origen stated, "Scripture contains many contradictions, and many statements which are not literally true, but must be read spiritually and mystically."

3. Regarding Jesus' entry into Jerusalem, Origen states, "Jesus is the word of God which goes into the soul that is called Jerusalem," "the ass and the foal are the old and the new Scriptures, on which the Word of God rides," etc. (Froom, *PFF1*, pp. 316, 317).

Such nonsense might be laughed off, except that Origen's method of tri-level interpretation (literal, moral, and mystical) came to dominate preaching in the Roman Church for a millennium. As de Kock convincingly documents, Origen molded his pupil Eusebius, who in turn appears to have influenced the most celebrated Roman Catholic Church father, Augustine (see de Kock, *The Use and Abuse of Prophecy*, pp. 14–17). As indebted as the Roman Church is to Augustine, it is no wonder that its teachings are so tragically mired in error.

This horseman is given a great dagger, the Greek word for dagger being the same as found in Ephesians 6:17, referring to the Word of God as the dagger of the Spirit. Hence, the great dagger that this horseman wields is primarily a counterfeit Word of God. Rather than focusing the attention of the unconverted multitudes on the slaughtered Lamb of Revelation 5:6, *wooing* them by His great love for them revealed in His (true) Word, churchmen wrested the Scriptures, employing literal force of arms to "compel them to come in" (Luke 14:23), grossly misinterpreting Jesus' words that He "came not to bring peace, but a dagger" (Matt. 10:34). This points especially to the time of Constantine (see comments regarding the church of Pergamos in Revelation 2:12–17). Constantine brought about that great union of church and state, in which the church employed the strong arm of the state to force people's consciences.

It is a sad commentary that the church, the apple of God's eye, was the very entity to take peace from the earth. The compromise during the period of Pergamos allowed all manner of idolatry to enter the church, and the allegorical method of interpretation could justify it all, as the method permits Scripture to be interpreted any way that suits the interpreter. It is entirely fitting that the calf-like living creature summons this horse, for the false worship promoted by the burgeoning false church corresponds well to the Israelites' false worship of the golden calf at Horeb, Jeroboam's idolatrous 2 golden calves at Dan and Bethel, and Jezebel's introduction of Baal (calf) worship to Israel (see Exod. 32:15–24; 1 Kings 12:26–33; 16:31–33).

The opening of the third seal reveals a black horse. The contrast with the initial white horse could not be greater; the church is no longer pure.

By this time, the pillars of truth in God's Word have been so thoroughly mixed with error that the pure truth can hardly be discerned. Notable among these, of course, was the move to transfer the Sabbath to Sunday (recall Constantine's edict of AD 321, establishing Sunday as a public festival throughout the Roman Empire). The immortality of the soul was another major error introduced. "The concept of the Innate Immortality of the soul as a 'Christian' doctrine did not appear in patristic literature until toward the close of the second century" (Froom, *CFF1*, pp. 928, 929).

To maintain this impure mixture of error with truth, the church held herself capable of interpreting the Scriptures and withheld its study from the people. The Bread of Life, God's Word, is represented as wheat and barley sold at famine prices,[59] indicating the near impossibility for the average person to study the Word for oneself. With this removal of the Word, it is no wonder that doctrinal errors, however incredible, were foisted upon the people and maintained by the church.

Note that the olive oil and wine were not to be priced unjustly. The wine represents Christ's new covenant via His death (see 1 Cor. 11:25), and the olive oil represents the Holy Spirit (see 1 Sam. 16:13). No matter how great the effort to suppress God's Word, the truth of Jesus' atoning death and the impressions of the Holy Spirit upon those seeking for truth could not be entirely obfuscated.

Note that these items—wheat, barley, olive oil, and wine—were used as payment for the building of Solomon's temple (see 2 Chron. 2:10, 15). All were key to the success of the building project. That the grains are priced beyond reason suggests that completion of God's temple could not be completed at this point in church history, the Dark Ages. On the other hand, that the vintage items are not perverted by the corrupt church means that hope was not lost, but merely delayed. Eventually, God's temple—His sanctuary—would be permitted to move forward to completion. "None can stay His hand" (Dan. 4:35, KJV).

---

[59] A *choinix* was a person's daily portion of grain (ANLEX and BDAG, p. 1086, s.v. χοινιξ); a denarius was a day's wage.

These items also point the reader to a related scriptural theme: Israel's harvest festivals. The firstfruits of the earliest grain, barley, was harvested at the time of the Feast of Unleavened Bread, commencing the 7 Weeks (see Exod. 34:18; 23:15; Lev. 23:6–14). The Feast of Weeks (Pentecost) marked the end of the 7 Weeks, when the firstfruits of wheat were harvested (see Exod. 34:22; 23:16; Lev 23:15–22). Finally, the Feast of Ingathering (Booths) in the fall followed the gathering in of fruit such as olives and grapes (see Exod. 34:22; 23:16; Lev 23:34–43). The fulfillment of these feasts comes in Revelation 14: the 144,000 are the firstfruits of the barley harvest; Jesus reaps the firstfruits of wheat harvest following the proclamation of the 3 angels' messages; the wicked are trampled in the winepress of God's wrath at the second coming.

Since Jesus' work in the heavenly sanctuary could not move into its finishing work in the Holy of Holies during the Dark Ages of Roman Catholic dominance, there was no significant harvest of souls. Nevertheless, the transgressors of God's Word during this period are sure to receive His wrath in the end.

The horseman holds in his hand the balance scale, hearkening back to Daniel 5, in which Belshazzar was weighed in the heavenly balances and found wanting. Judgment is the prerogative of heaven alone, a work to be done by Jesus in the Holy of Holies during the end-time day of atonement. In seeking to usurp Jesus' role as Judge during the time of the third horse, the Roman Church is simply continuing Lucifer's attempt to displace God as Judge in heaven (see Isa. 14:12–14).

The third living creature has the face of a man, representing God's aim to restore His image in mankind as at the beginning (see Gen. 1:26, 27). The irony is that the false church has developed its own man-made, counterfeit system of salvation to ensure that humanity perpetuates the fallen image inherited from Adam (see Gen. 5:3). Satan's aim is for people to put their faith in this earthly system, and hence not be prepared to stand free of the bondage of sin prior to the second coming.

The fourth seal reveals the last of the 4 horses. This particular horse presents a radical contrast: while the horse itself is a vibrant, grass-green color, its rider has the name Death. The horse is usually pictured as a sickly, pale green color ("pale horse," KJV). As footnote 41 points out, Scripture does not support this understanding. Instead, χλωρος is consistently used in the Septuagint and New Testament to refer to healthy green vegetation (chlorophyll-colored). A survey of the other Scriptural uses reveals a number of God's judgments, with devastation so bad that no green vegetation remains.[60]

Scripture regularly describes God's righteous people as trees (see Psalm 92:12–15) or a spreading vine (see Isa. 5:2; Jer. 2:21; 6:9). Even Jesus is described as a tender shoot (see Jer. 23:5; Zech. 3:8; 6:12) and the True Vine (see John 15:1, 5). Hence, Death on the green horse represents the near extinction of righteousness and righteous people at the hands of the Roman Catholic Church as it succeeded to supremacy during the Dark Ages.

Its follower, the Grave, represents the full maturation of the papal apostasy during the Dark Ages. This combination of a green horse, Death, and the Grave is the polar opposite of what we meet in Revelation 19:11 and 14: the white horse, with faithful armies following its Rider Jesus, who is the Life (see John 14:6) and has the keys to unlock death and the grave (see Rev. 1:18). This vivid description is a stark indictment of the Roman Catholic system and is meant to drive us all to seek Jesus and His righteousness.

Why does the horseman have authority to kill the fourth part of the earth? Recall that the horn from insignificance (Rome) arose from 1 of the 4 horns of Hellas, as well as 1 of the 4 winds (see Dan. 8:8, 9). Thus, the horseman (representing Roman Catholicism) has power to devastate that part of earth under his dominion. By contrast, God's 4 angels stand at all 4 corners of the earth, holding back the 4 winds of strife over all the earth (see Rev. 7:1).

---

[60] E.g., Exod. 10:15 (locusts of eighth plague decimated remaining flora); Deut. 29:23 (nothing green remains in the land of those who forsake *Yahweh's* covenant); 2 Kings 19:26 (Sennacherib wiped out peoples as easily as grass and vegetation).

When one recognizes that the fourth seal is an indictment of the Roman Catholic Church of the Dark Ages, one can appreciate the tremendous irony of the fourth horse being summoned by the flying eagle. God once saved His people from the idolatry of Egypt by a flying eagle (see Exod. 19:4), and during the Dark Ages, God used a flying eagle to watch over His faithful people while they were persecuted by spiritual Egypt (see Rev. 12:14). In light of the tens of millions that the Roman Catholic Church martyred (not to mention the souls misled spiritually, who will suffer the second death as a result of her sophistries), it is well to remember that Scripture points to the eagle as a bird of prey as well (see Matt. 24:28).

The agencies employed by Death in verse 8 refer the reader back to Ezekiel 5:17, where these same entities are outlined. A study of Ezekiel 5 confirms that the message of the fourth seal is indeed an indictment against an apostate church. Table 4 outlines the key points of Ezekiel 5:

Table 4: Relation of Ezekiel 5 to Revelation 6:8

REFERENCE	SUMMARY	RELATION TO REVELATION 6:8
Ezek. 5:5, 6	Jerusalem changed God's judgments into wickedness more than Gentiles did.	Roman Catholicism has apostatized from pure gospel more than any others have.
Ezek. 5:7, 8	Jerusalem worse than others → *Adonai Yahweh* will judge her openly.	Roman Catholicism worse than all others, but condemns faithful "heretics" openly.
Ezek. 5:11	Jerusalem defiled earthly sanctuary.	Roman Catholic Church supplants heavenly sanctuary with pagan earthly counterfeit.
Ezek. 5:17	God sends famine, beasts, deadly disease, and bloodshed against Jerusalem.	Satan gives Roman papacy authority to kill "heretics" by any and all means.

The counterfeit church is so corrupt during the time of the fourth seal that God must judge her severely. Her authority over the fourth part of the earth contrasts with the final judgment of the wicked, when all 4 corners of the wicked world are judged and destroyed (see Rev. 20:7–10).

To appreciate the fifth seal, recall that during the Dark Ages, the Roman Catholic Church slaughtered those true to the Word of God, those who held the testimony of the Lamb. These martyrs loved not their lives unto the death, preferring to lay them down rather than sin against God. The blood of these martyrs cries out to Him for vindication like that of Abel (see Gen. 4:10).

The martyrs of verse 10 are crying for judgment on their blood. "How long?" is a plea for judgment (see Ps. 74:10; 82:2; 94:2, 3). Reference to Daniel 8:13–14 shows it to be identical to Gabriel's question, to which Jesus responds that 2,300 evening-mornings are allotted until the heavenly sanctuary will be "restored to its righteous condition." Here in Revelation 6:10, the word translated "vindication" is εκδικεω, a derivative of δικαιοω, which means "make righteous." The holy people recognize that *Adonai*—Jesus—is responsible for vindicating the sacrifice of their lives, so the query "How long?" is a *legal* plea before their Judge. In reply, they are told to "cease for a time longer," i.e., until their cases are settled in the judgment.

Those whose blood cries out for vindication are each given a white robe, indicating that, at the resurrection day, they will walk with Jesus, for they are worthy (see Rev. 3:4). They must *cease* from the cares of this life for a time. This is a most interesting choice of words, for the word αναπαυω shares the same root as the word καταπαυω in Genesis 2:2–3 (Septuagint) to specify that God *ceased* from His creative work on the Sabbath day. The Hebrew word *shabbat* refers to cessation, as well as subsequent refreshment (see Exod. 31:17). These holy people are to cease from their faithful service to God and look forward to the refreshment they will receive when resurrected and gloriously transformed at the second coming of Jesus (see 1 Cor. 15:51–53).

Is it a stretch to assert that dead people are directed to cease, i.e., keep Sabbath? Observe that the wicked sleep in their graves for 1,000 years while the earth lies desolate, during which time Satan is sealed (see Rev. 20:3–6). Our study of Revelation 7 will show that the living God places His seal upon those who faithfully observe the seventh-day Sabbath, so for Satan to receive such a seal means that he is caused to cease (keep Sabbath) from his wicked work for 1,000 years. Likewise, all the wicked dead who sleep in the grave cease from their wicked works; they too will keep Sabbath, as it were. To be sure, Satan and all of the wicked don't keep Sabbath *holy*; they simply *cease* from their wicked course for a "time" (1,000 years). The earth has existed for approximately 6,000 years, so one can see how these 1,000 years serve as a millennial Sabbath (compare Ps. 90:4; 2 Peter 3:8), the antitype to the jubilee land rest of Leviticus 25.

The sixth seal indicates that during the time his servants have been directed to wait, God is working out the answer to their plea. The earthquake and signs in the sun and moon were prophetic signposts that occurred approximately 42 and 18 years before the end time, respectively. The falling of the stars occurred *during* the end time, but 11 years prior to the commencement of the end-time judgment. The final four verses jump to the conclusion of the pre-advent judgment, the second coming of Jesus.

The beginning of the end time was Sabbath, February 10, 1798, the date of the capture of Pope Pius VI by Napoleon's general, Berthier. The prophesied earthquake was the great Lisbon earthquake of 1755, which occurred on Sabbath, November 1. Lisbon "was one of the last centers of the Inquisition. People were still being burned at the stake in 1755 in Lisbon. The house of the Inquisition actually collapsed during the earthquake, and many people, particularly Protestants, saw this as the work of God."[61]

Could there be a more fitting *location* for this judgment than in this hotbed of the Roman Catholic Spanish Inquisition? Could there be a more fitting *time* to begin cataclysmic events leading to the vindication of God's true saints than the Sabbath, this *particular* Sabbath having been designated by the apostate church responsible for their deaths as All

---

[61] Robert Siegel and Mark Molesky, "'This Gulf Of Fire' Examines The Lisbon, Portugal, Earthquake In 1755," Interview, *All Things Considered*, National Public Radio, November 2, 2015, https://1ref.us/138 (accessed June 24, 2018). In the interview, Molesky discusses his book, *This Gulf of Fire—The Destruction of Lisbon, or Apocalypse in the Age of Science and Reason*. The book is all the more credible because he is an associate professor at Seton Hall University—a Roman Catholic institution.

Saints Day? It is regarded as one of the most devastating earthquakes of history, estimated as an 8.7 on the moment magnitude scale (successor to the better known Richter magnitude scale), wiping out a quarter of Lisbon's estimated 250,000 residents.[62] The most cursory Internet search will provide the interested student a wealth of information about this well-documented earthquake.

The sun becoming black as hairy sackcloth and the full moon becoming like blood was prophesied by Old Testament prophets and Jesus alike as a sign of the end (see Amos 8:9; Isa. 13:10; Matt. 24:29). This answers to the Great Dark Day in New England of Friday, May 19, 1780. Reports agree that the darkness began around 10:00 a.m., continuing into the Sabbath evening hours, marking the transition from May 19 to May 20. As the following make clear, this was no mere eclipse; this was *miraculous* darkness:

> The darkness of the following evening was probably as gross as has ever been observed since the Almighty fiat gave birth to light. I could not help conceiving at the time that if every luminous body in the universe had been shrouded in impenetrable darkness, or struck out of existence, the darkness could not have been more complete. A sheet of white paper held within a few inches of the eyes, was equally invisible with the blackest velvet. (Samuel Tenny, *Collections of Massachusetts Historical Society for the Year 1792*, vol. 1, pp. 97, 98, quoted in Smith, *Daniel and the Revelation*, p. 422)

> In the evening ... perhaps it never was darker since the children of Israel left the house of bondage. This gross darkness held till about one o'clock, although the moon had fulled but the day before. (*Boston Gazette*, May 29, 1780, quoted in Smith, *Daniel and the Revelation*, p. 422)

---

[62] "Historic Earthquakes Lisbon, Portugal 1755 November 01 10:16 UTC Magnitude 8.7," United States Geological Survey, https://1ref.us/139 (accessed June 24, 2019).

That the sun should be described as black as hairy sackcloth is very appropriate. During the 1,260 years of the Dark Ages, God's witnesses were described as dressed in sackcloth (see Rev. 11:3). This simple garb was the dress of prophets, e.g., John the Baptist (see Zech. 13:4; Matt. 3:4). Apparently, the martyrs are considered prophets, and their cry for vindication is answered by the sun dressed in prophetic garb.

There is another quite relevant reason for the sun being described as black as hairy sackcloth. The Greek word τρίχινος ("hairy") appears elsewhere only in Exodus 26:7 and Zechariah 13:4. Of interest here is Exodus 26:7 (Septuagint), which states that the wilderness sanctuary was covered with "hairy skins," the Greek rendering of the underlying Hebrew "goat [skins]." During the 1,260 years of papal supremacy, the heavenly sanctuary was lost sight of, and Roman Catholicism developed an elaborate earthly counterfeit, with human priests claiming the right to forgive sins and a re-enactment of Christ's death (the so-called "unbloody sacrifice"[63]) at every mass. To be sure, an eyewitness on May 19, 1780 would likely not immediately think of the wilderness sanctuary, but its *description* in Revelation 6:12 is meant to lead the historicist student (one who studies the fulfillment of prophecy in history) to recognize the connection. Just as the papacy had masked the truth of the heavenly sanctuary and elevated the sun as an object of worship by transplanting God's Sabbath with the pagan day of the sun, so in 1755, as the end time drew near, God masked the pagan object of worship, the sun, with a reminder that the truths of salvation being worked out in his heavenly sanctuary had long been covered in darkness.

The third sign was the falling of the stars. Some sources report that this occurred 3 successive nights, beginning November 10/11, 1833, but all agree that the astronomical display of November 12/13 was the most spectacular ever witnessed in recorded history. Contemporary scientist Denison Olmsted reports:

---

[63] "Why is the Mass called the 'unbloody' sacrifice of our Lord on his cross?", Catholic Answers, https://1ref.us/13a (accessed June 24, 2019).

After collecting and collating the accounts given in all the periodicals of the country, and also in numerous letters addressed either to my scientific friends or to myself, the following appeared to be the *leading facts* attending the phenomenon. The shower pervaded nearly the whole of North America, having appeared in nearly equal splendor from the British possessions on the north, to the West India Islands and Mexico on the south, and from sixty-one degrees of longitude east of the American coast, quite to the Pacific Ocean on the west. Throughout this immense region, the duration was nearly the same. The meteors began to attract attention by their unusual frequency and brilliancy, from *nine to twelve o'clock* in the evening; were most striking in their appearance from *two to five*; arrived at their maximum, in many places, about *four* o'clock; and continued until rendered invisible by the light of day. (Olmsted, *The Mechanism of the Heavens*, pp. 327, 328)

Another contemporary comments on the aptness of the prophetic description concerning this event:

The stars fell "even as a fig tree casteth her untimely figs, when she is shaken of a mighty wind." Here is the exactness of the prophet. The falling stars did not come, as if from several trees shaken, but from *one:* those which appeared in the east fell toward the east; those which appeared in the north fell toward the north; those which appeared in the west fell toward the west; and those which appeared in the south (for I went out of my residence into the park), fell toward the south; and they fell, not as *ripe* fruit falls. Far from it. But they flew, they were *cast*, like the unripe fruit, which at first refuses to leave the branch; and, when it does break its hold, flies swiftly, *straight off*, descending; and in the multitude falling, some cross the track of others, as they are thrown with more or less force. (*New York Journal of Commerce,*

Nov. 14, 1833, vol. 8, no. 534, p. 2, quoted in Smith, *Daniel and the Revelation*, p. 422)

Numerous accounts report that people of the day felt certain that the day of judgment had arrived, based on Revelation 6:13. Uriah Smith records many more firsthand accounts of this meteoric shower (see *The Daniel and the Revelation*, pp. 422–425).

The description of verse 14 is ironic, for it is to be remembered that throughout Revelation 6, the Lamb has been unsealing the scroll, which He took in 5:7. Now the striking revelation of Himself is itself described as a scroll being rolled up. This marks the time of the seventh plague, for "every mountain and island were moved out of their places," just as "every island disappeared; likewise, the mountains were not found" (Rev. 16:20). Having completed His work of atonement in the Holy of Holies, having fulfilled the everlasting covenant, Jesus comes at midnight to consummate His marriage. He arrives just at the time the wicked plan to eradicate His bride from the earth. Those who cower before the face of the Lamb in verses 15–17 are the wicked who have recently gathered for the battle of Har Megiddon in the sixth plague and will very soon be destroyed by the sword of Jesus at the second coming (see Rev 16:12–16; 19:15, 21).

In most translations, the wicked cry out concerning the "wrath of the Lamb." We must be careful, for Revelation employs two different Greek words that are commonly translated "wrath": θυμος refers to God's "intolerance for sin," used of the 7 last plagues (see 15:1); οργη might better be translated "retribution," referring to the final, irreversible judgment awaiting the obstinate sinner, i.e., death (see John 3:36). The arrival of Jesus during the sixth seal occurs at the conclusion of the 7 last plagues. Nothing awaits the sinner but terminal "retribution."

The cry for the mountains and rocks to fall on the wicked hearkens back to Isaiah 2:19, in which the wicked go into rocks and caves, fleeing from the glory of *Yahweh* when He shakes the earth. The whole of Isaiah 2 makes clear that these people have clung to idols, which *Yahweh* destroys. Throughout Revelation, the Sabbath of the fourth commandment appears in tandem with the second commandment forbidding idolatry. In this section dealing with the seals, the cry of the wicked, indicating their idolatry, is preceded and followed by Sabbath references: the fifth seal made allusion to the Sabbath when the righteous martyrs were told to cease for a time longer, and there is a most striking connection between the Sabbath and the seal of the living God in Revelation 7:1–8.

The sixth seal closes with the agonizing cry of the wicked, "Who is able to stand?" The question points *back* to Revelation 5:6, wherein the Lamb was seen standing firm, as though in the act of pouring out His blood, as well as *forward* to chapter 7, in which a people termed the 144,000 are able to stand.

The question about standing signals imminent destruction for the wicked at the second coming (compare Rev. 19:21), but it also signifies deliverance for God's people. "Who will stand before You once Your anger is roused? You cause judgment to be heard from heaven; earth fears and is quiet when God arises unto judgment, to deliver all the afflicted of earth" (Ps. 76:7–9). Who exactly are these "afflicted" that Jesus delivers at His return? "Who among us shall dwell with everlasting burnings? He that walketh righteously, and speaketh uprightly; he that despiseth the gain of oppressions, that shaketh his hands from holding of bribes, that stoppeth his ears from hearing of blood, and shutteth his eyes from seeing evil" (Isa. 33:14, 15, KJV). Thus, those who can stand when Jesus comes in awful majesty are those who have allowed themselves to be purified of every evil, those who have assimilated the very character of the Lamb who delivers them.

The Seal of the Living God

Revelation is meant to prepare its readers to stand faithful though the heavens may fall, so in answer to the question at the close of chapter 6, Revelation 7 provides a description of those very people, taking the reader back to a time *preceding* the close of probation and the outpouring of the plagues, when the angels are still restraining the winds of strife. "Angels are holding the four winds, represented as an angry horse seeking to break loose and rush over the face of the whole earth, bearing destruction and death in its path" (White, *20MR*, p. 217).

Why is the wind said to not blow upon the earth or sea or against any tree? The Sabbath commandment plainly states that *Yahweh* is the Maker of heaven, earth, and the sea—all realms of life. The reference here to earth and sea only limits the scope to life on this planet. The prohibition against blowing upon the planet is to give everyone a chance to learn what comprises true worship: honoring the Creator by keeping holy His seventh-day Sabbath. Those who stand are to worship God in spirit and truth (see John 4:23, 24).

As for the trees, Revelation refers to many different types: citron tree (ξυλον θυινος, see Rev. 18:12), tree of life (το ξυλον της ζωης, see 2:7; 22:2, 14, 19), fig tree (συκη, see 6:13), olive tree (ελαια, see 11:4), and simply "tree" (δενδρον, see 7:1, 3; 8:7; 9:4). To properly understand δενδρον in Revelation 7:1 and 3, Table 5 summarizes its Septuagint and New Testament usages:

Table 5: "Tree" in the Septuagint and New Testament

δενδρον IN LXX & NEW TESTAMENT	REFERENCES
Tree cut down lives again. Figure of resurrection and regeneration.	Job 14:7; Dan. 4:10, 11, 14, 20, 23, 26
Dashed hope is like an uprooted tree.	Job 19:10
Leafy/shady trees used in idolatrous worship.	Deut. 12:2; Isa. 57:5; Hosea 4:13; Ezek. 6:13
Trees in honor of Asherah (heathen goddess).	Isa. 17:8; 27:9
Not to destroy trees when besieging city, for they provide fruit.	Deut. 20:19
Tree is place for rest.	Gen. 18:4, 8
Test of a prophet: tree (prophet) bears good fruit or bad.	Matt. 7:17, 18; 12:33; Luke 6:43, 44
Every evildoer like a tree with bad fruit.	Matt. 3:10; 7:19; Luke 3:9
Immoral people like trees without fruit.	Jude 12

(*continued*)

Table 5: "Tree" in the Septuagint and New Testament (*continued*)

δενδρον IN LXX & NEW TESTAMENT	REFERENCES
As trees bud when summer is near, so signs of times show kingdom of heaven is near.	Luke 21:29–31
Kingdom of heaven like mustard seed grain that grows into large tree.	Matt. 13:32; Luke 13:19
Tree branches broken off to welcome Jesus.	Matt. 21:8; Mark 11:8

Table 5 indicates that trees often represent people (good and bad), and they help sustain life. In calling for the wind not to blow against them, the people of earth are being given the chance to bud and bring forth fruit, indicating clearly who they represent in the great controversy, whether Christ or Satan. God allows His people to be sorely tried, and they may feel like trees cut down, but he allows their stump to remain in the ground that they may yet blossom (see Job 14:7; Dan. 4:10–26). If the wind were to blow too soon, everybody would be cut off before any could blossom and bear good fruit for the harvest (the second coming). Those who bring forth good fruit are to be sealed with the seal of the living God.

Will God's people bring forth good fruit? Yes, they must, for this is the sure sign that summer harvest is near, and the harvest is the end of the age (see Luke 21:29–31; Matt. 13:39). "This gospel of the kingdom shall be preached in all the world for a witness unto all nations; and then shall the end come" (Matt. 24:14, KJV). Earth's probation can close only when the gospel has been preached in all the world. This preaching is not to be a collection of sermons, though; it will be given through *living* epistles—lives that are transformed by the gospel and bear good fruit (see 2 Cor. 3:2, 3). Psalm 92 (the only psalm designated "A Psalm, a Song for the Sabbath day") pictures God's people—those who manifest His character—as robust palm trees and cedars, putting forth abundant fruit, manifesting His righteous character. By contrast, trees thick with leaves, yet apparently devoid of fruit, were used in idolatrous worship.

One of the most illuminating texts is Deuteronomy 20:19, which states that in besieging a city, the fruit-bearing trees are to be left alone. Revelation highlights two cities: Jerusalem, comprised of God's people, and

Babylon, home to the wicked of earth. In Revelation, it is as though God is besieging wicked Babylon, issuing a warning to the inhabitants of earth, calling them to come out, that they not be destroyed when it collapses in the end. As His agents, though, faithful members of the remnant church need to be discrete and tactful in all their efforts to expose error and win souls, for unlike God, we cannot read the heart and may not recognize just how close someone is to the kingdom (see Mark 12:34). We dare not lose souls by wounding them through misguided zeal.

At this point, an angel arrests John's attention, coming from where the sun rises. This particular designation for the east directs our attention to the entrance to the sanctuary "eastward, toward the sunrise," as well as Jesus, the "Sun of righteousness who will arise with healing in His wings" (see Exod. 27:13; Mal. 4:2). Putting these texts together, the angel is coming from the heavenly sanctuary with a message of healing for those who are willing to let Jesus "save His people from their sins" (Matt. 1:21). The message heals our character, fully restoring God's image in us, that we may stand when the plagues are poured out.

The seal that the angel carries makes this character restoration *permanent* in God's remnant people. With that said, what is the seal? It is placed upon the forehead, showing it to be equivalent to the name of the Lamb and His Father (see Rev. 14:1). God changes people's names when their *characters* are changed by taking hold of His everlasting covenant (see Gen. 17:4, 5; 32:27, 28). Hence, those who are sealed are given that new name that no one but the recipient knows: God's name, the name of God's city New Jerusalem, and Jesus' new name (see Rev. 2:17; 3:12).

To fully appreciate the significance of the seal of the living God, we must observe that the word "seal" first appears in Exodus 28 in the description of the high priest's apparel. As one engraves a *seal*, so the *names* of the 12 sons of Israel are engraved upon the stones on the high priest's shoulders and the 12 stones of his breastplate. The title "Holiness unto *Yahweh*" was engraved as a seal upon the plate that the high priest wore on his turban over his *forehead*. The names of the tribes express *Yahweh's holy character*, which he *indelibly seals* in the minds of His people.

Paul informs us that the Holy Spirit seals us upon conversion until the day of redemption (see Eph. 1:13; 4:30), however, the seal of Revelation 7:2 is uniquely styled the "seal of the living God." In Acts 14:15, Paul refers to God as "the living God, He who made the heaven, the earth, the sea, and all things therein." This language is drawn directly from the Sabbath commandment (see Exod. 20:11). Hence, the living God gives life to His creation, and His seal is His Sabbath. Ceasing from earthly cares on His appointed day, the seventh day of the week, honors God as our Creator and is vital in the experience of His people as He prepares them to stand in the day of the plagues.

Those who are sealed are called servants, for they have surrendered all to a Master that, by experience, they have come to know cares for them better than they themselves do (comp. Exod. 21:5, 6). Those who stand in the day of God's wrath have not been pre-determined to stand in that great day apart from the exercise of their own free will, as Calvinism erroneously teaches. These people exercise a *living* faith, consciously choosing to surrender all. Indeed, "the righteous shall live by his faith" (Hab. 2:4).

Next, John hears the number of those sealed: 144,000. To some, the natural reading of this statement is that there are precisely 144,000 people who are sealed.[64] Before proceeding, we need to allow Scripture to explain whether the truth of this number is *literal* or *symbolic*.

The number 144,000 next appears in Revelation 14:1, where it is immediately preceded by and juxtaposed with that infamous number of the beast, 666 (see Rev. 13:18). Obviously, there are not 666 beasts. Rather, Revelation 13:17 relates this number to the name of the beast, i.e., its wicked *character*; so it is with the 144,000: the number informs us of their righteous *character*, not the number of individuals.

---

[64] One group that strongly advocates this understanding is the Jehovah's Witnesses. They assert that precisely 144,000 will live in heaven proper, while the rest of the saved are to experience eternal life on the earth made new (*What Does the Bible Really Teach?*, p. 74). Our study of Revelation 21 will make clear that the new earth is *part* of heaven. In fact, it becomes the very capital of God's entire creation, so such a distinction between final locales is without foundation.

What has the number 144,000 to do with righteousness? Observe that the 144,000 are composed of 12 units of 12,000 apiece from *the sons of Israel*, pointing us back to the 12 tribal names engraved on the stones of the high priest's costume. However, who is Israel? It is the people with whom God establishes His covenant (see Exod. 34:27). It is the people whose *hearts* are circumcised (see Deut. 10:16; 30:6; Jer. 4:4; Rom. 2:29). Circumcision is the sign of the everlasting covenant (see Gen. 17:9–14), established with Abram and his Seed, which is Christ (see Gal. 3:16). Those who belong to Christ are reckoned as Abraham's seed and therefore as heirs of the covenant promise (see v. 29).

In seeking out the significance of the 144,000, we must examine the covenant cut with Abram in Genesis 15:13–21. Abram's seed were to be afflicted in Egypt 400 years. A biblical year consists of 360 days (see Gen. 7:11; 8:3, 4), so this 400-year-period was 144,000 days.

This afflicted seed would be delivered in the 4th generation. This is explained by the second commandment, which states that God's people are not to make and worship any image (idol), for such iniquity will be visited unto the fourth generation (see Exod. 20:4–6). *Yahweh's* aim is not only deliverance from slave labor, but from all the idolatry they adopted during their 144,000-day sojourn in Egypt.

Hence, the number 144,000 refers to Abram's seed, those who partake of *Yahweh's* covenant and are thereby delivered from the idolatry of spiritual Egypt so that they may inherit the covenant promises, including the promised land, heavenly Canaan. Like everyone in history, the 144,000 have previously been slaves to sin (see 1 Kings 8:46; Ps. 14:2, 3; Rom. 3:23), in bondage to the idolatry of spiritual Egypt. The 144,000 are a unique group in the judgment hour of the end time, those who fully surrender to God *as* a united group. In turn, God fully ripens the character of these firstfruits. Through their character transformation, the gospel of the kingdom goes to all the world for a witness, leading to the conversion of a multitude of others.

One last observation regarding the 144,000: their release from spiritual Egypt and enumeration in Revelation 7:5–8 parallel Numbers 2, in which the 12 tribes of the sons of Israel are enumerated following their release from Egypt. A typical description is as follows: "Those encamped eastward toward the sunrise, of the standard of the camp of Judah according to their hosts [or 'armies']" (v. 3). Following their release from Egypt, God referred to His people in military language, expecting them to go forth to conquer the land of Canaan. Therefore, the 144,000 are His end-time, everlasting gospel army, a highly organized, non-combatant search-and-rescue party.

After hearing the number of those sealed, John sees a vast multitude that no one can number. Their white robes indicate a spotless character, and the palm branches in their hands, victory. The text points out that they are standing "before the throne and before the Lamb," a perfect contrast with the wicked at the close of chapter 6, who cried out, "Who is able to stand?"

The question is much debated whether the 144,000 and the vast multitude are the same group or distinct. In the following quotation, if "the number of them that shall be sealed" means the 144,000, then the subsequent quotation from Revelation 7:10 (referring to the vast multitude) would seem to equate both groups:

> Of the number of them that shall be sealed will be those who have come from every nation and kindred and tongue and people. From every country will be gathered men and women who will stand before the throne of God and before the Lamb, crying, "Salvation to our God which sitteth upon the throne, and unto the Lamb." (White, *CT*, p. 532)

To arrive at a decision based on more definite reasoning, let us begin by examining *why* some see the 144,000 and the vast multitude as the same group. The reason has to do with what John *hears* and *sees* in Revelation. Consider Table 6:

Table 6: What John Hears and Sees: Different Views of the Same Thing

JOHN HEARS	JOHN SEES	HARMONY
Rev. 1:10: Loud trumpet-like voice.	Rev. 1:12, 13: Son of man.	Trumpet-like voice → Ten Commandments given at Sinai (see Exod. 19:13–19; 20:18). Ten Commandments are the basis of the judgment (see Eccl. 12:13, 14.) Son of man is the Judge (see Dan. 7: 9, 10, 13).
Rev. 5:5: "Behold, Lion from tribe of Judah."	Rev. 5:6: A Lamb standing.	Jesus pleads His blood (as Lamb) while serving as the mediating Judge (Lion).

This leads some to posit a general principle concerning hearing and seeing in the book of Revelation, hence, the group whose number John *hears* in verse 4 is identical with the vast multitude he *sees* in verse 9. Before rushing to conclusions, note the following:

1. The examples in Table 6 both deal with Jesus; Revelation 7:4 deals with His followers.
2. For the examples in Table 6, John is given a command; there is no command in Revelation 7:4.
3. In Revelation 4:1–2, John again hears the trumpet-like voice of *Jesus*, but he beholds the *Father* on the throne. What is heard and what is seen are not the same entity.

The final point above is sufficient to discredit the hearing-seeing argument as an unsound rule for interpretation. To arrive at a satisfactory answer, we must compare Scripture with Scripture. We begin by noting that the 144,000 come from the 12 *tribes* of Israel, whereas the vast multitude comes from every nation, tribe, people, and tongue—a much greater swath of the human race. The vast multitude would seem to include the tribes composing the 144,000, *as well as* those from every nation, people, and tongue—the very groups called by Babylon to worship the golden image (see Dan. 3:4).

The makeup of the vast multitude becomes clearer when we compare it with Revelation 14. In the first five verses, we have a glimpse of 144,000, the "firstfruits" of earth's harvest, sealed in their foreheads. They in turn go forth to proclaim the first angel's message of Revelation 14:6, announcing the everlasting gospel to "every nation, tribe, tongue, and people"—the same groupings that comprise the vast multitude. Thus, taken together, chapters 7 and 14 suggest a distinction between the 144,000 and the vast multitude. The message given by the 144,000 to "every nation, tribe, tongue, and people" (the 3 angels' messages of Revelation 14:6–12) ripens the earth for the wheat harvest, leading to the *formation* of the vast multitude from "every nation, all tribes, peoples, and tongues":

> [John] records the closing message which is to ripen the harvest of earth, either as sheaves for the heavenly garner, or as fagots for the fires of the last day. ...
>
> The most solemn warning and the most awful threatening ever addressed to mortals is that contained in the third angel's message. ...
>
> The message containing this warning is the last to be proclaimed before the revelation of the Son of man. (White, *ST*, November 1, 1899)

These early (144,000) and later (vast multitude) harvests are both precious grain. Both "have passed through the time of trouble such as never was since there was a nation; they have endured the anguish of the time of Jacob's trouble; they have stood without an intercessor through the final outpouring of God's judgments. But they have been delivered" (White, *GC*, p. 649) from spiritual Egypt, having partaken of the everlasting covenant.

Observe that the vast multitude stands before the throne, just like the 144,000 in Revelation 14:3 do. Thus, they too have conquered in the battle with self and sin. This is confirmed by the white robes they wear, denoting their pure character, and the palm branches they have in their hands. At His triumphal entry just days before His crucifixion, "a vast multitude" heralded Jesus by waving palm branches (see John 12:12, 13). Likewise, the vast multitude waves palm branches as they welcome Jesus at the second coming, His triumphal return. In Psalm 92, the psalm for the Sabbath day, the righteous are said to "flourish as the date palm" (verse 12), indicating how vital the Sabbath experience is in preparing the people whose characters will indeed grow to full maturity.

How do we know that Revelation 7:9–10 pictures the second coming? The vast multitude provides the final, living demonstration in answer to the question, "Who is able to stand?" They stand before the throne and the Lamb, while at the second coming, the wicked seek to hide from the One seated on the throne and the Lamb's retribution (see Rev. 6:16). Their palm fronds point to the Feast of Ingathering (also called the Feast of Booths), at which time the Israelites were to erect temporary shelters from palm fronds (see Lev. 23:39–43). As the vast multitude sees Jesus arriving in the clouds, they wave the palm branches of their temporary booths in anticipation of their arrival into the eternal Promised Land.

Why does the text say the multitude is so vast that "no one was able to number" it? This points to the Abrahamic covenant, which refers to the seed of Abraham as the numberless stars of heaven and the sand of the sea shore (see Gen. 15:5; 22:17). At the height of the conflict just before Jesus returns, a vast number of people take their stand for Him and experience the fulfillment of the everlasting covenant—salvation to the fullest, i.e., character perfection. "Wherefore he is able also to save them to the uttermost that come unto God by him, seeing he ever liveth to make intercession for them" (Heb. 7:25, KJV).

One of the elders now directs John's attention to the white robes worn by the vast multitude, inquiring as to their *identity* and place of *origin*. These questions hearken back to the story of Jonah, in which the mariners inquire of the disobedient prophet *who* is responsible for the storm they are experiencing, and from *where* he comes (see Jonah 1:8). To this, Jonah replies that he is a Hebrew, one who serves the living God, the one who made both sea and dry land—an allusion to the Creator and the Sabbath (see Acts 14:15; Exod. 20:11).

It is critical for the end-time remnant to understand the vital role the Sabbath plays in perfecting their characters. However, just as Jonah's reply to the mariners lacked power and was betrayed by the fact that the storm was brought on by him running away from his God-appointed task, so Sabbath-keeping without the exercise of a *living* faith in Jesus lacks vital power. It was only when Jonah was truly converted in the belly of the great fish that he could preach the world's shortest sermon, resulting in the mass, and nearly instantaneous, conversion of wicked Nineveh (see Jonah 2; 3:4, 10).

John responds to the elder's question with, "My lord, *you* know." This points back to Ezekiel 37:1–14, in which Ezekiel is asked whether the very dry bones he sees can live, and he responds, "*Adonai Yahweh, You* know." He is told to prophesy unto the dry bones, which come together into skeletons with flesh covering them. However, the key ingredient is missing— the breath of life. Only when Ezekiel commands the wind to breathe on them do the bodies live, stand upon their feet, and form a great army. The passage explains that God resurrects His spiritually dead people, Israel, by putting His Spirit in them.

The allusion to Ezekiel 37:1–14 informs us that the vast multitude has not always been victorious. Until their pleas for God's Spirit are answered, they lack the courage and power necessary to make it through the final test unscathed; filled with the Spirit, they emerge victorious from the "great tribulation" (compare Dan. 12:1).

> At that time, while the work of salvation is closing, trouble will be coming on the earth, and the nations will be angry, yet held in check so as not to prevent the work of the third angel. At that time the "latter rain," or refreshing from the presence of the Lord, will come, to give power to the loud voice of the third angel, and prepare the saints to stand in the period when the seven last plagues shall be poured out. (White, *EW*, pp. 85. 86)

> They were clothed with an armor from their head to their feet. They moved in exact order, like a company of soldiers. Their countenances expressed the severe conflict which they had endured, the agonizing struggle they had passed through. Yet their features, marked with severe internal anguish, now shone with the light and glory of heaven. They had obtained the victory, and it called forth from them the deepest gratitude and holy, sacred joy. …
>
> I heard those clothed with the armor speak forth the truth with great power. It had effect. Many had been bound … The honest who had been prevented from hearing the truth now eagerly laid hold upon it. All fear of their relatives was gone, and the truth alone was exalted to them. They had been hungering and thirsting for truth; it was dearer and more precious than life. I asked what had made this great change. An angel answered, "It is the latter rain, the refreshing from the presence of the Lord, the loud cry of the third angel." (White, *EW*, p. 271)

The process of obtaining this victory over every besetting sin is what is meant by "they washed their robes and whitened them with the blood of the Lamb." It was *necessary* for Jesus to die in our place upon Calvary to make the atoning sacrifice, but that act in and of itself is not *sufficient* to fully cleanse our characters of sin. His blood must actually *do* something for the believer. "The life of the flesh is in the blood … for the blood, it makes atonement for the life" (Lev. 17:11). During the end-time day of atonement, Jesus actually pleads His shed blood before the Father, and as He does so, it really, truly, tangibly purifies us.

Many people think that justification by faith is merely forgiveness for their past sins, a whitewashing of an otherwise black record, and that this is sufficient to secure eternal life. Not so. The Greek word for "justification" is identical with the word translated "righteousness." Hence, "justification by faith" is "righteousness by faith," which includes not only God's imputed righteousness (the common understanding of justification), but also His imparted righteousness (the process of sanctification). His people are not simply *declared* righteous while they continue on in a life of transgression—God performs no such dishonest transaction. By exercising faith in His promise to fulfill His everlasting covenant, God's people actually *become* righteous beings this side of heaven. Note the following:

> But forgiveness has a broader meaning than many suppose. When God gives the promise that He "will abundantly pardon," He adds, as if the meaning of that promise exceeded all that we could comprehend: "My thoughts are not your thoughts, neither are your ways My ways, saith the Lord. For as the heavens are higher than the earth, so are My ways higher than your ways, and My thoughts than your thoughts." Isaiah 55:7–9. God's forgiveness is not merely a judicial act by which He sets us free from condemnation. It is not only forgiveness *for* sin, but reclaiming *from* sin. It is the outflow of redeeming love that transforms the heart. David had the true conception of forgiveness when he prayed, "Create in me a clean heart, O God; and renew a right spirit within me." Psalm 51:10. And again he says, "As far as the east is from the west, so far hath He removed our transgressions from us." Psalm 103:12. (White, *MB*, p. 114)

Our trouble is that we often forget a key attribute of God brought out in the life of faithful Abraham: "God, who makes the dead alive, calling the things which are not as though they are" (Rom. 4:17). God's spoken promises carry with them the creative power to bring about their own truth (see Ps. 33:6, 9). When we are born again, we start out as babes and begin the steady process of maturation. Hence, we may continue to *see* only a lack of righteousness, yet by *faith*, we may look unto Jesus, the Finisher of our faith, accepting that what He has begun He will carry through to completion (see Heb. 12:2; Phil. 1:6). The only power in the universe that can thwart God's purpose to make us righteous is our own free will.

The victorious vast multitude serves Him *continually* ("day and night") in His temple, not only when they are finally in heaven, but while on this sin-stained earth. In *this* life, they dwell in heavenly places with complete devotion to Him (see Eph. 2:6), for their physical *bodies* are truly temples of the Holy Spirit (see 1 Cor. 3:16, 17; 6:19, 20). They experience the Spirit's victory over the flesh, the divine nature subduing the carnal *continuously* (see Rom. 8:4; 2 Peter 1:4).

The text says that "He who sits upon the throne will spread His tent over them." This is pilgrim/covenant language, referring back to the days of Abraham, to whom was given the covenant while he was an itinerant tent dweller on this earth (see Heb. 11:9, 13). Except for the promises of God, it might have seemed that He was forsaken, not having a permanent place to call his own. As Abraham would pitch his tent in each new locale, God Himself pitched about him. According to Psalm 91, God's tent is a shadow, a refuge, a fortress, a protective mother bird—and He will protect His people in the final conflict.

Verse 16 quotes from Isaiah 49:10. The entirety of Isaiah 49 is a beautiful picture of God's tender regard for His people. When Zion moans, "*Yahweh* has forsaken me, *Adonai* has forgotten me," He responds with, "Would a woman forget her nursing child, that she would not show compassion on the son of her womb? Indeed, these may forget, but I will not forget you" (Isa. 49:14, 15). In His sermon on the mount, Jesus uses hungering and thirsting to refer to the insatiable desire for righteousness, providing assurance that this longing *will be filled* (see Matt. 5:6). Here in Revelation 7:16, the elder assures John that the vast multitude—Jesus' corporate bride—will be absolutely filled with righteousness.

While the impenitent under the fourth plague are *literally* scorched by the sun (see Rev. 16:8, 9), the vast multitude will no longer be burned by the sun, i.e., they will not be deceived by false worship practices revolving around Sunday in opposition to God's Sabbath. Those comprising the vast multitude have been sealed (the seal of God's holy law being the Sabbath), forever protected from idolatry, epitomized by the most ancient object of pagan worship, the sun.

The Lamb leads them to springs of living water, for *Yahweh* has dried up the springs that spiritual Babylon affords (see Jer. 51:36). These are fountains "of water, springing up into everlasting life" (John 4:14), from which we are to drink freely (see Rev. 21:6). Hence, though sin is overcome fully *before* the second coming, the righteousness of our characters will develop throughout eternity:

> The religion of Christ is of a character that demands constant advancement. The Lord does not design that we shall ever feel that we have reached to the full measure of the stature of Christ. Through all eternity we are to grow in knowledge of him who is the head of all things in the church. If we would draw upon his grace, we must feel our poverty. Our souls must be filled with an intense longing after God, until we realize that we shall perish unless Christ shall put upon us his Spirit and grace, and do the work for us" (White, *ST*, May 9, 1892).

The promise to wipe away every tear comes from Isaiah 25:8, at the time when "He has swallowed up death forever." Of course, this occurs at "that day"—the second coming—when the righteous of all ages unite in proclaiming, "Lo, this is our God; we have waited for him, and he will save us: this is the LORD; we have waited for him, we will be glad and rejoice in his salvation." (Isa. 25:9, KJV).

The Seventh Seal

The seals conclude with a mysterious silence that lasts "for about half an hour." The end-time judgment is referred to as "the hour of His judgment" (Rev. 14:6). This judgment hour consists of two halves of unequal duration: the first half, when probation is open, and all are tried to see of what sort their characters are; the second half, when mankind's probation closes, and the 7 last plagues commence, is the final test that demonstrates before all beings the irreversibly hard hearts of the wicked (see 3:10).

At this point, Jesus stops interceding on our behalf and comes forth from the Holy of Holies—the throne room, which Revelation repeatedly calls heaven (e.g., Rev. 4:1–3). Since no prayers may now enter the throne room, and Jesus is not there to plead His blood on our behalf, heaven is absolutely silent. Consider the following:

> Hab. 2:20: *Yahweh* is in the temple, His sanctuary; Hush before Him, all the earth.
>
> Zech. 2:13: Hush, all flesh, before *Yahweh*, for He is roused from His holy dwelling.
>
> Zeph. 1:7: Hush before *Adonai Yahweh*, for the day of *Yahweh* is near, for *Yahweh* has prepared a slaughter. He has set apart those whom He has called.

God gathers all the wicked for slaughter during the sixth plague, then miserably destroys them during the seventh plague at His coming (see Rev. 16:16, 21; 19:17–21). The slaughter prepared by *Yahweh* referred to in Zephaniah 1:7 find its fulfillment in the great supper of God (see Rev. 19:17), when the birds feast on the wicked. In one sense, the wicked are set apart for this feast, in which they are the fare; in the primary sense, though, He has sealed His righteous bride, setting her apart so that the plagues do not touch her, just as He promised in Revelation 3:10.

An hour of prophetic time is 15 days. The second coming marks the beginning of the antitype of the Feast of Ingathering, an 8-day celebration (see Lev. 23:39). Without being dogmatic, it *might* be that the plagues last 7 days, followed by 8 days (approximately ½ prophetic hour) for the Feast of Ingathering (1 day for the second doming and 7 days for the journey to heaven). "We all entered the cloud together, and were seven days ascending to the sea of glass" (White, *EW*, p. 16).

PART 3: THE KEY POINTS

REVELATION 4:1–8:1: JESUS

Jesus is the slaughtered Lamb who comes before the Father to begin receiving His kingdom at the commencement of the wedding judgment, when He serves as High Priest and Judge. In chapter 6, He opens the scroll. In chapter 7, the vast multitude worships Jesus, who has delivered them from the power of sin.

REVELATION 5:6: JESUS STANDS FOR HIS BRIDE

As High Priest during the end-time day of atonement, Jesus stands as the Lamb before the Father (seated as Supreme Judge in chapter 4) and the 24 elders (the grand jury) in the Holy of Holies, pleading His shed blood (defense attorneys always stand when making their case before the judge and jurors) as sufficient ransom for His bride. Simultaneously, He applies it to each willing believer's life, developing his or her character to the point that sin is no longer indulged.

REVELATION 4:1–8:1: THE WEDDING THEME AND THE SABBATH

The setting for these chapters is through the open door, in the Holy of Holies, Jesus' wedding takes place. The Sabbath is introduced in chapter 4, in which God is worshipped as Creator, in harmony with the fourth commandment (see Exod. 20:8–11). In chapter 5, the Lamb is worshipped, who was slain to redeem us, again in harmony with the fourth commandment (see Deut. 5:12–15). The focus on the Sabbath goes hand-in-hand with the wedding theme, for "thy Maker is thine husband … thy Redeemer the Holy One of Israel" (Isa. 54:5). The Sabbath is God's ever-lasting covenant (see Exod. 31:16), His pledge to marry His people, for marriage itself is an everlasting covenant (see Mal. 2:14–16).

Beginning in chapter 5, the focus is on the sealed scroll which the Lamb unseals. This is a further link with the Sabbath and marriage. In the first seal, the rider on the white horse holds a bow, the sign of God's ever-lasting covenant (see Gen. 9:16). The Lisbon earthquake of the sixth seal took place on Sabbath, November 1, 1755. At the return of Jesus for His bride, the wicked ask who can stand. Chapter 7 answers the question—it is those who have the seal of the living God in their forehead. The high priest wore the phrase "holiness for *Yahweh*" on his forehead (see Exod. 28:36–38), and the Sabbath is likewise called "holiness for *Yahweh*" (see Exod. 16:23; 31:15). Hence, when the seal of the living God is placed on the forehead of believers, it signifies that they are of one mind with the High Priest, Jesus, perfectly holy in character. Their marriage with their Redeemer is now complete.

Most of the professing Christian world is unaware of God's holy Sabbath, instead keeping Sunday in honor of His resurrection. In view of this, note the following: 1) In the beginning, God pronounced a blessing on the Sabbath day (see Gen. 2:3); 2) in Revelation 4, the heavenly beings nearest the throne honor the Sabbath and Him who instituted it; 3) the second commandment states that we are not to worship anything that *we* make, while the fourth commandment states that we *are* to worship Him who made us. Sunday sacredness is an invention of mankind; history books are clear on this point. The reader is encouraged to research this to one's own satisfaction (e.g., *PFF1*, pp. 376–381). On March 7, AD 321, Constantine instituted the first law enjoining Sunday observance, with no mention of exalting Christ. It was simply a political ploy to court the favor of *non*-believers in his realm, pagans who adored the day of the sun:

> All judges and city people and the craftsmen shall rest upon the venerable Day of the Sun. Country people, however, may freely attend to the cultivation of the fields, because it frequently happens that no other days are better adapted for planting the grain in the furrows or the vines in trenches. So that the advantage given by heavenly providence may not for the occasion of a short time perish. (Ayer, *A Source Book for Ancient Church History*, div. 2, per. 1, ch. 1, sec. 59[g], pp. 284, 285)

REVELATION 4:1–8:1: DECISION QUESTIONS

Is victory over sin possible? The wedding theme enables us to rephrase the question so as to forever settle the matter: Is Jesus able to have a successful marriage, one in which His bride is truly one flesh with Him? Those who are accounted as part of Jesus' bride will have the seal of the living God—"holiness for *Yahweh*"—written in their forehead, their mind.

Do you want to be of one mind with Him, in perfect harmony with your Maker? The Lamb is standing for His bride before the throne right now. If you accepted His wedding invitation earlier, is it now your desire to stand for *Him* in the pre-advent wedding judgment, honoring your Creator and Redeemer in all that you say, think, and do?

If so, choose now to permit God to fully work out His everlasting covenant—the new covenant—in your life. Let Him seal you with the sign of that everlasting covenant, the seventh-day Sabbath. Perhaps you need to study out the matter of the Sabbath to be fully persuaded, or learn *how* to keep it holy. Are you willing to begin learning right now?

4A:
WEDDING
ANNOUNCEMENT

REVELATION 8:2–6:
JESUS INTERCEDES

8 ²Then I saw the 7 angels who stand before God; 7 trumpets were given to them.

³Then another Angel came and was **standing** over the altar, holding a golden censer. Much incense was given to Him, that He might offer it with the prayers of all the holy people upon the golden altar which is before the throne. ⁴The smoke of the incense, with the prayers of the holy people, ascended from the hand of the Angel before God. ⁵The Angel had taken the censer, filled it with fire from the altar, then cast it into the earth; there were thunderclaps, voices, lightning flashes, and an earthquake.

⁶Then the 7 angels, those holding the 7 trumpets, prepared themselves to trumpet forth.

COMMENTARY

Chapter 7 answered the question of the sixth seal as to who could stand in the day of God's judgment. The 7 trumpets of Revelation 8–11 show the steps Jesus takes throughout sacred history to answer the plea of the fifth seal for vindication of the blood of the martyrs. The seventh trumpet marks the commencement of the end-time judgment, when God will finally vindicate His martyrs' shed blood.

In verse 2, John observes 7 angels who are given 7 trumpets. They prepare to blow in verse 6, but in the intervening verses, John's attention is directed to yet *another* Angel standing over the altar. When we recall that Jesus took His stance at the door (see 3:20), and the Lamb stood before the throne as though being slaughtered (see 5:6), we conclude that this Angel is in fact Jesus.

An angel, properly understood, is a messenger. From Revelation 12, we learn that sin began in heaven, with Satan and his angels warring against Michael and His angels in an attempt to unseat Jesus and assume His prerogatives. Scripture is plain that Jesus consented to be made a little *lower* than the angels (see Heb. 2:9; Ps. 8:5), choosing to become what He was not by nature, i.e., human flesh (see John 1:14), in order to teach the human race the true character of God. Is it any surprise that Jesus would condescend to take upon Himself the nature of angels to answer the questions *they* have concerning the character of God?

Let us examine the work of this Angel. First, He comes with a golden censer to the altar—the altar of burnt offering, for the altar of incense is consistently described as *golden* (see later in Rev. 8:3; Exod. 40:5, 26). A fire burned continuously on the altar of burnt offering (see Lev. 6:12), so it was here the high priest would go to obtain the fire necessary to burn incense at the golden altar of incense. After this, he would enter the Holy of Holies on the Day of Atonement (see Lev. 16:12, 13). We conclude that Revelation 8:3 pictures Jesus before the golden altar during the centuries intervening His ascension and the start of judgment on October 22, 1844 (see Rom. 8:34; Heb. 7:25).

Why does Jesus offer incense with peoples' prayers in verses 3 and 4, specifically those reported under the fifth seal of Revelation 6:9–11? This is explained in Psalm 141, a psalm of David. Since Jesus is the true David, the psalm can be read as Jesus' own plea. Thus, in verse 2, He presents His *own* prayer before *Yahweh* as incense. He lifts His hands and pleas the merits of His own evening self-sacrifice. Jesus so identifies with His people that their afflictions are as though done to Him (see Matt. 25:40, 45), so He intercedes for them, with the Holy Spirit transforming their prayers so that they may be acceptable before a perfectly holy God (see Rom. 8:26, 27).

Verses 3 and 4 picture Jesus interceding in the centuries leading up to the judgment that began October 22, 1844. The thunderclaps, voices, lightning flashes, and earthquake at the close of verse 5 mark the beginning of the seventh plague (see Rev. 16:18; note also that the first plague is poured "into the earth," Rev. 16:12), after probation has closed and just before Jesus returns at the second coming. This suggests that the early part of Revelation 8:5, in which the Angel takes the censer and casts it into the earth, must deal with the intervening judgment and close of probation. Does the Bible confirm this?

According to Leviticus 16:12, the high priest *took the censer with him into the Holy of Holies on the Day of Atonement*. To get a more complete picture, we turn to the book of Numbers:

> Num. 16:46, 47 (KJV): Moses said unto Aaron, Take a censer, and put fire therein from off the altar, and put on incense, and go quickly unto the congregation, and make an atonement for them: for there is wrath gone out from the LORD; the plague is begun. And Aaron took as Moses commanded, and ran into the midst of the congregation; and, behold, the plague was begun among the people: and he put on incense, and made an atonement for the people.

Note that Aaron took a censer and put fire therein to *make atonement*. Thus, the beginning of Revelation 8:5 refers to Jesus beginning His work during the end-time day of atonement. Were Aaron to cast the censer to the earth (i.e., no longer hold it in his hand), he would cease this work of atonement. Does the Bible support this understanding?

To answer, we turn to Ezekiel 9 and 10, which deal with the close of probation on the Day of Atonement. In Ezekiel 9:6, God seals His faithful people. When this is complete (verse 11), one dressed in the linen of the high priest on the Day of Atonement is told to take coals of fire from between the cherubs, fill the hollows of his hands (same language as Leviticus 16:12, when the high priest moved *into* the Holy of Holies on the Day of Atonement), and scatter it over the city (as by casting down the censer) as judgment upon all the unfaithful (see Ezek. 10:2, 7). Thus, casting the censer into the *earth* in Revelation 8:5 implies that God's faithful remnant have been sealed and marks the close of probation for the *earth*. In harmony with this understanding, the close of Revelation 8:5 moves to the start of the seventh plague.

Following this summary of Jesus' intercessory work in both its Holy Place and Most Holy Place phases, the 7 angels prepare to trumpet forth, providing a detailed look at how Jesus works to answer the plea of his faithful martyrs.

REVELATION 8:7–11:19: THE 7 TRUMPETS

Trumpets 1–4

8 ⁷So the first [angel] trumpeted: there was hail and fire mixed with blood, and these were cast into the earth. The third part of the earth was burned up, the third part of the trees was burned up, and all green grass was burned up.

⁸Then the second angel trumpeted: something like a great burning mountain was cast into the sea. The third part of the sea became blood, ⁹the third part of the living creatures in the sea died, and the third part of the ships was ruined.

¹⁰Then the third angel trumpeted: a great star, burning like a lamp, fell from heaven. It fell upon the third part of the rivers and upon the water springs. ¹¹The name of the star is Wormwood. The third part of the waters turned into wormwood, and many men died due to the waters, for they were made bitter.

¹²Then the fourth angel trumpeted: the third part of the sun, the third part of the moon, and the third part of the stars were struck, such that the third part of them were darkened; the day did not shine forth for the third part of it, and the night likewise.

Trumpets 5–7: The 3 Woes

¹³Then I saw and heard 1 eagle flying in mid-heaven, saying in a loud voice, "Woe, woe, woe to those dwelling upon the earth, on account of the remaining trumpet voices of the 3 angels who are about to trumpet forth!"

The Fifth Trumpet: Woe #1

9 [1]Then the fifth angel trumpeted, and I saw a star which had fallen from heaven unto the earth, and to him was given the key of the well of the abyss. [2]Then he opened the well of the abyss, and smoke ascended from the well, like smoke of a blazing furnace; the sun and the air were darkened by the smoke of the well. [3]Out of the smoke, locusts came forth upon the earth; authority was granted them, authority like the scorpions of the earth have. [4]However, it was told them that they were not to corrupt[65] the grass of the earth, nor any greenery, nor any tree, but only those men who do not have the seal of God upon their foreheads. [5]To them it was granted, not that they kill them, but that they be tormented 5 months; their torment was like a scorpion's torment, when it stings a man. [6]So in those days, men will seek death, yet there is no possibility they will find it; they will long to die, but death will flee from them.

[7]The likenesses of the locusts were like horses prepared for war. Upon their heads was something like golden crowns. Their faces were like the faces of men, [8]yet they had hair like the hair of women, and their teeth were like those of lions. [9]They had chests like iron breastplates, and the sound of their wings was like the sound of many horse-drawn chariots galloping unto war. [10]They have tails like those of scorpions, that is, stingers; in their tails, they have authorization to corrupt[66] men 5 months. [11]These have a king over them, the angel of the abyss: his name in Hebrew is Abaddon, while in the Greek, he has the name Apollyon.

[12]Woe 1 is past. Behold, there are still 2 woes coming afterward.

The Sixth Trumpet: Woe #2

[13]Then the sixth angel trumpeted, and I heard 1 voice from the 4 horns of the golden altar which is before God [14]saying to the sixth angel who was holding the trumpet,

---

[65] See footnote 48.
[66] See footnote 48.

"Loose[67] the 4 angels who are bound by the great river Euphrates."
[15]Then the 4 angels who were prepared for the hour, and for the day, month, and year,[68] were released that they should kill the third part of men.

[16]The number of horse-based forces[69] was myriads of myriads;[70] I heard their number. [17]Thus I saw the horses in the vision, and those seated upon them: they had fiery red, hyacinth blue, and sulphurous yellow breastplates; the horses' heads were like lions' heads, and out of their mouths were proceeding fire, smoke, and brimstone. [18]By these 3 plagues, the third part of men was killed—by the fire, smoke, and brimstone proceeding out of their mouths—[19]for the authority of the horses was in their mouths and in their tails, for their tails were like serpents, having heads, and with them they corrupt.[71]

[20]Yet the rest of men, those not killed by these plagues, did not repent of the works of their hands, that they should not worship the demons, that is, golden, silver, bronze, stone, and wooden idols, which are not able to see, nor hear, nor walk. [21]They did not repent of their murders, nor their sorceries, nor their fornication, nor their thefts.

The Strong Angel

10[1]Then I saw a strong Angel coming down from heaven, clothed with a cloud, the arch of light over His head, His face like the sun, and His lower legs[72] like fiery pillars. [2]He was holding in His hand an open scroll. He placed His right foot upon the sea, while His left

---

[67] Or "release." "Loose" points to the loosing of the fifth seal, the cry of the martyrs in Revelation 6:10.

[68] TR & NTG read, "for the hour, day, month, and year."

[69] TR & NTG read, "cavalry-based forces," emphasizing the riders instead of horses.

[70] TR & NTG read, "2 myriads of myriads."

[71] See footnote 48.

[72] Greek, "his feet," but the lower legs are better represented by pillars than are feet, as recognized by many translations (e.g., CJB, ESV, HCSB, MIT, NET, NJB, RSV, NRSV). In 1 Samuel 17:6, Goliath has bronze armor on his "feet," though nearly all translations, KJV included, properly render this as "legs" ("shins," HCSB).

[he placed] upon the earth. [3]He cried out in a loud voice, just as a lion roars; when He cried out, the 7 thunders spoke with their own voices. [4]When the 7 thunders spoke, I was about to write, but I heard a voice from heaven saying, "Seal up those things the 7 thunders spoke. You may not write them."

[5]The Angel which I saw **standing** upon the sea and the earth raised His right hand toward heaven [6]and swore by Him who lives forever and ever—Him who created the heaven and the things therein, the earth and the things therein, and the sea and the things therein—"Time will be no longer. [7]Instead, in the days of the voice of the seventh angel, when he is destined to trumpet forth, the mystery of God is to be brought to completion, according to the good news He proclaimed to His servants the prophets."

[8]The voice which I heard from heaven began speaking with me again, saying, "Go, take the little scroll, the one open in the hand of the Angel **standing** upon the sea and upon the earth." [9]So I went to the Angel, telling him to give me the little scroll. He said to me, "Take it, and eat it. It will make your stomach bitter, but in your mouth it will be sweet like honey."

[10]I took the scroll from the hand of the Angel and ate it: it was in my mouth like sweet honey; and once I swallowed it, my stomach was made bitter. [11]They told me, "You must prophesy again unto[73] many peoples, unto many nations, tongues, and kings."

---

[73] The Greek word επι, in the dative case, generally translates as "at," "over," or "against." The source of this passage is Ezekiel 2:8–3:11, in which Ezekiel is directed to eat a scroll and speak "to" (Hebrew 'el, Greek προς, both used in an adversative sense) the rebellious house of Israel. Translations that read "against" (EBR, NJB) understand that the message concerns the following four people groups and are likely confrontational; those that read "before" (KJV, MIT) understand the message is addressed to the four people groups, but don't capture the confrontational nature of it; those that read "about" (ESV, NKJV, NASB, NAB, YLT, RSV, NRSV, HCSB, NET, CJB) understand that the message *concerns* the following four people groups, but not that the message is spoken *directly to* them.

The Temple Measured and 2 Witnesses During the Dark Ages

11

¹Then there was given me a reed like a rod while He was saying, "Arise, measure the temple of God, the altar, and those who worship therein. ²However, the outer court of the temple, exclude it, do not measure it, for it is given to the nations. The holy city they will trample underfoot 42 months. ³Yet I will commission My 2 witnesses, and they will prophesy 1,260 days clothed in sackcloth. ⁴These are the 2 olive trees and the 2 menorahs which stand before the Lord of the earth.[74] ⁵If anyone wishes to corrupt them, fire comes out of their mouth and devours their enemies; if anyone wishes to corrupt them, he must be killed in this manner. ⁶These have authority to lock heaven, that rain not fall the days of their prophecy; they have authority over the waters, to turn them into blood, and to strike the earth as often as they wish with every plague.

Beast Versus the 2 Witnesses

⁷"When they finish their testimony, the beast which comes up from the abyss will make war with them, conquer them, and kill them. ⁸Their corpse[75] will lie upon the public square of the great city, which is spiritually called Sodom and Egypt, where also their Lord was crucified. ⁹Then those of the peoples, tribes, tongues, and nations see[76] their corpse[77] 3.5 days, and they will not permit their corpses to be put in a grave. ¹⁰Those who dwell upon the earth rejoice over them; they will celebrate and give gifts to each another, for these 2 prophets tormented those who dwell upon the earth."

---

[74] TR reads, "God," and BYZ and NTG read κυριος ("Lord"), used to translate *Adon(ai)* in the Hebrew Scriptures. The 2 olive trees come from Zechariah 4:11–14, which refers to "*Adon* of the whole earth." Hence, "Lord" in Revelation 11:4 is correct.

[75] TR reads, "corpses," and BYZ and NTG read, "corpse." "Corpse" is fine, since the 2 witnesses together comprise the 1 Bible.

[76] TR reads, "will see," and BYZ and NTG read, "see."

[77] See footnote 75.

[11]After the 3.5 days, the spirit of life[78] from God entered into them, they stood upon their feet, and great fear fell upon those beholding them. [12]Then I heard a loud voice from heaven saying to them, "Come up here." So they went up into heaven in the cloud, and their enemies beheld them. [13]In that day[79] a great earthquake occurred, and the tenth part of the city fell. In the earthquake, the names of 7,000 men were killed. The rest became terrified, and gave glory to the God of heaven.

[14]The second woe is past. The third woe—behold!—is coming quickly.

The Seventh Trumpet: Woe #3

[15]The seventh angel trumpeted, and there were loud voices in heaven saying, "The kingdom of the world has become [the kingdom] of our Lord and His Anointed, and He will reign forever and ever." [16]Then the 24 elders who sit upon their thrones before the throne of God fell upon their faces and prostrated themselves in worship of God, [17]saying, "We thank you, *Yahweh* God of hosts,[80] He who is and He who was, for You have assumed Your great power and begun to reign.

[18]"The nations were infuriated,[81] and Your retribution[82] came, as well as the appointed time for the dead to be judged, to give the reward to Your servants—the prophets, the holy people, those who fear Your name, small and great—and to ruin those who ruin the earth."

[19]The temple of God in heaven was opened, and the ark of the covenant of the Lord[83] was seen in His temple. There were lightning flashes, voices, thunderclaps, [an earthquake,] and great hail.[84]

---

[78] One might expect "breath of life" here. Job 27:3 (LXX) harmonizes the expressions: "Indeed, while my *breath* is still in me, God's *Spirit* remains in my nostrils."

[79] TR and NTG read, "In that hour."

[80] Greek, "Lord God the Almighty"

[81] Greek οργιζομαι, related to οργη, God's "retribution" during the end-time judgment (see Rev. 6:16, 17; 14:10; 16:19; 19:15).

[82] See footnote 46.

[83] The end-time judgment commencing in verse 15 and ending in verse 19 matches well with Malachi 3:1, in which the LXX translates the Hebrew *ha'adon* ("the *Adon*" or "the Lord," a variant of *Adonai*) with κυριος (usually translated "the Lord").

[84] BYZ lacks "an earthquake," while TR and NTG have it.

COMMENTARY

To fully appreciate the imagery employed in the trumpets, one needs to consider matters from two vantage points: 1) historical fulfillment that matches the prophecies *literally*, and 2) appropriate references from the Hebrew Scriptures to learn the *spiritual significance* of the historical fulfillment.

Trumpets 1–4

Historically, the first trumpet focuses primarily on the historical window of AD 405 to 410, dealing with the invasions of Alaric and the Visigoths under his command, and secondarily, Radagaisus and his barbarians.

Alaric wished to invade Gaul, and this was accomplished under Radagaisus' army. December 31, AD 406 marked the fall of the Roman Empire east of the Alps. Alaric pressed into Italy and besieged Rome in the years 408, 409, and 410. In 410, the city succumbed and, for 6 days, suffered all manner of atrocity. Alaric continued further south into Italy and would have continued his conquest, had not his heaven-appointed role as agent of judgment against Rome ended with his death that same year.

It is fascinating to note what the non-Christian historian Gibbon said concerning Alaric's Visigothic conquest of Rome: "The union of the Roman Empire was dissolved; its genius was humbled in the dust; and armies of unknown barbarians, issuing from the frozen regions of the North, had established their victorious reign over the fairest provinces of Europe and Africa" (Gibbon, *The History of the Decline and Fall of the Roman Empire*, vol. 5, ch. 33, p. 362) It will prove amazing how this secular historian confirms the prophetic message of trumpets 1–4 regarding Western Rome.

The prophecy says that only one third of the earth and trees was to be burned up. The Roman Empire had 3 capitals: Rome, Constantinople, and Ravenna. Only Rome was affected during the period of the first trumpet.

As for the trees and green grass, the gardens of Sallust, in which were pleasure gardens with forests, were burned up (see Treiyer, *The Mystery of the Apocalyptic Trumpets Unraveled*, p. 41). Gibbon's reference to the "frozen regions of the North" answers well to the hail of the prophecy.

As for the spiritual significance of the prophetic description, let us begin with "hail and fire mixed with blood." This points us to Exodus 9:13–26, the record of the seventh of the 10 plagues, in which God called for hail mixed with fire to fall upon all in Egypt who did not heed His warning to take cover. Revelation is full of allusions to the exodus from Egypt, establishing a connection between idolatrous Egypt of old and Rome. Just as the hail fell only upon those who rebelled in Egypt, and not upon God's followers, so the Visigoths, themselves Germanic Christians, did not attack Christian temples, but only pagan Romans (Treiyer, *Apocalyptic Trumpets*, p. 41).

The additional mention of blood may point back to the first plague, when the waters were turned to blood (see Exod. 7:17), but there is a stronger link to the end-time battle with Gog. In Ezekiel 38:21–22, it says that God will rain down overflowing rain, hail, fire, and brimstone on Gog. The hail coincides with Jesus' second coming during the seventh plague (see Rev. 16:21), while Revelation 20:10 explicitly mentions fire and brimstone in the final showdown against Gog following the 1,000 years. The first trumpet against pagan Rome typifies the final judgment against Satan and those who side with him.

How do "earth," "trees," and "green grass" relate to the siege and burning of pagan Rome? Throughout Revelation, the earth is associated with the target of God's judgment, associated as it is with worldliness, pleasure-seeking, idolatry, and evil thinking. In our discussion of Revelation 7:1–3, it was noted that trees are often associated with pagan worship. As for the green grass, Deuteronomy 29:23 indicates the totality of the destruction of Sodom and Gomorrah and the cities of the plain by noting that no "grass" (Hebrew) or "greenery" (Septuagint) remained. Together, "earth," "trees," and "green grass" picture pagan Rome sunken in self-pleasing idolatry, hinting at her ultimate demise.

The second trumpet focuses on the conflict between Rome and Genseric the Vandal, who died in AD 477, one year after the collapse of the Western Roman Empire.

In AD 428, Genseric became king of the Vandals, succeeding his brother Gunderic to the throne. Genseric moved the Vandals from Spain to northern Africa. Bonifacius (a Roman general and governor of the Diocese of Africa[85]) transported his vessels across the Straits of Gibraltar, after which Genseric concentrated his efforts on building ships, building the strongest naval power in the Mediterranean (see Jones, *The Great Nations of Today*, p. 29). In October of AD 439, he conquered Carthage, which became his base of operations.

As a Germanic Christian, Genseric had no use for paganism, so he was a threat to both the pagan Roman Empire and the Catholic Church, with its importation of pagan practices. In AD 455, Emperor Maximus was killed by the mob, and his body was thrown into the Tiber River. Recognizing his opportunity, Genseric, three days later, came boldly to pillage Rome. He paid no mind to the pleas of Pope Leo the Great to spare the city, pledging only that he would not kill the populace, burn buildings, or torture captives. Over the course of two weeks, all the goods were plundered, including the implements of the Jewish sanctuary, which had been held at Rome since the fall of Jerusalem in AD 70 at the hands of Titus' army. Nearly 400 years later, the sacred vessels were transported by barbarians to Carthage (see Jones, *Great Nations*, pp. 30, 31).

In AD 457, Emperor Majorian began assembling a naval fleet to destroy Genseric. The fleet was kept in the harbor of Carthagena in Spain. In a single day in AD 460, Genseric sunk and burned most of the fleet (which had taken 3 years to build), appropriating the remainder for his own fleet (see Jones, *Great Nations*, p. 32).

The position of Rome was even more precarious now. Its resources seriously weakened, appeal was made to the *Eastern* Empire. Constantinople assembled a staggeringly massive fleet—1,113 ships with crew and

---

[85] "Bonifacius," Wikipedia, https://1ref.us/13b (accessed June 28, 2019).

soldiers exceeding 100,000 people. Ever artful, Genseric represented that he desired 5 days in order to arrange a truce. The Roman Commander agreed, and this delay proved ruinous to Rome. He assembled his own most massive ships, filled with explosives, and when the winds proved favorable, drove right into the midst of the Roman fleet. The combination of nighttime, winds, the closeness of the ships, and the experience of Genseric and his navy, proved devastating to the Roman fleet. In this single encounter, half of the Roman army was lost (see Treiyer, *Apocalyptic Trumpets*, p. 42; Jones, *Great Nations*, pp. 33–35).

Infidel historian Gibbon recognized the importance of Genseric in the fall of Western Rome:

> After the failure of this great expedition [the Constantinopolitan fleet], Genseric again became the tyrant of the sea: the coasts of Italy, Greece, and Asia, were again exposed to his revenge and avarice; Tripoli and Sardinia returned to his obedience; he added Sicily to the number of his provinces; and, before he died, in the fulness [sic] of years and of glory, he beheld the final extinction of the empire of the West. (Gibbon, *Decline and Fall*, vol. 6, ch. 36, p. 130)

> The terrible Genseric—a name which, in the destruction of the Roman empire, has deserved an equal rank with the names of Alaric and Attila. (Gibbon, *Decline and Fall*, vol. 5, ch. 33, pp. 343, 344)

Verse 8 focuses attention on the sea, which is where Genseric conducted his campaigns. The "great burning mountain" refers not to Genseric, but to Rome, which he attacked, for Jeremiah 51:25 refers to spiritual Babylon (end-time Rome) as a "mountain of destruction … destroying all of the earth" that *Yahweh* will make a "burnt mountain." This pictures Rome as an active volcano, destroying everything it contacts, yet in the end, it is itself burned by God's sea-faring instrument of judgment. In consequence of His judgments via Genseric, Rome was weakened, but not yet destroyed, hence only a third of the sea became blood, a third of the creatures died, and a third of its ships were ruined.

It is only fitting that this partial demise of Rome takes place in the *sea* at the hands of Genseric. Rome is represented as a beast arising from the sea (see Dan. 7:3; Rev. 13:1), which refers to wicked people (see Is. 57:20; 60:5), and it is the final depository of sin (see Mic. 7:19).

The third trumpet began to sound in AD 451, ending soon thereafter in 453. If it seems odd that the third trumpet ends *before* Genseric destroys the Roman fleets in 460 and 468 under the second trumpet, observe that only the *initial sounding* of the trumpets is successive; the text says nothing about the conclusion of each trumpet in relation to the start of the next. The agent of judgment under the third trumpet is the infamous Attila the Hun.

The relatively brief career of Attila under the third trumpet is characterized in verse 10 as a falling star, singularly bright for a moment, gone the next. It was prophesied to fall upon a third of the rivers and water springs, aptly describing Attila's career in the Alps, that great source of water for Europe:

> It is said particularly that the effect would be on "the rivers," and on "the fountains of waters." ... We may suppose that this refers to those portions of the empire that abounded in rivers and streams, and more particularly those in which the rivers and streams had their origin—for the effect was permanently in the "fountains of waters." As a matter of fact, the principal operations of Attila were in the regions of the Alps, and on the portions of the empire whence the rivers flow down into Italy. The invasion of Attila is described by Mr. Gibbon in this general language: "The whole breadth of Europe, as it extends above five hundred miles from the Euxine to the Adriatic, was at once invaded, and occupied, and desolated, by the myriads of barbarians whom Attila led into the field," ii. 319, 320. (Barnes, *Notes on the Old Testament*, comments on Rev. 8:11)

Attila and his host moved west from Hungary, wreaking havoc upon Gaul. In AD 451, Roman general Aetius and the Visigothic king Theodoric I waged war against and overcame Attila and his barbarian host at the Battle of Chalons (also known as the Catalaunian Plains). This curbed Attila's Gallic expedition, changing the course of this "great star, burning like a lamp."

It is to be noted that Attila desired and sought the hand of Honoria, sister of Emperor Valentinian III, prior to his Gallic expedition. The offer was repulsed at the time and then again following the Battle of Chalons. To avenge his defeat at Chalons and frustrated attempt to secure Honoria as wife, Attila successfully obliterated Aquileia in AD 452 (see Gibbon, *Decline and Fall*, vol. 6, ch. 35, pp. 66, 67). His courage renewed by this victory, he considered inflicting the same upon Rome. During the course of these deliberations, a Roman delegation came to Attila's camp, headed up by the same Pope Leo the Great who would later plead with Genseric in AD 455 to spare Rome (see Jones, *Great Nations*, p. 43). "The barbarian monarch listened with favourable, and even respectful, attention; and the deliverance of Italy was purchased by the immense ransom or dowry of the princess Honoria." This respite, while no doubt welcome on the part of the Roman envoy, was more permanently secured upon the soon death of Attila. While awaiting delivery of Honoria, Attila took another wife, Ildico, and sometime during the wedding night (AD 453), Attila expired when an artery burst, filling his lungs and consequently suffocating him (Gibbon, *Decline and Fall*, vol. 6, ch. 35, pp. 73–75).

Before considering the fourth trumpet, one must understand the references to "bitter" water and Wormwood. In God's economy, water springs describe His Torah and the fear of *Yahweh*, both of which preserve His people from death (see Prov. 13:14; 14:27). Said another way, water springs represent eternal life (see Ps. 36:9; John 4:14). By contrast, bitter waters and wormwood are sources of complaint and great suffering (see Exod. 15:23, 24; Lam. 3:15, 19). Attila's course brought death and destruction along the waterways in the region of the Alps, making them bitter. This is a most appropriate judgment, for Revelation identifies the root problem with Rome as idolatry, and turning from God to foreign gods is a root producing gall and wormwood (see Deut. 29:17, 18).

Identifying Attila as Wormwood is also quite ironic, for wormwood is a medicinal herb that kills intestinal worms.[86] Earlier in Rome's history, when Herod Agrippa I accepted praise due only to God, God struck him, and he was eaten by worms (see Acts 12:21–23). All throughout Rome's history, pagan and papal, worship goes to self and not God, which eats out one's spiritual connection with Him, making one fit only as food for worms (see Isa. 66:24). In striking Rome, Attila served as needed herb to attack the intestinal worm of Rome.

The fourth trumpet signals the demise of the Western Roman Empire. The sun, moon, and stars were common references to the Roman emperor, consuls (governors in modern parlance), and senate, respectively (see Treiyer, *Apocalyptic Trumpets*, p. 45; Jones, *Great Nations*, p. 47). This designation for pagan Rome's leadership is most apt, for Scripture warns against imitating pagans in their worship of the sun, moon, and stars (see Deut. 4:19; 17:3; 2 Kings 23:5; Jer. 8:2).

Only a third of these were to be stricken. Earlier, Constantine had transferred imperial power to Constantinople, and later this power was divided between there and Rome. Further, Constantinople had an exarch in Ravenna, serving as a third capitol of the Roman Empire. In AD 476, one of these fell, namely, the Western Roman Empire. Interestingly, while the *state* of the Western Roman Empire was extinguished during the fourth trumpet, the Roman *church* survived, and as the bishop of Rome was elevated, Western Rome reemerged as a power different from all predecessors (see Dan. 7:24). Papal Rome will be dealt with in the last 3 trumpets, the death blow coming via the 7 last plagues of the seventh trumpet.

How were the various heavenly bodies darkened? Flavius Odoacer was a soldier who wished to do away with the office of emperor. He led a revolt that deposed Romulus Augustulus from office on September 4, AD 476. He resigned before the Roman senate, which in turn drafted a letter to

---

[86] See GELNTBSD, sec. 3.21, s.v. αψινθος.

Emperor Zeno of Constantinople, in which they "consent[ed] that the seat of universal empire shall be transferred from Rome to Constantinople" (Gibbon, *Decline and Fall*, vol. 6, ch. 36, p. 148). Odoacer was made the first barbarian king of Italy, subordinate to Emperor Zeno. With Rome's renunciation of the office of emperor, a third of the sun was stricken.

The prophecy predicts that next, the moon, or consuls, should be darkened. This occurred during the reign of the Eastern (i.e., Byzantine or Constantinopolitan) Emperor Justinian, when his general Belisarius brought Italy into subjection. "The succession of consuls finally ceased in the thirteenth year of Justinian [AD 541], whose despotic temper might be gratified by the silent extinction of a title which admonished the Romans of their ancient freedom" (Gibbon, *Decline and Fall*, vol. 7, ch. 40, p. 82).

Next, the stars, or Roman senate, were to be darkened. This occurred in AD 552, when Belisarius' successor Narses defeated the Goths and conquered Rome (see Jones, *Great Nations*, p. 53).

Following the striking of the third part of the sun and the darkening of the third part each of the moon and stars, the fourth trumpet concludes with the curious remark that the third part of the day's and night's light did not shine forth. This highlights the successive extinguishing of the 3 different luminaries. Interestingly, this slow extinguishing of the "light" of the Western Roman Empire did not forever extinguish these parties, for as previously noted, Western Roman influence would reemerge under the guise of the papacy. In this phase, the pagan worship of sun, moon, and stars is replaced with veneration of the pope (as successor of the Caesars, he is the sun), the virgin Mary (Catholic theology holds Mary to be the woman standing on the moon in Revelation 12:1), and the host of canonized saints that replaced the senators, the stars of pagan Rome (Treiyer, *Apocalyptic Trumpets*, p. 45).

Trumpets 5–7: The 3 Woes

Now that Western Rome has been dealt with, an eagle is seen flying in mid-heaven, announcing 3 woes (the last 3 trumpets). The *Textus Receptus* reads, "angel" rather than "eagle." While this might seem to agree well with the angel seen flying in mid-heaven in Revelation 14:6 announcing the first of 3 angelic messages, the reading "eagle" in the Majority and critical texts is likely correct. Why? Recall that the 4 living creatures include a flying eagle, highlighting deliverance via God's everlasting covenant (see Exod. 19:4; Rev. 12:14), and of course the trumpets are marching forward to the commencement of the end-time judgment of the seventh trumpet, culminating in the great jubilee deliverance when Jesus returns for His faithful bride.

This eagle issues a warning to those "dwelling upon the earth" on account of the 3 remaining trumpet voices. This warning anticipates the 3 angels' messages of Revelation 14:6–12: the first angel addresses his message to those who are seated (synonymous with "dwelling," *Textus Receptus*) upon the earth. Those who reject *that* message will experience the 7 last plagues of the seventh trumpet.

The first 4 seals detailed the development of the corrupt church, while the remaining 3 seals dealt with the martyrs' cry for justice and God's response (the end-time judgment). The trumpets have a corresponding arrangement: the first 4 detail God's judgment on Western Rome, while the last 3 are set apart as "woes." The fifth and sixth trumpets deal with the Eastern Roman Empire, ruled from Constantinople, which was responsible for elevating the papacy above all bishops, while the seventh trumpet disposes of the papacy once and for all.

The Fifth Trumpet: Woe #1

In the third trumpet, Attila the Hun was represented as a great star. Here in the fifth trumpet, the principal agent of God's judgment is also represented as a star fallen to the earth. The star of the third trumpet was "burning like a lamp," signifying its very brief period of activity. The absence of such a description here suggests a longer judgment.

The first four trumpets foretold the demise of the Western Roman Empire in AD 476, and the fourth trumpet mentioned the darkening of the stars, foretelling the end of the Roman senate in 552. Hence, the activity of the fifth trumpet, which begins the history of the fall of the *Eastern* Roman Empire, is expected to begin sometime *after* 552.

This star was given the key to the "well of the abyss." To the modern western reader, this may not immediately suggest the appropriate image to deduce which part of the world we are to examine following AD 552. When we turn to the creation account, we learn that "the earth was formlessness and emptiness, and darkness was upon the face of the deep" (Gen. 1:2), which the Septuagint translates as "abyss." This informs us that an "abyss" is an undeveloped area. Further, the "well" of said abyss suggests that this undeveloped area is a desert region.

At this point, we will simply assert the time, location, and people in view, and let the remainder of the commentary on verses 1–12 validate the following identification: the fifth trumpet details the rise of Islam, specifically focusing on the spread of Mohammed's religion following his death on June 8, AD 632. Gibbon confirms the connection between Islam and Eastern Rome:

> While the state was exhausted by the Persian war, and the church was distracted by the Nestorian and Monophysite sects, Mahomet, with the sword in one hand and the Koran in the other, erected his throne on the ruins of Christianity and of Rome. The genius of the Arabian prophet, the manners of his nation, and the spirit of his religion, involve the causes of the decline and fall of the Eastern empire; and our eyes are curiously intent on one of the most memorable revolutions, which have impressed a new and lasting character on the nations of the globe. (Gibbon, *Decline and Fall*, vol. 9, ch. 50, p. 1)

Under the fourth trumpet, the third part of the sun was struck and darkened, signifying the end of the Western Roman emperor. The darkening of the sun under the fifth trumpet suggests that the activity of Islam will culminate in the end of the *Eastern* emperor. The word for "air" (verse 2) is used in the Septuagint only in 2 Samuel 22:12 and its parallel, Psalm 18:11, stating that *Yahweh's* tent (His heavenly sanctuary) is in "clouds of air." Three verses earlier, smoke comes from *Yahweh's* nose, and fire from His mouth; the smoke from the well in Revelation 9:2 is like "smoke of a blazing furnace." This suggests that this verse refers to a masking, as it were, of the true Sun of righteousness (see Mal. 4:2) and His heavenly sanctuary. Indeed, papal Christianity was so focused on battling Islam during the long centuries of the Dark Ages that a true knowledge of God was lost.

There are locusts seen emerging from the smoke of this conflict. Locusts are known for swarming, as in the eighth plague upon Egypt (see Exod. 10:12–15), indicating that the introduction of Islam would be rapid and extensive. History confirms this:

> In the ten years of the administration of Omar, the Saracens reduced to his obedience thirty-six thousand cities or castles, destroyed four thousand churches or temples of the unbelievers, and edified fourteen hundred moschs for the exercise of the religion of Mahomet. One hundred years after his flight from Mecca, the arms and the reign of his successors extended from India to the Atlantic Ocean, over the various and distant provinces, which may be comprised under the names of I. Persia; II. Syria; III. Egypt; IV. Africa; and V. Spain. (Gibbon, *Decline and Fall*, vol. 9, ch. 51, pp. 116, 117)

Unlike the swarms that befell Egypt under the eighth plague, devouring the plants of the field and the fruit of the trees, these locusts are specifically commanded to *not* damage the grass, plants, or trees. In Revelation 7:1–3, a similar restriction is given in the end time to not harm trees until God's servants, the 144,000, are sealed in their foreheads, i.e., have their characters perfected. Revelation 9 refers to a sealing work in prior centuries. People were sealed who *left nothing undone* of what God had revealed concerning their characters up to that point.

History provides an astounding confirmation of the command given these "locusts." Ten years after he entered Medina in AD 622, Mohammed died June 8, 632 and was immediately succeeded by Abu Bakr. Abu Bakr sent forth his army of Saracens with these words:

> "Remember," said the successor of the prophet, "that you are always in the presence of God, on the verge of death, in the assurance of judgment, and the hope of paradise. Avoid injustice and oppression; consult with your brethren, and study to preserve the love and confidence of your troops. When you fight the battles of the Lord, acquit yourselves like men, without turning your backs; but let not your victory be stained with the blood of women or children. Destroy no palm-trees, nor burn any fields of corn. Cut down no fruit-trees, nor do any mischief to cattle, only such as you kill to eat. When you make any covenant or article, stand to it, and be as good as your word. As you go on, you will find some religious persons who live retired in monasteries, and propose to themselves to serve God that way: let them alone, and neither kill them nor destroy their monasteries: And you will find another sort of people, that belong to the synagogue of Satan, who have shaven crowns [Even in the seventh century, the monks were generally laymen: they wore their hair long and dishevelled, and shaved their heads when they were ordained priests. The circular tonsure was sacred and mysterious; it was the crown of thorns; but it was likewise a royal diadem, and every priest was a king, &c. (Thomassin, *Discipline de l'Eglise*, tom. i. p. 721–758, especially p. 737, 738)]; be sure you cleave their skulls, and give them no quarter till they either turn Mahometans or pay tribute." (Gibbon, *Decline and Fall*, vol. 9, ch. 51, pp. 135, 136)

Abu Bakr unwittingly issued the command given in Revelation 9:4, ordering that Christians were to be spared, while the monks, representing a paganized Christianity in his mind, were to be dealt with as infidels. It is prophesied in verse 5 that the locusts have power to torment for 5 months, answering to the common life cycle of the desert locust. From the issuance of this decree in AD 632 by Abu Bakr until the signing of a peace treaty between Caliph Harun al-Rashid and Constantinople in 782 was 150 years, or 5 prophetic months of 30 prophetic days each (see Treiyer, *Apocalyptic Trumpets*, pp. 50, 51).

Rome would think to change "appointed times and law" (Dan. 7:25). Constantine initiated the first Sunday law in AD 321, yet "generally speaking, the day of the sun did not occupy the place of Sabbath as the day of rest until the 6th century" (Treiyer, *Apocalyptic Trumpets*, p. 52), and of course, the papacy was not formally inaugurated as a counterfeit high priest until 538 (see *THE STAND*, comments on Daniel 7, 8, and 12). The papal system takes credit for changing the 10 Commandments by virtue of altering the fourth commandment, which commands keeping holy God's seventh-day Sabbath:

> Q. *What is the Third Commandment?*
>
> A. The Third Commandment is: Remember that thou keep holy the Sabbath day.
>
> Q. *Which is the Sabbath day?*
>
> A. Saturday is the Sabbath day.
>
> Q. Why do we observe Sunday instead of Saturday?
>
> A. We observe Sunday instead of Saturday because the Catholic Church transferred the solemnity from Saturday to Sunday. (Geiermann, *The Convert's Catechism of Catholic Doctrine*, p. 50)

Reference to the current Roman Catholic catechism confirms that the papacy has made three major changes to God's law: 1) the change of the Sabbath to Sunday, 2) the removal of the second commandment prohibiting idolatry, and 3) splitting the prohibition concerning coveting of the tenth commandment into two pieces to retain 10 Commandments (see *Catechism of the Catholic Church*, pp. 496, 497).

The seal of God is in His law (see Isa. 8:16), which is written in the hearts of believers in fulfillment of His everlasting covenant (see Jer. 31:31–34; Ezek. 36:26, 27). Islam, in Revelation 9, attacks those who know the claims of God's law but live contrary to it. This is true especially of Roman Catholic leadership.

The locust army of verses 7–11 draws on the imagery of Joel 1:6, which describes the enemy of *Yahweh's* people as an immense number of locusts with lions' teeth. Since Scripture uses the lion to represent judgment, this army is God's agency to punish apostasy in the Roman Catholic Church and bring down the Eastern Roman Empire, for they have retarded the fulfillment of His everlasting covenant.

The locusts are compared to war horses in appearance, just as Joel 2:5 refers to the locust army as warriors with chariots. This is well suited to the Islamic armies on their horses. The golden crowns atop their heads answer to the golden helmets worn by the Muslims. Likewise, the description of "chests like iron breastplates" matches the historical fact that Muslim soldiers and their horses wore iron armor (see Treiyer, *Apocalyptic Trumpets*, pp. 49, 50).

The horses' tails are described as scorpion stingers. "The prophet who teaches lies, he is the tail" (Isa. 9:15). The arch deceiver, Satan, deceived a third of the heavenly angels with his tail (see Rev. 12:4), referring to the lies he trafficked against God's government (see Ezek. 28:16). Thus, God identifies Islam as a movement characterized by a lying prophet (Mohammed), one speaking for the father of lies, Satan himself (see John 8:44).

Reference is made once again to 5 months in verse 10. One might suppose this is the same 5-month period of verse 5, but verse 11 specifies that the locusts now have a king over them. This was not true of Islam at its inception or for many centuries afterward. Not until Othman I was there an Ottoman Empire or organized government of the Muslims, of which he was the Caliph. Note Gibbon's description:

It was on the twenty-seventh of July, in the year twelve hundred and ninety-nine of the Christian aera, that Othman first invaded the territory of Nicomedia; and the singular accuracy of the date seems to disclose some foresight of the rapid and destructive growth of the monster. (Gibbon, *Decline and Fall*, vol. 11, ch. 64, p. 157)

Remarkably, Gibbon refers to the work of Islam from Othman I onward as "destructive," which harmonizes with verse 11, in which the king's name is said to be Abaddon ("destruction") in Hebrew, and Apollyon ("destroyer," a variant of the Greek *apoleia*, meaning "destruction"). Table 7 summarizes where the Septuagint uses *apoleia* to translate the Hebrew *'abaddon*:

Table 7: *Abaddon* **(Hebrew) and** *Apollyon* **(Septuagint)**

REFERENCE	SIGNIFICANCE
Job 28:22	*Abaddon* equated with death
Job 26:6; Prov. 15:11; 27:20; Ps. 88:11	*Abaddon* equated with the grave
Job 31:12 (see also verses 11, 14, 33)	*Abaddon* linked with judgment for covering sin

Putting the foregoing verses together, it becomes clear that the locust king, the angel of the abyss, Apollyon ("Destroyer") brings *death* ("destruction") as God's *judgment* via the Muslim conquests. Othman I was the earthly agent of death, while the one with true dominion over death is the devil (see Heb. 2:14). Ironically, Satan is locked in the abyss and ultimately destroyed in Revelation 20.

Gibbon provided us a precise date, July 27, 1299, permitting us to check for an historical terminus 150 years later. On October 31, 1448, Emperor John VIII Palaiologos died, leaving vacant his throne. Historian Gibbon states:

The empress-mother, the senate and soldiers, the clergy and people, were unanimous in the cause of the lawful successor [Constantine]: and the despot Thomas, who, ignorant of the change, accidentally returned to the capital, asserted with becoming zeal the interest of his absent brother. An ambassador, the historian Phranza, was immediately despatched to the court of Adrianople. Amurath received him with honour and dismissed him with gifts; but the gracious approbation of the Turkish sultan announced his supremacy, and the approaching downfall of the Eastern empire. By the hands of two illustrious deputies, the Imperial crown was placed at Sparta on the head of Constantine. (Gibbon, *Decline and Fall*, vol. 11, ch. 67, p. 322)

Constantine XI was installed as Byzantine emperor on January 6, 1449, 150 years after Othman I's invasion of Nicomedia in 1299. The fall of the Eastern Empire's capitol, Constantinople, was now assured.

The Sixth Trumpet: Woe #2

The sixth trumpet opens with Jesus still in the Holy Place, ministering at the golden altar of incense. The direction given to "loose" the 4 angels points back to the loosing of the fifth seal, in which the martyrs cry out for justice. The sixth trumpet is a continuation of the answer to that plea.

Revelation is symbolic, so one need not assume that these 4 angels are winged, heavenly creatures. Angels represented teachers and ministers—church leadership—in Revelation 1:20; so here, the angels represent Islamic leadership, specifically the 4 sultans/sultanates of the Turkish Empire: those of Baghdad, Damascus, Iconium, and Aleppo (see Jones, *Great Nations*, p. 72; Treiyer, *Apocalyptic Trumpets*, p. 55) at the *beginning* of the hour-day-month-year prophetic time period, as well as the 4 powers to which the Ottoman Empire yielded itself at the end of this same time period.

The mention of the Euphrates points one to the river flowing through Babylon. When its lifegiving waters were diverted during Belshazzar's reign, Babylon fell (see Isa. 45:1, 2; Dan. 5:30). In this context, *spiritual* Babylon is in view, namely Rome. Since the Western Roman Empire fell during the fourth trumpet, this can refer only to the remaining Eastern Roman

Empire and the papacy. All support for the Eastern Roman Empire will be cut off under the sixth trumpet. Support for papal Rome will be weakened, yet its final destruction awaits the conclusion of the seventh trumpet, when the sixth and seventh plagues are poured out, the Euphrates dries up completely, and God pronounces its doom (see Rev. 16:12–21).

The 5 prophetic months of Revelation 9:10 terminated in 1449, with the crowning of Constantine XI Palaiologos as emperor of Constantinople upon securing the permission of Sultan Murad II. Murad II died in 1451, and his son, Mehmed II, determined to take Constantinople. The city fell May 29, 1453, as did Emperor Constantine XI and his soldiers in their last stand. One might see in this event a fulfillment of Revelation 9:15: the hour (of judgment) for Constantinople occurred on that very day, month, and year, for the Eastern Roman Empire ceased. As there were 3 empires at the time—the Eastern (Byzantine) Roman Empire, papal Rome, and now the non-Roman Muslim Ottoman Empire—this would represent the death of the third part of men (see Treiyer, *Apocalyptic Trumpets*, p. 55).

Of course, the foregoing event, while historical, leaves a few loose ends in terms of the prophecy. First, there is no apparent way in which to link the dates January 6, 1449 (the installation of Constantine XI as emperor) or July 27, 1449 (the end of the 150 years that commenced July 27, 1299) to May 29, 1453 (fall of Constantinople) by the expression "for the hour, and for the day, month and year." Second, in what way do the 4 angels play into the downfall of Constantinople? Third, can it really be said that Constantinople *fell* at this point? True, the Eastern Roman Empire did fall, but it was simply replaced by the Ottoman Empire, which took Constantinople as its seat of empire.

The event toward which Revelation is pointing us must account for 1) the time period, 2) the 4 angels, and 3) the death of the third part of men. Thus, the phrase "for the hour, and for the day, month, and year" refers not to the point in time at which the *Eastern Roman Empire* fell, but rather the *period* of prophetic time during which Islam would carry on its destructive work against *papal Rome* (the papacy, not the Eastern Roman Empire, is the principal, earthly antagonist in the book of Revelation). At the end of this period, the *Muslim Ottoman Empire* would fall. Hence, the first third of men to fall was the Western Roman Empire (fourth trumpet), while the second third of men to fall refers to the fall of Constantinople as the seat of the Muslim Ottoman Empire.

Applying the prophetic-day-for-a-literal-year principle, this works out to 15 days plus 1 year plus 30 years plus 360 years, or 391 years and 15 days. The terminus of the fifth trumpet was July 27, 1449; marching ahead 391 years and 15 days takes one to August 11, 1840.

Did anything happen on August 11, 1840 to confirm this understanding? After studying this prophecy, Millerite preacher Josiah Litch published a book in 1838, in which he *predicted* that the fall of the Ottoman Empire "will take place about 1840" (Litch, *The Probability of the Second Coming of Christ About A.D. 1843*, p. 189). Litch grew more convinced as time drew near, writing more specifically, "the 391 years 15 days … will end in the 11th of August, 1840, when the Ottoman power in Constantinople may be expected to be broken. And this, I believe, will be found to be the case" (Litch, *Signs of the Times*, August 1, 1840).

When this highly specific and seemingly absurd prediction came to pass, many were astounded and began to take prophetic preaching seriously. The Eastern Roman Empire's fate was sealed when it *subordinated* itself to the Ottoman Empire's sultan. Likewise, the Ottoman Empire's demise was marked when it *subordinated* itself: "At the very time specified [by Josiah Litch, namely August 11, 1840], Turkey, through her ambassadors, accepted the protection of the allied powers of Europe, and thus placed herself under the control of Christian nations. The event exactly fulfilled the prediction" (White, *GC*, p. 335).

The 4 angels at the beginning of this 391-year-15-day period were the 4 sultans of the Ottoman Empire in Baghdad, Damascus, Iconium, and Aleppo. At the end of this period, the 4 angels refer to those to whom the Ottoman Empire yielded in 1840, namely, Britain, Russia, Austria, and Prussia (see Jones, *Great Nations*, pp. 76, 77). The third of men to be killed was not those killed *by* the Ottoman Empire, but the Ottoman Empire itself. With the Western Roman Empire defunct and Constantinople no longer a power with which to be reckoned, papal Rome has yet to meet its end.

Attention is now given to the Muslim warriors during this prophetic period. Their numbers were beyond count, being "myriads upon myriads," hearkening back to the description of the angelic host at the commencement of judgment in Daniel 7:10 and Revelation 5:11. This language confirms that the Islamic hordes served as God's agent of judgment at this time.

The prophecy records the colors of the horsemen's breastplates as "fiery red, hyacinth blue and sulphurous yellow," precisely matching what history records the Turkish warriors wore (Treiyer, *Apocalyptic Trumpets*, p. 57). Their heads are said to be like lions, similar to the description of the Saracen hosts in verse 8, showing them to be God's instrument of judgment, as well as their great strength. However, this time there is no mention of their teeth; instead, "fire, smoke, and brimstone" were proceeding out of their mouths. Innate, natural, lion-like strength of earlier centuries has given way to mankind's invention of gunpowder. Gunpowder is composed of 2 fuels—sulfur (brimstone) and charcoal— as well as an oxidizer—saltpeter (potassium nitrate).[87] John's description highlights the brimstone of gunpowder, its ignition upon firing, and the resultant smoke upon firing a shot, apparently in line with the heads of the warriors' horses. Gibbon confirms the use of gunpowder in the conquest of Constantinople in 1453:

> Among the implements of destruction, he [Turkish sultan Mohammed] studied with peculiar care the recent and tremendous discovery of the Latins [firearms]; and his artillery surpassed whatever had yet appeared in the world. ...
>
> A foundry was established at Hadrianople: the metal was prepared; and at the end of three months, Urban produced a piece of brass ordnance of stupendous, and almost incredible

---

[87] "Gunpowder," Wikipedia, https://1ref.us/13c (accessed June 30, 2019).

magnitude; a measure of twelve palms is assigned to the bore; and the stone bullet weighed above six hundred pounds. A vacant place before the new palace was chosen for the first experiment; but to prevent the sudden and mischievous effects of astonishment and fear, a proclamation was issued, that the cannon would be discharged the ensuing day. The explosion was felt or heard in a circuit of a hundred furlongs: the ball, by the force of gunpowder, was driven above a mile; and on the spot where it fell, it buried itself a fathom deep in the ground. (Gibbon, *Decline and Fall*, vol. 12, ch. 68, pp. 13, 14)

There are two sources of authority for this army of horsemen: their mouths and tails. The gunpowder came from their mouths, pointing to military coercion. The tail refers to the lying of a false prophet (see remarks on verse 10), hence the deceitful message through Mohammed (and ultimately Satan—note the description of the tails as serpents) that impelled the warriors forward, giving them confidence in the success of their enterprise.

With the conquest of Constantinople in 1453, a defense against the Muslims was lost. Papal Rome was distracted by fighting off the Muslim hordes during this time period, and this providentially permitted the rise and spread of the Protestant Reformation. Catholic monarchs could not assert their power to quash the growing Protestant Reformation because they required the support of German princes (who favored the Protestant cause) to ward off the Muslim encroachment (see Treiyer, *Apocalyptic Trumpets*, pp. 55, 56).

The last two verses of Revelation 9 confirm that papal Rome is in view. The principal sin against which Scripture warns is idolatry, the divinely prescribed antidote being God's holy Sabbath and the system of salvation outlined in the sanctuary (see Lev. 26:1, 2). The principal changes papal Rome has made to God's 10 Commandments are the removal of the second commandment (forbidding idolatry) and the alteration of the fourth commandment to commend Sunday—rather than Sabbath—worship.

Regarding the sanctuary, the mass is a counterfeit of salvation outlined in the heavenly sanctuary (see *THE STAND*, comments on Daniel 8). The list of idol-making materials in verse 20 alludes to Belshazzar's idolatrous revelry (see Dan. 5:4, 23). The conspicuous omission of iron—representing Rome in Daniel 2:32–33—only highlights the Roman papal power all the more.

The foolhardiness of clinging to the papal system, being in every respect a perversion of Christianity and salvation through faith in Christ alone, is highlighted by the observation that the various idols are "not able to see, nor hear, nor walk." Daniel confirmed the inability of idols to see or hear (see 5:23), and Jeremiah their inability to walk (see 10:5). The end of the verse calls idol worship exactly what it is—the worship of demons.

The last verse draws attention to God's downtrodden law, citing commandments 6, 7, and 8, as well as the "sorceries" that hold adherents of the papal system in disobedience. What are these "sorceries" (Greek φαρμακεια)? During the time period of the sixth trumpet, this could very simply refer to mind-altering drugs, as opium was widely used within the Ottoman Empire, both for medicinal purposes and recreational use.[88] More broadly, sorcery amounts to anything and everything that distracts people from prayer and studying and meditating upon God's Word; those things that prevent the seat of their moral decision-making, the frontal lobe, from being completely under God's control. Today, this goes well beyond drugs and alcohol to include the cinema, so-called "social" media, pornography, video games, and of course, the proliferation of mind-altering psychotropic drugs compounded in medical pharmacies. All of these can be so addicting that they are nearly impossible to give up apart from the power of Jesus' enabling grace. They medicate and confuse minds, making people practically incapable of comprehending truth and heeding God's voice.

---

[88] "Opium," Wikipedia, https://1ref.us/13d (accessed June 30, 2019)

The Strong Angel

The progress of the sixth trumpet is apparently interrupted as John's attention is arrested by the appearance of a strong Angel coming down from heaven. However, this "interlude," as scholars style it, actually continues the prophetic timeline without interruption.

The word "Angel" has been capitalized. Let us examine the evidence to determine His identity. "His face like the sun" is word-for-word identical to Matthew 17:2, describing Jesus' face when He was transfigured before Peter, James, and John. The angel's lower legs are described with the very language Exodus 13:21 uses for the pillar of fire by night that led the Israelites in the wilderness. "Clothed with a cloud" suggests the pillar of cloud by day in the same passage, identified as the Angel of God, Jesus Himself (see Exod. 14:19). Recall also that the Son of man, Jesus, came before the Ancient of Days with the clouds of heaven for His role in the end-time judgment. With that said is the angel of Revelation 10 Jesus?

What about the arch (iris) of light about His head? This detail hearkens back to Revelation 4, in which the Father's throne was banded with an arch of light. We discovered that the iris points back to the anointing oil of Exodus 30:22–33, used for anointing the sanctuary, its various articles, and ultimately Aaron as high priest, as well as his sons. It also suggested the bright bow surrounding Jesus' throne in Ezekiel 1:28. Finally, it points back to the rainbow as the sign of the everlasting covenant between God and every living creature in Genesis 9:16. Together, these observations put beyond all doubt that the strong Angel is Jesus, who desires to marry His people, fulfilling the everlasting covenant.

Jesus holds in His hand an open scroll. The language of verse 2 points us to Daniel 12:4,[89] in which Daniel is commanded to seal his scroll until the end time, which began February 10, 1798. Since Jesus now holds *open* the time prophecies of Daniel, February10, 1798 is past. In Revelation

---

[89] BYZ uses the same Greek word for "scroll" as does Daniel 12:4 (LXX and Theodotion), while TR and NTG employ a modified word, meaning "little scroll."

10:7, the seventh trumpet—during which the wedding begins, and the 2,300 days conclude—is referred to as future. Since Revelation 9:15 took us to August 11, 1840, chapter 10 concerns events that take place just prior to the commencement of Jesus' wedding on October 22, 1844.

Following 1798, there was an explosion of interest in the time prophecies. William Miller arrived at his understanding of the prophecies in 1818 and began to preach them publicly in 1831. In 1821, Joseph Wolff, the "missionary to the world," began to preach the soon coming of Jesus. Lacunza, a Jesuit priest writing under the pseudonym Rabbi ben-Ezra, wrote about the second advent, and in the mid-1820s, his work reached England and was translated into English. Following Josiah Litch's astonishing prediction that the Ottoman Empire would fall on August 11, 1840, interest soared in the time prophecies (see White, *GC*, pp. 331, 334, 335, 357, 363).

Why are His feet on the sea and earth? "The Angel's position, with one foot on the sea, the other on the land, signifies the wide extent of the proclamation of the message. It will cross the broad waters and be proclaimed in other countries, even to all the world" (White, 19*MR*, p. 321). "The mighty angel who instructed John was no less a personage than Jesus Christ. Setting His right foot on the sea, and His left upon the dry land, shows the part which He is acting in the closing scenes of the great controversy with Satan. This position denotes His supreme power and authority over the whole earth" (White, *1MR*, p. 99).

Jesus cries with a voice like a lion roaring. In our study of chapter 5, we learned that the lion is associated with judgment, hence His message concerns judgment.

Concerning the 7 thunders, no better understanding can be given than that which follows:

John heard the mysteries which the thunders uttered, but he was commanded not to write them. The special light given to John which was expressed in the seven thunders was a delineation of events which would transpire under the first and second angels' messages. It was not best for the people to know these things, for their faith must necessarily be tested. In the order of God, most wonderful and advanced truths would be proclaimed. The first and second angels' messages were to be proclaimed, but no further light was to be revealed before these messages had done their specific work. (White, *1MR*, pp. 99, 100)

The 7 thunders outlined events to follow under the first and second angel's messages of Revelation 14:6–8. We are not told what these events were, but we do know about the timing of the messages:

In these cities [Boston, others of the East] the message of the first angel went with great power in 1842 and 1843. (White, *Ev*, p. 390)

The second angel's message of Revelation 14 was first preached in the summer of 1844, and it then had a more direct application to the churches of the United States, where the warning of the judgment had been most widely proclaimed and most generally rejected, and where the declension in the churches had been most rapid. But the message of the second angel did not reach its complete fulfillment in 1844. The churches then experienced a moral fall, in consequence of their refusal of the light of the advent message; but that fall was not complete. (White, *GC*, p. 389)

Since the 7 thunders outlined events to follow under these messages, and the second angel's message did not reach its culmination in 1844, we conclude that not everything the 7 thunders spoke was fulfilled when judgment commenced on October 22, 1844. Apart from the 7 thunders of Revelation 10:3–4, the word "thunders" occurs another 7 times in Revelation. Table 8 provides a synopsis of each occurrence:

Table 8: The 7 Thunders of Revelation (Outside Revelation 10:3–4)

REFERENCE	SUMMARY OF VERSE(S)	HISTORICAL (OR FUTURE) FULFILLMENT OF THUNDER
Rev. 4:5	A: Thunders proceed from throne.	A: End-time judgment convenes. Marriage ceremony to begin.
Rev. 6:1	B: With voice of thunder, lion-like creature shows John white horse.	B: First seal opens (judgment begins). True church began victoriously.
Rev. 8:5	C: Thunders follow angel casting censer into earth.	C: Intercession ceases. Probation closed.
Rev. 11:19	D: Lightning, voices, thunder, earthquake, hail.	D: Seventh plague poured out on wicked (see Rev. 16:17, 21).
Rev. 14:2	C': John hears voice like many waters, great thunder, harpists.	C': 144,000 sealed—their probation has closed—in full harmony with God.
Rev. 16:18	B': Thunders follow voice from the temple saying, "It is over!"	B': Onset of seventh plague. Harlot Babylon collapses.
Rev. 19:6	A': John hears voice of vast multitude, many waters, thunderclaps.	A': End-time judgment (marriage) complete. Jesus to come for His bride.

Table 8 reveals that the 7 thunders all concern the end-time judgment. They are arranged in a chiastic structure; the focal point is the judgment poured out upon the wicked during the seventh plague.

As an Angel, Jesus stands for the fourth time in Revelation, and His fifth stance follows in verse 8 (the previous stances were in Revelation 3:20; 5:6; 8:3). He takes an oath in verse 5 with language reminiscent of Daniel 12:7. A key difference is that the reference to the 1,260 days is lacking. The 1,260 and 1,290 days terminated in 1798. On the other hand, the 1,335 days extended to the beginning of 1844, and the 2,300 evening-mornings to October 22, 1844, when the judgment wedding commenced. Jesus' left hand is no longer raised, as the first two prophecies have reached their fulfillment; His right hand remains raised, a pledge that the cleansing of the sanctuary will be brought to completion during His wedding.

Jesus swears by "Him who lives forever and ever," a reference not only to Daniel 12:7, but also Deuteronomy 32:40, in which *Yahweh* lifts

His hand to heaven and swears that He lives forever. Study of this passage, particularly verses 36 and 43, reveals that *Yahweh vindicates* His people when every earthly support is gone and *provides atonement* for His land, i.e., His people. The remainder of Revelation 10:6 identifies Him who lives forever and ever as the Creator of heaven, earth, the sea, and everything therein, using the language of the Sabbath commandment (see Exod. 20:11). Hence, Jesus' oath focuses attention on Himself as Creator, the one who makes atonement for His people, as well as the Sabbath, the memorial of His everlasting covenant and His pledge to marry His people (see Exod. 31:16, 17; Isa. 54:5; 56:1–6).

Let us note how critical it is to understand and be able to chart the Bible's time prophecies. Some may be content with a simple "Jesus only" message, but remember that Revelation opens with the assertion that the entire book is a revelation of Jesus Christ. Satan knows the value of these prophecies, so he has done all he can to discredit God as Creator. The father of modern geology, James Hutton, put forth a new theory before the Royal Society of Edinburgh on July 4, 1785, published in full in 1788 as *Theory of the Earth*. He proposed that geological processes in the past were as slow as what he observed in his day, leading him to suppose that the exposed rock he saw took vast amounts of time to form. He concluded, "The result, therefore, of our present enquiry is, that we find no vestige of a beginning, no prospect of an end."[90] This was not well-received, being perceived as atheistic. Not deterred, he expanded his theory and republished it as *An Investigation of the Principles of Knowledge and of the Progress of Reason, from Sense to Science and Philosophy* (comprising an astonishing 2,138 pages) in 1795, just 3 years prior to 1798.[91]

In October 1844, the very month in which the 2,300 evening-mornings terminated and the end-time day of atonement began, publisher and scientist Robert Chambers anonymously published *Vestiges of the Natural*

[90] James Hutton, "Theory of the Earth," Transactions of the Royal Society of Edinburgh, vol. I, part II, pp. 209–304, plates I and II, https://1ref.us/13e (accessed July 1, 2019).

[91] "James Hutton," Wikipedia, https://1ref.us/13f (accessed July 1, 2019).

History of Creation, a work that denied the biblical creation account, promoting instead the notion of transmutation of species. Darwin himself felt that this work prepared the way for his own work, *The Origin of Species*, completed in 1844, though not published until 1859.[92] For the student of Bible prophecy, it should be plain that Satan masterminded such works, timing them to inspire disbelief in the prophecies being fulfilled at the time of their publication.

Jesus swears that "time will be no longer." In Daniel 12:6, the question is asked, "Until what point [till one finally reaches] the end of these wonders?" In response, verses 7–13 delineate the 1,260, 1,290, 1,335-day, and 2,300-evening-morning prophecies. Jesus' words in Revelation 10:6 mean that the last of these time prophecies, the 2,300 evening-mornings, is about to conclude. Time prophecies stop at this point, highlighting the marriage between the Son of man and His bride as the crowning event in salvation history. Jesus is *not* predicting a point beyond which time ceases to be part of our existence, for His very next words speak of the mystery of God being completed "in the *days* of the voice of the seventh angel," during which time the wedding takes place.

The trumpets are an answer to the cry of the martyrs of the fifth seal, who were told to "cease for a *time* longer." That waiting time is now over, when "time will be no longer." Reference to Revelation 11:15 confirms that the trumpeting forth of the seventh angel corresponds to the opening of the end-time judgment. The focus is no longer on *when* events will transpire, but on the *nature* of the greatest event to follow Jesus' death on the cross—the completion of the "mystery of God," the full maturation of the character of God in His people, the fulfillment of the everlasting covenant.

When the mystery of God is completed, God's people will finally be a perfect reflection of His character. According to 2 Peter 3:9–18, this

---

[92] "Vestiges of the Natural History of Creation," Wikipedia, https://1ref.us/13g (accessed July 1, 2019).

very transformation hastens Christ's return.[93] Beyond that point, Christ's return can be just as quick as the members of His corporate bride are willing to *unite* in submitting to His will (see Eph. 4.13). No one knows when probation will close and Jesus will return (see Matt. 24:29–39), for this is not fixed to a particular *date*, but rather a *condition* or *state* of character. Many pooh-pooh the idea of character perfection in God's people, confounding it with the heresy of perfectionism,[94] but Jesus essentially counters, "The mystery of God is to be brought to completion, according to the good news He proclaimed to His servants the prophets." If we deny character perfection before Jesus returns, we deny Jesus's ability to prepare His bride for a perfect marriage.

John is now directed to eat the little scroll. Though it would be sweet in the mouth like honey, it would make his stomach bitter. The language hearkens back to Ezekiel 2:8–3:11, in which *Adonai Yahweh* hands Ezekiel a written scroll and commissions him to speak the words therein to rebellious Israel. That it is to be sweet in his mouth like honey indicates that the message concerns *Yahweh's* judgments, words, and wisdom (see Ps. 19:9, 10; 119:102, 103; Prov. 24:13, 14). When *Yahweh* brought his people out of Egypt, He gave them the test about gathering manna each day except the Sabbath. The manna was sweet like honey; hence, eating the scroll hints at the Sabbath.

Ezekiel was told that Israel would refuse to listen to his message, and it is this rejection that makes the sweet message so bitter in one's stomach. The Millerites who initially proclaimed the message described in Revelation 10 did not recognize in it the Sabbath message. However, following the Great Disappointment of October 22, 1844, there were some

---

[93] " 'When the fruit is brought forth, immediately he putteth in the sickle, because the harvest is come.' Christ is waiting with longing desire for the manifestation of Himself in His church. When the character of Christ shall be perfectly reproduced in His people, then He will come to claim them as His own" (White, *COL*, p. 69).

[94] Perfectionism teaches that God's people reach a point beyond which they cannot be tempted. The Bible teaches that, just like Jesus in His earthly life, God's people *will* be tempted—indeed, sorely so—until Jesus comes, but they will be brought into perfect harmony with God, no longer *indulging* sin in thought, word, or deed, or omitting any good works that they ought to do.

who began to see the Sabbath truth contained in the first angel's message of Revelation 14:6–7.

Ezekiel's scroll was written on both sides (see Ezek. 2:10), in turn pointing to the two-sided flying scroll Zechariah saw in vision (see Zech. 5:1–4). This flying scroll contained the 10 Commandments, one side containing humanity's duty to God, the other side, our duty to each other. Further, the dimensions of Zechariah' scroll correspond to the porch of Solomon's temple (see 1 Kings 6:3), hinting that the scroll John receives concerns the (heavenly) temple (see Rev. 11:1–6).

Once he has digested the scroll and found it to be bitter, John is directed to proclaim the message *again*. Why? A clue is found in the book of Ezekiel, for immediately following Ezekiel's commission to eat the scroll and preach to rebellious Israel, he hears a voice proclaiming, "Blessed be the glory of *Yahweh* from his place" (Ezek. 3:12). This place is of course the heavenly sanctuary, the location of the judgment. The book of Ezekiel centers around God's work of atonement, with chapters 40–48 devoted exclusively to a picture of the temple, given to Ezekiel on "Rosh Hashanah, on the tenth of the month" (40:1), which is none other than the Day of Atonement (see Lev. 23:27). The message of final atonement and end-time judgment must go forth to the world.

John's experience eating the scroll typifies the Millerites in their experience as October 22, 1844 came and went. History confirms that the first and second angels' messages went forth from 1842–1844 as the Millerite preachers proclaimed the second advent was near. Conviction settled on many hearts, working reformation in the believers who wished to be ready for the very soon coming of Jesus. The Millerite preachers proclaimed the cleansing of the sanctuary on October 22, 1844, which they misunderstood to refer to Jesus' cleansing the earth by fire at His return. These preachers were correct as to the date and event (the cleansing of the sanctuary), but they misunderstood the *nature* of the cleansing.

The experience of the Millerites was like that of Jesus' disciples at the time of His crucifixion. The disciples recognized Jesus as a conquering king, so His death came as a crushing blow. In fact, He *was* a conquering king, but they misunderstood the *nature* of His kingdom and the manner in which He conquers. He does not employ force of arms, but woos people with the promptings of his Spirit (see Hos. 2:14; Zech. 4:6). After His resurrection, their hopes revived; they began to understand the Scriptures rightly and once again went forth proclaiming Jesus.

Likewise, the Millerites' hopes were blasted on October 22, 1844, but following a season of prayer for an understanding of what happened, Hiram Edson was given a glimpse of heaven in which he saw Jesus ministering as High Priest in the Holy of Holies. While many Millerites promptly fell away from their belief as a result of this Great Disappointment and joined the ranks of those who mocked, making the experience that much more bitter for the rest, those who maintained their faith were motivated by Edson's vision to study the matter out thoroughly from Scripture. This study led them to understand that the sanctuary referred not to the earth (the Bible never calls the earth God's sanctuary), but to God's sanctuary in *heaven*. The cleansing of the heavenly sanctuary in Daniel 8:14 refers to its purification from the records of sins, with a corresponding purification in the hearts of believers (see Lev. 23:27; 1 Cor. 3:16, 17; 6:19, 20).

This correct understanding of the sanctuary unlocked the mystery of the Great Disappointment, inspiring the faithful Millerites to go forth once again, heralding the invitation to come to the wedding of the ages. It also provided the extra key to make their preaching effective. Merely preaching the time prophecies of Daniel or the permanence of the 10 Commandments is not enough to change peoples' *hearts* so that they are ready for the return of Jesus; there must be a radical change in the character that comes from an intimate knowledge of the Father and Son (see John 17:3). Such intimate knowledge comes from a proper understanding of the plan of salvation as outlined in the wedding chamber—the heavenly sanctuary. It is here that Revelation 11 next focuses our attention.

The Temple Measured and 2 Witnesses During the Dark Ages

The answer to the Great Disappointment lay in a correct understanding of the sanctuary. Thus, the antidote to John's bitter stomach is to measure the temple of God. What does it mean to measure the temple? The answer lies in the temple description of Ezekiel 40–48.

In Ezekiel 40–42, the angel makes extensive measurements of the temple. The setting for these chapters is specified in 40:1 as the Day of Atonement, the great day of judgment. The sole standard of the judgment is God's character as expressed in the 10 Commandments (see Eccl. 12:13, 14). In Ezekiel 43:10, the angel instructs Ezekiel to describe this temple to the house of Israel with the intent that they may be ashamed of their deviant lifestyle as they measure its perfect pattern. Ezekiel is to "write [out the pattern] before their eyes, that they may preserve its entire design and all of its ordinances, *and do them*" (see 43:11).

Ezekiel is next given the measurements of the altar of burn offering (see v. 13), just as John is next told to measure the altar. This directs attention to Jesus' perfect atoning sacrifice upon the cross.

Finally, in Ezekiel 47:1–12, the angel measures the water flowing from the sanctuary, a picture of God's law flowing forth from Zion (compare Isa. 2:3; Mic. 4:2). The water of God's law is so pure that it heals the waters of the sea and the creatures therein, the sea being a symbol of sin and those drowning therein (see Mic. 7:19; Isa. 57:20). Those who have been transformed during the Day of Atonement are described in Ezekiel 47:10 as fishers of men, saving the now healthy fish with the gospel net. This is the result of Jesus *applying* His life-giving blood, shed at Calvary, during the end-time judgment. As He writes His law upon the heart, we partake of the divine nature (see 2 Peter 1:4). Likewise, John's direction to measure "those who worship therein" is a measurement of their *character*.

Hence, John's measurements direct attention to the Day of Atonement, Jesus' atoning sacrifice, and the character of God's professed people. It must be noted that the Day of Atonement provides atonement for the temple, altar, and people (see Lev. 16:16, 18, 19, 30).

Next, John is directed *not* to measure the outer court, for it is given to the nations, those who do *not* profess to be God's people. His faithful people are termed "the holy city," a designation common in Scripture (see Isa. 62:12; Dan. 9:16, 24). It is prophesied that the nations will trample God's people for 42 prophetic months—the 1,260 years of papal supremacy, AD 538–1798. During that period, millions were to be tortured and put to death, yet God promised that His 2 witnesses would continue to prophesy and the knowledge of that truth would not be wholly extinguished. They were to do this in sackcloth, a representation of both mourning and true repentance during this period (see Amos 8:10; Joel 1:13; Jonah 3:5–8).

Who are *Yahweh's* 2 witnesses? "These are the 2 olive trees and the 2 menorahs which stand before the Lord of the earth"—language drawn from Zechariah 4:14, which says "these are the 2 sons of pressed oil, standing by the Lord of all the earth." The 2 olive trees are spoken of as the conduit of the Holy Spirit in verses 2–6. Note the clear explanation of the olive trees and menorahs:

> Concerning the two witnesses the prophet declares further: "These are the two olive trees, and the two candlesticks standing before the God of the earth." "Thy word," said the psalmist, "is a lamp unto my feet, and a light unto my path." Revelation 11:4; Psalm 119:105. The two witnesses represent the Scriptures of the Old and the New Testament. Both are important testimonies to the origin and perpetuity of the law of God. Both are witnesses also to the plan of salvation. The types, sacrifices, and prophecies of the Old Testament point forward to a Saviour to come. The Gospels and Epistles of the New Testament tell of a Saviour who has come in the exact manner foretold by type and prophecy. (White, *GC*, p. 267)
>
> The oil is a symbol of the Holy Spirit. Thus the Spirit is represented in the prophecy of Zechariah. ...
>
> From the two olive trees the golden oil was emptied through the golden pipes into the bowl of the candlestick, and thence into the golden lamps that gave light to the sanctuary. So from the holy ones that stand in God's presence His Spirit is imparted to the human instrumentalities who are consecrated to His service.

The mission of the two anointed ones is to communicate to God's people that heavenly grace which alone can make His word a lamp to the feet and a light to the path. "Not by might, nor by power, but by My Spirit, saith the Lord of hosts." (White, *COL*, pp. 407, 408)

We have now identified all 10 menorahs of Solomon's temple: 7 menorahs represented the church in 7 different periods of history (see Rev. 1:20); 1 menorah of 7 fiery lamps burning before the throne represented the 1 Holy Spirit in all 7 ages of the church (see Rev. 4:5); 2 menorahs represent the Old and New Testaments.

Though largely hidden from the people during the Dark Ages, God's Word was never wholly eradicated from the earth.[95] Revelation 11:5–6 presents the 2 witnesses under the figures of Moses (representing the Torah, or Law) and Elijah (representing the Prophets). The phrase "the Law and the Prophets" refers to all of Scripture (see John 1:45; Matt. 5:17; 7:12; 22:40), confirming our identification of the 2 witnesses. Fire coming from their mouths and devouring their enemies alludes to Elijah, who called down fiery judgment that consumed his enemies (see 2 Kings 1:9–12). Likewise, Elijah predicted no rain during the days of his prophesying (see 1 Kings 17:1), which Jesus and James specify as 3.5 years or 1,260 literal days (see Luke 4:25; James 5:17), matching the 42 months of

---

[95] "During the greater part of this period, God's witnesses remained in a state of obscurity. The papal power sought to hide from the people the word of truth, and set before them false witnesses to contradict its testimony. ... When the Bible was proscribed by religious and secular authority; when its testimony was perverted, and every effort made that men and demons could invent to turn the minds of the people from it; when those who dared proclaim its sacred truths were hunted, betrayed, tortured, buried in dungeon cells, martyred for their faith, or compelled to flee to mountain fastnesses, and to dens and caves of the earth—then the faithful witnesses prophesied in sackcloth. Yet they continued their testimony throughout the entire period of 1260 years. In the darkest times there were faithful men who loved God's word and were jealous for His honor. To these loyal servants were given wisdom, power, and authority to declare His truth during the whole of this time" (White, *GC*, pp. 267, 268).

Revelation 11:3. Moses was the instrument whom *Yahweh* used to turn the Nile to blood, the first of the 10 plagues (see Exod. 7:14–12:30).

All these references to Elijah and Moses are *judgments*. Elijah's fire was a purely *punitive* judgment that consumed *non-believers*. Elijah's 1,260 days of drought was meant as a *corrective* judgment upon *idolatrous Israel* (professed believers). The plagues fell upon the sons of Israel *and* Egypt (the first 3 fell upon God's people and unbelievers, while the last 7 fell only upon unbelievers, with the dual intent of turning people's hearts to *Yahweh* and revealing what was in their hearts).

Beast Versus the 2 Witnesses

"The beast which comes up from the abyss" points to a kingdom (beasts and kingdoms are equated in Daniel 7:1–8), one which rises up against the Scriptures toward the end of the 1,260-year period, effectively killing them for a time. According to Revelation 11:8, the great city of this nation is characterized as Sodom and Egypt, whose pre-eminent characteristics were sexual depravity and atheistic defiance of the true God, *Yahweh*, respectively (see Gen. 19:4, 5; Exod. 5:2).

"In the persecution which France had visited upon the confessors of the gospel, she had crucified Christ in the person of His disciples" (White, *GC*, p. 271; compare Matt. 25:40). Their bodies were to lie in the public square, hearkening back to the public square in Sodom, as well as that of Gibeah, when God's people fell to the same state of depravity as the Sodomites did (see Gen. 19:2; Judges 19:15, 22). In our discussion of Daniel 9:25 (see *THE STAND*, comments on Daniel 9), we learned that the public square was a public area where judgment was rendered. Hence, the kingdom in view here was so bold as to pass sentence against the 2 witnesses, i.e., the Word of God. There would be (apparent) triumph over the Word of God for 3.5 prophetic days, or 3.5 literal years. All of these characteristics were satisfied in the nation of France. A law banning religion was passed in the capital city of Paris on November 10, 1793.

Due to the unimaginable chaos and license that followed, such restrictions were removed June 17, 1797.

Why is the French Revolution mentioned in Revelation? Consider the following astute observation:

> The war against the Bible, carried forward for so many centuries in France, culminated in the scenes of the Revolution. That terrible outbreaking was but the legitimate result of Rome's suppression of the Scriptures. ... It presented the most striking illustration which the world has ever witnessed of the working out of the papal policy—an illustration of the results to which for more than a thousand years the teaching of the Roman Church had been tending. (White, *GC*, pp. 265, 266)

The giving of gifts in Revelation 11:10 signifies the joy the people felt when first "liberated" from the restraints of Scripture. At variance with all nations in the history of the world, the worship of God was done away, baptism and communion were forbidden, and the weekly rest was replaced with a day of self-indulgence every tenth day; the Goddess of Reason was enthroned (portrayed as a dancing girl of the opera); death was declared an eternal sleep; Bibles were gathered up and burned (see White, *GC*, pp. 273–276).

What ignited the French Revolution? The following is very insightful:

> It was popery that had begun the work which atheism was completing. The policy of Rome had wrought out those conditions, social, political, and religious, that were hurrying France on to ruin. Writers, in referring to the horrors of the Revolution, say that these excesses are to be charged upon the throne and the church. ... In strict justice they are to be charged upon the church. Popery had poisoned the minds of kings against the Reformation, as an enemy to the crown, an element of discord that would be fatal to the peace and harmony of the nation. It was

the genius of Rome that by this means inspired the direst cruelty and the most galling oppression which proceeded from the
throne. (White, *GC*, pp. 276, 277)

Papal policy leads humanity to exalt itself and neglect (or even despise)
God. As the eighteenth century drew to a close and the bitter results of
the Revolution were seen, mankind recognized the frightful folly of its
unchecked course and saw the need for dependence upon God. Note the
reformation that followed:

> For the fifty years preceding 1792, little attention was given to
> the work of foreign missions. No new societies were formed, and
> there were but few churches that made any effort for the spread
> of Christianity in heathen lands. But toward the close of the
> eighteenth century a great change took place. Men became dis-
> satisfied with the results of rationalism and realized the neces-
> sity of divine revelation and experimental religion. From this
> time the work of foreign missions attained an unprecedented
> growth. (White, *GC*, pp. 287, 288)

In this sense, the 2 witnesses had the breath of life breathed into them.
Then they ascended on a cloud, while their enemies beheld them. Movement on a cloud hearkens back to Daniel 7:13–14, when the Son of man
comes to the end-time judgment on a cloud, and forward to Revelation
14:14, when He appears on a cloud for the reaping of the earth at the close
of human probation. The command is given, "Come up here," the very
same given to John in 4:1, when he was summoned to the throne room of
judgment. Mankind passed judgment on the Scriptures in 11:8, and now
heaven vindicates them in verse 12.

The section concludes with reference to a great earthquake and the
tenth part of the city falling. The combination of the earthquake and the
number 10 evoke the giving of the law at Sinai (see Exod. 19:18; 20:1–17).
The law is the basis of the end-time judgment (see Eccl. 12:13, 14).

Further, Abraham pled with *Adonai* to spare the city Sodom if only 10 righteous people could be found by investigation (see Gen. 18:21, 32). In Daniel 1, a 10-day trial was followed by investigation of the youths' faces, and later, the supreme judge, the king himself, investigated the youth and determined they were 10 hands above the officers in his kingdom.

The foregoing establishes that an investigative judgment was in view with the French Revolution. Ironically, the number 7,000 indicates that it was the faithful who perished at this time. *Yahweh* declared to Elijah that 7,000 who had not bowed the knee to the sun god Baal (see 1 Kings 19:18) still remained in Israel. In the very next chapter, Ahab is promised victory over Ben-Hadad, king of Syria, and this was accomplished with an army of precisely 7,000 faithful soldiers (see 1 Kings 20:15).

At this point, the description of the sixth trumpet, the second woe, concludes. Recall that the Ottoman Empire fell on August 11, 1840, followed by Jesus' appearance as a strong Angel in Revelation 10. Chapter 10 concluded with the prophecy that the Millerite experience would be sweet, then incredibly bitter with the passing of the time at the Great Disappointment on October 22, 1844. The faithful were commanded to go forth once more, in spite of the ridicule, and proclaim the truth. This truth concerned a *proper* understanding of the cleansing of the sanctuary: it was not identical with the second coming of Jesus for His bride, but instead the last great step Jesus was to take to *prepare* His bride for His return. This is why Revelation 11:1–6 opened with a survey of the sanctuary and verses 7–13 contrasted this with the French Revolution, illustrating the tragic outworking of papal policy in attempting to replace Jesus' role in the heavenly sanctuary with an earthly counterfeit.

The Seventh Trumpet: Woe #3

Jesus now begins to receive His kingdom. This reception began concurrent with the Day of Atonement on October 22, 1844 as He began to determine who would compose His kingdom. Said another way, the wedding between Christ and His church began at this time. A number of people have professed to accept Jesus' marriage proposal; the end-time judgment investigates the genuineness of each profession. As the names of the genuinely faithful come up in review, Jesus acknowledges their place as kings, judges, and priests in His kingdom (see Rev. 20:4, 6). Unlike preceding kingdoms, His kingdom will stand *forever*, for His subjects are completely devoted to His principles of righteousness.

One should not understand from verse 15 that the instant the seventh trumpet blows, the kingdom is established and the great controversy between Christ and Satan is over. Rather, the sounding of the seventh trumpet indicates that the final outcome of Christ's kingdom is certain. Consider His statement shortly before He was crucified: "Now the ruler of this world will be cast out" (John 12:31). Jesus did not mean that the very moment He spoke, or when He expired on the cross a few days later, the devil would immediately forfeit any claim to this world and the controversy would end; He meant that His imminent death on the cross made the end of Satan's reign inevitable. God calls "those things which do not exist as though they do exist" (Rom. 4:17). God's Word is so powerful that what He speaks comes to pass.

The kingdom is said to belong to "our Lord and His Anointed." This refers to Father and Son, respectively. Jesus was referred to as Lord in the context of His crucifixion (see Rev. 11:8), so why is the Father now referred to as Lord? Recall from Revelation 4:11 that the Father was called "our Lord and our God" while sitting on the throne. Jesus sat on the throne when He ascended on high (see Heb. 1:3; 10:12), but when the judgment began, He stood before the throne as a Lamb in the act of being slain (see Rev. 5:6, 13). When the judgment concludes, Jesus will once again sit on the throne, His kingdom fully made up (see 14:14).

Recall that the Father anointed Jesus a second time as discussed in the remarks on Revelation 5. Why anoint Jesus more than once? Much of Solomon's life is paralleled in Revelation. Solomon was made king a second time and anointed (see 1 Chron. 29:22). In fact, he was anointed as *Yahweh's* representative, and Zadok was anointed high priest. In antitype, Jesus was first anointed when He ascended to heaven and the Holy Spirit was poured out at Pentecost (see Acts 2:1–4). As He commenced His end-time work in the Holy of Holies, the Father anointed Him as King (since He began to receive the kingdom) and high-priestly Judge (to officiate during the end-time day of atonement).

Verse 16 parallels the scene in Revelation 4 and 5: the 24 elders sit on their thrones, fall on their faces, and worship God as well as His Anointed, and assert that He will reign forever and ever (see 4:4, 10; 5:8–10, 13). They refer to God as *Yahweh*, employing His covenant name, for the subjects of His kingdom are those who have experienced the everlasting covenant. They also refer to Him as "God of hosts," recognizing Him in advance as the victorious Commander of heaven's host, soon to come for His bride at the *end* of the pre-advent judgment (see 19:11–16).

The unbelieving nations are furious, for Satan sees his deceptive power over the end-time remnant is fast slipping away and urges on those in his service to blot them from the face of the earth. This fury is identical with that of the dragon against the end-time remnant of the church's seed in 12:17. The dragon represents both Satan (see 12:4a, 9; Isa. 27:1) as well as the kingdoms through which he works, including ancient Egypt (see Ezek. 29:3), ancient pagan Rome (see Rev. 12:4b; 13:2), and the end-time image of the beast that speaks as a dragon (see v. 11), also called the end-time king of the south, spiritual Egypt (see Dan. 11:40). The political leaders of the end-time coalition express the dragon's fury.[96]

No matter how furious these end-time political powers may be, they are subject to God's retribution, for He will "ruin those who ruin the earth." Verse 18 is a summary of the judgment, with the anger and destruction of the nations at either end of the verse, and the reward of the righteous at the center. Note that the judgment begins with the dead, terminating with the living just before Jesus returns. This pre-advent judgment, in session since October 22, 1844, is *investigative* in nature.[97]

---

[96] "Kings and rulers and governors have placed upon themselves the brand of antichrist, and are represented as the dragon who goes to make war with the saints—with those who keep the commandments of God and who have the faith of Jesus" (White, *TM*, p. 39).

[97] Scripture abounds with examples of investigative judgments (see Gen. 3:8–13; 4:9, 10; 11:5; 18:20, 21; Dan. 1:12–15, 18–20).

The final phase of the judgment, the executive phase, is *punitive* in nature, for it destroys those who have ruined the earth. The last part of verse 18 alludes to Genesis 6:11–12 (LXX), which reads, "Now the earth was ruined before God, and the earth was filled with unrighteousness. *Yahweh* God saw the earth, and it was ruined, for all flesh had ruined its way upon the earth." The ruin in Genesis 6 refers to the character of the people who no longer reflected the image of God. Likewise, Revelation 11:18 is primarily concerned with the character of earth's occupants, though a righteous character does involve exercise of proper dominion over the earth entrusted to us (see Gen. 1:26–28).

What does the open temple in verse 19 signify? The following is clear:

> "The temple of God was opened in heaven, and there was seen in His temple the ark of His testament." Revelation 11:19. The ark of God's testament is in the holy of holies, the second apartment of the sanctuary. In the ministration of the earthly tabernacle, which served "unto the example and shadow of heavenly things," this apartment was opened only upon the great Day of Atonement for the cleansing of the sanctuary. Therefore the announcement that the temple of God was opened in heaven and the ark of His testament was seen points to the opening of the most holy place of the heavenly sanctuary in 1844 as Christ entered there to perform the closing work of the atonement. (White, *GC*, p. 433)

Hence, the open temple in verse 19 marks the onset of the judgment. The lightning flashes, voices, and thunderclaps will appear at the onset of the seventh and final plague when the judgment has ended and probation has forever closed, with the great hail marking its climax (see Rev. 16:17, 21).

PART 4A: THE KEY POINTS

REVELATION 8–11: JESUS IN THIS PASSAGE

Jesus is the Angel who ministers at the altar of incense and the strong Angel with the scroll. He is anointed King at His ascension, then again as High Priestly Judge as the judgment commences.

REVELATION 8:3; 10:5, 8: JESUS STANDS FOR HIS BRIDE

Jesus stands before the altar of incense, interceding for His people throughout probationary time. When He casts the censer down, probation closes, and the plagues fall (compare Rev. 8:5 and 16:18). When the end-time day of atonement begins, Jesus stands upon sea and earth—the very places whence the end-time beasts of Revelation 13 arise—showing His sovereignty over earthly affairs.

REVELATION 8–11: THE WEDDING THEME

In Revelation 11:15, the seventh trumpet sounds, marking the opening of the end-time judgment—Christ's wedding—on October 22, 1844. As the wedding draws to its close, the mystery of God is to be finished. This mystery is Christ in us, the hope of glory (see Col. 1:27). In fact, the key to understanding the Great Disappointment (when Jesus did not come to earth on October 22, 1844) and being prepared for when Jesus *does* return at the second coming is a correct understanding and application of His work in the heavenly sanctuary—the work of reproducing His character perfectly in His people. This transformation must take place, for Christ's bride is to become one flesh with Him, meaning she has His character. The wedding invitation will be given in full power throughout the whole world as it sees Jesus in the transformed lives of His people (see Matt. 24:14).

4B:
DRAGON PERSECUTES
AND SON OF MAN COMES
FOR HIS BRIDE

REVELATION 12: DRAGON PERSECUTES

Two Signs in Heaven: The Woman and the Dragon

12 [1]A great sign appeared in heaven: a woman clothed with the sun, the moon under her feet, and upon her head a crown of 12 stars. [2]She was pregnant, crying out while in labor, tormented to give birth.

[3]Another sign appeared in heaven. Behold: a great, fiery red dragon, which had 7 heads and 10 horns, and upon its heads 7 diadems. [4]Its tail was drawing the third part of the stars of heaven, then it cast them into the earth. The dragon was standing before the woman who was about to give birth, so that when she should deliver, he would devour her Child. [5]She gave birth to a Son, a Male, who was destined to shepherd all the nations with an iron rod. Her Child was snatched up to God and to His throne. [6]Then the woman fled into the wilderness, where she has a place prepared by God, that there they should nourish her 1,260 days.

War in Heaven: Michael and the Dragon

[7]There was war in heaven: Michael and His angels went to war with the dragon; likewise, the dragon and his angels warred. [8]However, he was not strong enough, nor was a place found for him anymore in heaven. [9]So the great dragon was cast out—that ancient serpent, the one called [the] devil and Satan, who leads the entire world astray—he was cast into the earth, and his angels were cast out with him.

[10]Then I heard a loud voice in heaven saying, "Now salvation, power, the kingdom of our God, and the authority of His Anointed have come,

for the accuser of our brethren was cast out, the one who accuses them before our God day and night, [11]and they conquered him by the blood of the Lamb and by the word of their testimony. They did not love their life, even unto death. [12]Therefore rejoice, you heavens, and those who pitch their tent therein; woe unto the earth and unto the sea, for the devil has come down to you having great intolerance [for obedience],[98] for he knows he has a short season."

War on Earth: The Dragon, the Woman, and the Remnant

[13]When the dragon saw that he was cast into the earth, he persecuted the woman which gave birth to the Male. [14]There were given to the woman 2 wings of a great eagle, that she might fly unto her place in the wilderness, away from the presence of the serpent, so that she might be nourished there a time, [2] times,[99] and half a time.

[15]The serpent cast water like a river out of his mouth after the woman, that he might cause her to be swept away. [16]However, the earth helped the woman: the earth opened *its* mouth, and swallowed up the river which the dragon cast out of *his* mouth. [17]The dragon was infuriated by the woman and departed to wage war against the remnant of her seed, those who keep God's commandments and have the testimony of Jesus.

COMMENTARY

Two Signs in Heaven: The Woman and the Dragon

Having traversed 7 churches, 7 seals, and 7 trumpets, the book now provides a history of the woman who will ultimately become Christ's bride.

---

[98] Greek θυμος ("wrath," KJV). In Revelation, this refers to God's intolerance for sin and Satan's/Babylon's intolerance for obedience.

[99] The "2" is supplied, for 3.5 times equates to the 1,260 days of Revelation 12:6 and the 42 months of Revelation 11:2 and 13:5.

The word "woman" in verse 1 can in fact be translated "wife," provided we understand that the marriage proper is yet to take place during the antitypical day of atonement. Recall that Mary was considered Joseph's wife during the engagement period (see Matt. 1:18–25). Christ's wife is His church (see Eph. 5:22–33).

She is arrayed with the host of heaven. Just as the physical, heavenly bodies are to illuminate the earth (see Gen. 1:15), so the church in right relation to these bodies is to be a spiritual light for this earth. This contrasts with pagan Rome, which styled its emperors, consuls, and senate as sun, moon, and stars, respectively. In worshipping these bodies contrary to *Yahweh's* explicit direction to Israel (see Deut. 4:19; 17:3; 2 Kings 23:5), Rome effectively worshipped its own governing system.

How exactly does she give light to the earth? "His seed will be forever, His throne like the sun before me; like the moon it will be established forever, a faithful witness in the sky" (Ps. 89:36, 37). The woman of Revelation 12 is Christ's seed, while the church of the last days is called the remnant of her seed (see v. 17). She is clothed with the sun (Christ's throne), indicating that His rule and judgments envelop every aspect of her life. Her feet on the moon (the faithful witness) indicates that she, too, is seated on a throne (note that she is giving birth in verse 2, which is done on a birthstool; see Exod. 1:16). Just as the foundation of God's throne is righteousness and judgment as summarized in the 10 Commandments (see Ps. 97:2), so the footstool upon which her feet rest is *Yahweh's* faithful promise to fulfill His covenant.

Another passage sheds light on verse 1: Joseph's dream in Genesis 37:9–11. This enables us to identify the 12 stars as the 12 tribes of Israel. In other words, the 12 tribes of the Hebrew Scriptures continue on as the woman (the church)—spiritual Jews (see Rom. 2:28, 29; Gal. 3:26–29). These 12 stars form a crown, indicating that she will reign with Christ.

The woman is described as pregnant. Scripture likens the process of salvation—deliverance from sin, the development of Christian character—to bearing children (see 1 Tim. 2:14, 15). It may seem that it will not result in a successful birth, yet the Lord promises to bring the child forth (see Isa. 26:17, 18; 66:8, 9) and that the pain will be forgotten (see John 16:21, 22). The intensity of her labor indicates she is nearly ready to deliver—she nearly reflects God's character.

John's attention is now arrested by another sign: a great dragon with 10 horns. Verse 9 identifies this dragon as Satan. However, Satan works through human agencies to accomplish his purposes. In verses 4 and 5, the woman gives birth to the Son—Jesus—and it was Rome that sought to kill Him at that time (see Matt. 2:13–18). Its fiery red description links it to the fiery red horse of the second seal, when the church began to show signs of corruption, depending on force to accomplish her aims. The 7 heads are those on the 4 living creatures of Daniel 7:1–7, representing the kingdoms through which Satan worked to achieve dominion over the earth (note the diadems atop each head). The 10 horns are the same as those of the Roman beast of verse 8, namely, the 10 divisions of the Roman Empire.

Revelation 12:4–5 form an incredibly compact history, covering Satan's initial work of deception in heaven until the second coming. In our study of Revelation 9, we saw that the tail represents a lying prophet (see Isa. 9:15), and stars represent angels (see 1:20; Job 38:4–7). Satan is *the* false prophet who deceived a third of the heavenly angels "by the abundance of [his] trafficking," with the result that God "cast [him] out in disgrace from the mountain of God" (Ezek. 28:16).

Having mutinied in heaven, Satan thought to frustrate the prophecy of Jesus' birth on earth. He is called a great dragon in verse 4, and Jesus is referred to as a Male. These two descriptions point to the deliverance from Egypt, for Pharaoh is called the great dragon (see Ezek. 29:3), and Moses' mother Jochebed "conceived and gave birth to a male" (Exod. 2:2, LXX). Just as God delivered Moses, then used him to deliver His people into the wilderness, He delivered Jesus so that He would later deliver His people into the wilderness.

Following His resurrection, Jesus was taken to heaven (Acts 1:9–11), where He sat down upon His Father's throne (see Heb. 1:3; 10:12). He "is destined to shepherd all the nations with an iron rod." Jesus is given the nations under the seventh trumpet (see Rev. 11:15–19), and Psalm

2:9 indicates that He "shepherds" them by dashing them to pieces at the second coming. Hence, Revelation 12:5 covers events from Jesus' birth to the second coming.

In verse 6, the text transitions to the period of papal persecution, describing God's church as fleeing into the wilderness, where He has prepared her a place in which she is nourished for 1,260 days. This hearkens back to Exodus 19:4, in which *Yahweh* says He took Israel out of Egypt on wings of eagles and "brought [them] to Myself." Similarly, God ministered to the needs of Hagar and Jesus in the wilderness (see Gen. 21:15–19; Matt. 4:11). He brought the woman into the wilderness so that she could be with Him, and through her He would preserve a remnant. In spite of persecution, this church in the wilderness (largely the Waldensian church) kept alive the truths of God's Word.[100]

War in Heaven: Michael and the Dragon

We return to the controversy in heaven. The Greek word πολεμος, usually translated "war," is the source of our English word "polemics." The war in heaven was not physical combat, but rather a war of words concerning contrasting modes of government: God grants everyone *liberty* to choose to love Him and others supremely, while Satan coerces all to adopt *libertinism*, indulging self by doing what is right in one's own eyes.

Michael's name means "Who is like God?" The answer to the question is Jesus, of course. Michael is the one with whom Satan disputed concerning the resurrection of Moses (see Jude 9). Michael is the archangel whose voice resurrects the dead, but Jesus states that *His* voice wakes the dead (1 Thess. 4:16; John 5:25–29). Michael is Jesus, the Ruler of *Yahweh's* host (see Josh. 5:13–15).

Daniel and Revelation scholars recognize Michael as Jesus, and some Christians recognize this, but others may raise an eyebrow, questioning

---

[100] See Wylie's *Protestantism in the Waldensian Valleys* for the incredible manner in which God preserved His people.

Jesus' description as an angel. It will surprise some to learn that Christians for *centuries* have recognized Michael as Jesus. Commenting on Daniel 10:13, the Geneva Bible (published in 1560, pre-dating the 1611 King James Bible) states, "To assure his children of his love he sends forth double power, even Michael, that is, Christ Jesus the head of angels." Again, regarding Daniel 12:1, "God will send his angel to deliver it, whom he here calls Michael, meaning Christ, who is proclaimed by the preaching of the Gospel." It is no modern heresy to declare that Michael is Jesus!

In verse 9, the dragon is called "that ancient serpent," referring to Satan's use of a serpent as a medium to deceive Eve in the Garden of Eden (see Gen. 3:1–19; 1 Tim. 2:14). He led Eve to doubt God's assertion that if she ate the fruit of the tree of the knowledge of good and evil, she would surely die. He got her to disobey (and through her influence, Adam too) and has since led "the entire world astray" with the false belief in the immortality of the soul. Nearly everyone, Christian or otherwise, believes that at death, a person's soul wings its way to heaven, still alive, though the body is dead. The Bible is clear that when people die, they sleep (see John 11:11–14; 1 Thess. 4:13–18). In this state, they know nothing, their thoughts perish, and they do not praise, remember, or thank *Yahweh* (see Eccl. 9:5; Ps. 146:4; 115:17; 6:5). Paul declares that God alone has immortality and is imperishable (1 Tim. 6:15, 16; 1:17), and immortality is only bestowed on righteous mortals at the second coming (see 1 Cor. 15:51–55).

Some may object that Adam and Eve did not die the day they ate of the fruit. While true, this in no wise proves their immortality. God warned them that the day they disobeyed, their death was *certain*, and by definition, death comes only upon those who are *mortal*. In a similar vein, Satan's destruction was made certain at the cross, though his power did not cease that very day.

Until the day Jesus died upon the cross, Satan was not entirely barred from heaven. Scripture records that he continued to appear in the heavenly councils (see Job 1:6–12; 2:1–7; 1 Kings 22:19–22). Why would he have access to heaven if he no longer held his heavenly position? Jesus recognizes Satan as "ruler of this world" (John 12:31; 14:30; 16:11), for Adam forfeited his God-given dominion (see Gen. 1:26–28) in consequence of sin. In fact, this is why Satan was able to offer Jesus all authority over the kingdoms of the world when tempting Him in the wilderness (see Luke 4:5–7), for he is ruler of this world until Jesus returns.

Satan was cast out of heaven, referring to the throne room, where he had once been a covering cherub (see Ezek. 28:14, 16). Further, he was "cast into the earth." When Jesus casts His censer "into the earth" (see Rev. 8:5), probation closes, and the 7 last plagues began to fall. Hence, when Satan and his angels were cast into the earth, their probation forever closed.

There is a certain irony worth noting: the 4 living creatures praise God "day and night" (Rev. 4:8), while Satan accuses fallen humanity "day and night." The vast multitude serves God "day and night in His temple," while Satan is at last tormented in the lake of fire "day and night" (7:15; 20:10).

Good news rings out in 12:10. The heavenly host rejoices that God's kingdom and the authority of His Anointed have come. What does this mean? On the one hand, the accuser of the brethren (legal, courtroom language) was cast out at the cross, and following His ascension to heaven, Jesus was anointed King. Jesus is also called Anointed in Revelation 11:15, when He is anointed again at the commencement of the end-time judgment. The angels rejoice that their brethren (mankind) have conquered, prizing faithfulness to God above their own lives. Strictly speaking, this is true only at the completion of the end-time judgment, when God has restored His image perfectly in humanity. Hence, Revelation 12:10–11 takes us from Jesus' ascension to the close of the judgment.

During the judgment hour, Jesus gives to every sincere, repentant believer the ability to *conquer* in the battle with sin. He Himself knows what it is to feel the flesh recoil from doing God's will, for He agonized, "Father, if thou be willing, remove this cup from me," while in the same breath He voiced complete submission: "nevertheless not my will, but thine, be done" (Luke 22:42, KJV). Temptation is no excuse for sin, for He promises, "My grace is sufficient for you" (2 Cor. 12:9), and with any temptation that comes our way, He "will make also the way of escape, that [we] may be able to endure" (see 1 Cor. 10:13).

Such good news is enough to make *all* who choose to pitch their tent in heaven rejoice! Those who reject this good news choose instead to remain enslaved to sin (see Rom. 6:16). Theirs is a galling yoke, for the devil knows he has a short season in which to keep mankind enslaved to disobedience.

War on Earth: The Dragon, the Woman, and the Remnant

The text returns to the persecuted woman who gave birth to the Male. As in 12:5, this points us back to the birth of Moses. Like pagan Rome in verses 4 and 5, papal Rome is pictured as persecuting Egypt of old. During the 3.5 times (AD 538–1798), God delivered His people, largely the Waldenses, who were suffering papal persecution, by "2 wings of a great eagle" into the wilderness, just as with Israel of old (see Exod. 19:4). Such seclusion also served to remove countless temptations, making it easier to contemplate His handiwork in the beauties of nature. It also served to increase their faith by causing them to lean on God to make it through circumstances unaided by any earthly supports.

We next read of the serpent casting water out of his mouth like a river, the earth in turn helping the woman by swallowing this river. This continues the Egyptian imagery, as the following verses makes clear:

> Jer. 46:7, 8 (LXX): Who is it that will come up like [the] river, like rivers churning water? The waters of Egypt will come up like [the] river. He said, "I will go up, cover the earth, and destroy those inhabiting it."

> Jer. 46:7, 8 (Hebrew): Who is this coming up like the Nile? Like rivers, his waters are churning. Egypt comes up like the Nile. Like rivers, [his] waters are churning. He said, "I will go up, cover the earth, and destroy the city and those dwelling therein."

Ezek. 29:3: Behold, I am against you, Pharaoh, king of Egypt, the great dragon who lies in the midst of the Nile's streams, who has said, "My Nile is my own—I made it!"

Comparison of the Hebrew and Greek of Jeremiah 46:7–8 reveals that the "river" referenced in Revelation 12:15–16 is none other than the Nile. The dragon is none other than the Pharaoh of spiritual Egypt, i.e., the papacy. Just as the Pharaoh sought to kill all male Israelite babies by commanding that they be cast into the Nile (see Exod. 1:16, 22), so the papacy employed military might to sweep away the faithful Waldenses during the Dark Ages.

What was Satan's purpose in casting males into the Nile? He knew the 400 years of Egyptian bondage were drawing to a close (see Gen. 15:13–16), so he sought to prevent the promised deliverance by destroying the deliverer who must be raised up. In like manner, Satan knew that final deliverance awaited God's people as a result of the approaching, end-time judgment. If he could destroy them before the antitypical day of atonement commenced on October 22, 1844, Satan would emerge victorious in the great controversy.

When Israel crossed over the Red Sea, the Egyptians followed, but "the earth swallowed them up" (see Exod. 15:12). Likewise, here the earth swallows the Nile river, permitting the woman to survive in the wilderness throughout the 1,260 years of papal persecution.

This begs the question, What are the waters of the spiritual Nile? The waters of Babylon are peoples (see Rev. 17:15), so the waters of the Nile are the peoples of spiritual Egypt. The people of spiritual Egypt who tried to sweep away the Waldenses were the military forces that the papacy time and again sent to exterminate them in their mountain fastnesses. We might also note that physical persecution ceased before the 1,260 years were complete, at which point the devil tried another approach: spiritual Egypt (Paris, France) boldly denied God, like Pharaoh of old did (see Exod. 5:2), and exalted human reason. Hence, what we now call humanism was added to the arsenal of the Nile waters.

How does the earth help the woman in 12:16? First, God protected his faithful Waldensians throughout the centuries in the wilderness of the Alps. Wylie relates how Cataneo's expedition to exterminate the Waldenses failed in spectacular fashion (see *Protestantism in the Waldensian Valleys*, chs. 2, 3). Second, during the French Revolution at the close of the 1,260 years, another country was emerging, one relatively uninhabited for centuries, in which people could live without the religious intolerance of the Old World. Discussion of this will be deferred until Revelation 13:11–18.

The dragon is especially enraged in the last days, departing to wage war on the end-time remnant of the woman's seed. The "seed" hearkens back to *Yahweh's* covenant promises to Abram concerning his seed (e.g., Gen. 12:7; 13:15, 16; 15:5; 17:7–19). This remnant of the woman's seed is a people who keep God's commandments (the words of the everlasting covenant; see Exod. 34:28), which is in turn sealed with the sign of the everlasting covenant, His holy, seventh-day Sabbath (see Exod. 31:16, 17).

Those called the remnant also have the testimony of Jesus, defined in Revelation 19:10 as the spirit of prophecy. This means the end-time remnant are blessed with the prophetic gift. When Israel left Egypt of old, God entered into covenant with them, and they were blessed with a leader, Moses, who was a prophet (see Deut. 18:15). Likewise, the remnant of the woman's seed, God's end-time, commandment-keeping church, is expected to have a leader blessed with the prophetic gift. Paul enjoins us to seek that gift especially (see 1 Cor. 14:1), and Moses desired that *all believers* be blessed with that gift (see Num. 11:29). Whether or not a multitude of believers will possess this gift in the very end (see Joel 2:28, 29) remains to be seen. What *is* an established fact is that a pioneer of the remnant church *has* been blessed with the gift of prophecy, and it has been blessed by the guidance provided by that gift (details can be found on pages 261–262).

REVELATION 13 AND 14:
FINAL CONFLICT AND SON
OF MAN COMES

The Sea Beast

13 [^1]Then I stood[101] upon the sand of the sea. I saw a beast coming up out of the sea, having 10 horns and 7 heads. Upon its horns were 10 diadems, and upon its heads, blasphemous names. [2]The beast which I saw was like a leopard, its feet were like those of a bear and its mouth was like a lion's mouth. The dragon gave it his power, his throne, and great authority. [3]One of its heads was as if slaughtered unto death, yet its mortal wound was healed, and the entire earth marveled, [following] after the beast. [4]They worshipped the dragon who had given his authority to the beast, and they worshipped the beast, saying, "Who is like the beast? Who is able to wage war against it?"

[5]It was given a mouth speaking great things, that is, blasphemy; also, it was given authority to wage war 42 months. [6]It opened its mouth in blasphemy against God, to blaspheme His name and His tent, that is, those pitching their tents in heaven. [7]It was permitted to wage war with the holy people, even to conquer them.

It was given authority over every tribe, people, tongue, and nation. [8]All those who dwell upon the earth will worship it, those whose name is not written in the scroll of life of the Lamb slaughtered from the foundation

---

[101] BYZ and TR read, "I stood," while NTG reads, "He [i.e., the dragon] stood."

of the world. [9]If anyone has an ear, let him hear: [10]If one has a band of captives, he so goes [into captivity]; if anyone will kill by the dagger, he must be killed by the dagger. Here is the endurance and the faith of the holy people.

The Lamb/Dragon Beast

[11]Then I saw another beast coming up out of the earth, having 2 horns like a lamb, yet speaking as a dragon. [12]It exercises all the authority of the first beast on its behalf. It requires the earth and those who dwell therein to worship the first beast, which was healed of its mortal wound. [13]It performs great signs, even that fire should come down from heaven upon the earth before men. [14]It leads astray [my peoples],[102] those who dwell upon the earth, by the signs which it was permitted to do on behalf of the beast, telling those who dwell upon the earth to make an image to the beast, the one which had the wound from the dagger—yet lived. [15]It was permitted to give breath to the image of the beast, that the image of the beast should both speak, and require as many as would not worship the image of the beast be killed. [16]It requires that everyone—small and great, both rich and poor, both free and slaves—give themselves marks upon their right hand or upon their forehead, [17]that no one be able to buy or sell, unless he has the mark, the name of the beast, or the number of its name.[103]

Wisdom Riddle: The Number 666

[18]Here is wisdom: he who has a mind is to compute the number of the beast, for it is a man's number, and his number is 666.

---

[102]BYZ brackets "my peoples" as doubtful. In Revelation, "those who dwell upon the earth" consistently refers to the wicked.

[103]TR reads, "unless he has the mark, or the name of the beast, or the number of its name." BYZ lacks "or" before "the name of the beast," but the editors supply a comma following "mark." NTG lacks "or," and the editors supply no comma, suggesting the translation "the mark: the name of the beast or the number of its name." See commentary for defense of three separate descriptors, as in TR and the much older Chester Beatty Papyrus III.

The Lamb and the 144,000: Firstfruits of Barley Harvest

14 ¹Then I looked, and behold, the Lamb was **standing** upon Mount Zion, and with Him a number—144,000—those who have His name and the name of His Father written upon their foreheads. ²Then I heard a voice from heaven, like a voice of many waters and like a voice of great thundering; the voice which I heard was like harpists harping upon their harps. ³They were singing a new song before the throne, and before the 4 living creatures and the elders. No one was able to learn the song, except the 144,000, those who had been redeemed from the earth. ⁴These are those who were not defiled with women, for they are virgins. These are those who follow the Lamb wherever He goes. These were redeemed by Jesus from among men, a firstfruits offering to God and to the Lamb. ⁵No lie was found in their mouth, for they are without blemish.

Proclamation of 3 Angels' Messages: Ripening Earth for Harvest

⁶Then I saw an angel flying in mid-heaven, having the everlasting gospel to proclaim to those sitting[104] upon the earth: to every nation, tribe, tongue, and people, ⁷saying in a loud voice, "Fear the Lord,[105] and give Him glory, for the hour of His judgment has come! Worship Him who made heaven, the earth, the sea, and water springs."

⁸Then another, a second angel, followed, saying, "Babylon the great has fallen![106] Due to the wine of intolerance [for obedience][107] of her fornication, she has intoxicated all the nations."

⁹Then another angel, a third, accompanied them, saying in a loud voice, "If anyone worships the beast and his image, and takes [his] mark

---

[104] BYZ and NTG read, "sitting"; TR reads, "dwelling." Either Greek word can translate the Hebrew *yashav* ("sit, dwell").

[105] TR and NTG read, "God"; BYZ reads τον κυριον ("the Lord").

[106] TR and NTG read, "fallen, fallen"; BYZ reads, "fallen."

[107] See footnote 98.

upon his forehead or upon his hand, [10]then he will drink of the wine of God's intolerance [for sin],[108] which has been mixed undiluted in the cup of His retribution,[109] and he will be tormented by fire and brimstone before the holy angels and before the Lamb. [11]The smoke of their torment ascends forever and ever; those who worship the beast and his image have no cessation, day nor night, nor anyone who takes the mark of his name.

[12]"Here is the endurance of the holy people: they keep God's commandments and Jesus' faith."

[13]Then I heard a voice from heaven saying, "Write: 'Blessed are the dead, those who die in [the] Lord from now on.' Indeed," says the Spirit, "that they may cease from their labors, while their works accompany them."

Son of Man Reaps Earth's Wheat Harvest

[14]Then I looked, and behold, a white cloud. Upon the cloud One like the Son of man was seated, having upon His head a golden crown, and in His hand a sharp sickle. [15]Another angel emerged from the temple, crying out in a loud voice to the One seated upon the cloud, "Send forth your sickle and harvest, for the hour to harvest has come since the harvest of the earth is dry."[110] [16]So the One seated upon the cloud cast His sickle over the earth, and the earth was harvested.

Trampling the Winepress

[17]Then another Angel emerged from the temple in heaven, He too having a sharp sickle. [18]Yet another angel emerged from the altar, having authority over the fire,[111] and called with a loud cry to the One holding the sharp sickle, saying, "Send forth Your sharp sickle and gather the clusters

---

[108] See footnote 98.

[109] See footnote 46.

[110] "Dry" grain refers to grain ready for harvest. "Dry" is a different word from "ripened" in verse 18.

[111] Or "over the wheat." See remarks on this verse.

of the vine of the earth, for her grapes have ripened." **[19]**So the Angel cast His sickle into the earth, and gathered the vine of the earth, and cast [it] into the great winepress of God's intolerance [for sin].[112] **[20]**The winepress was trampled outside the city; blood came out of the winepress unto the bridles of the horses for 1,600 stadia.

COMMENTARY

The Sea Beast

At the end of Revelation 10, we learned that John's behavior in eating the scroll typified the experience of the Millerites; so here, his stance upon the sand of the sea typifies the tiny remnant of God's people standing among the teeming multitudes who claim to be part of Israel but truly are not (see Rom. 9:6). He typifies the remnant people who partake of the everlasting covenant, the very ones whom the dragon seeks to destroy at the close of chapter 12. As they watch the beasts of Revelation 13 come to full maturity, it will look as though their doom is certain. However, just as He has throughout sacred history, God will surely deliver the remnant when He comes to rescue His bride.

John sees a beast emerging from the sea. The 10 horns and 7 heads, as well as the mention of leopard, bear, and lion point unmistakably to Daniel 7:1–8, in which 4 beasts emerged from the great sea, the Mediterranean. Making this connection is vital to understanding Revelation 13 properly. There are 4 beasts in Daniel 7, of which the Babylonian lion, Medo-Persian bear, and fearsome Roman beast have 1 head apiece, while the leopard of Hellas has 4 heads, giving the requisite 7 heads of Revelation 13:1. Comparison with Daniel 7:7–8 shows that the 10 horns are associated with the fourth beast, Rome.

The imagery John uses enables us to see where he is in the stream of prophetic time. Note that verse 2 lists the beasts as leopard, bear, and

---

[112] See footnote 98.

lion—exactly the reverse of Daniel 7. This shows that Babylon and Medo-Persia have already come and gone in succession, and Hellas has already arisen. The beast has only 10 horns, hence, the horn from insignificance referred to in Daniel 7:8—papal Rome—has not yet arisen. On the other hand, all 7 heads *are* present, and the 10 horns associated with the fourth beast *are* present.

In *THE STAND*, we noted that the 4 heads of the third beast (Hellas) correspond to the 3 kingdoms that arose from the breakup of Alexander's kingdom, as well as the kingdom that pre-dated Alexander, that to which all Greek philosophy traces its roots—the western Greeks of Magna-Grecia. The 3 kingdoms following Alexander's reign—the Seleucid (Syrian), Ptolemaic (Egyptian), and Antigonid empires—all passed away before Jesus' birth. On the other hand, the book of Daniel provides several indicators that Greece and Rome overlapped a great deal,[113] so we correctly deduce that John is living in the days of the fourth head of the leopard beast: the Greco-Roman empire.

The Babylonian, Medo-Persian, Seleucid, Ptolemaic, and Antigonid empires have all passed away, while papal Rome is yet future. Nevertheless, the beast still retains the mouth of a lion, the feet of a bear, and the body of the leopard (which includes its 4 wings and 4 heads), for "they took away their dominion, yet an extension of their lives was granted them until [the] appointed time" (Dan. 7:12) of the end-time judgment. In other words, the beast of Revelation 13:1–10 is indeed Rome, itself an amalgamation of the prior kingdoms, built on a foundation of Greek philosophy (dualism being especially important), Medo-Persian Mithraic worship, and Babylonian polytheism.

The dragon at the end of 13:2 who gives his power, throne, and great authority to the beast represents both Satan (see 12:9) and the agency through whom he worked, pagan Rome (see vs. 4, 5). From John's vantage point, this transfer of power from pagan to papal Rome is yet future.

---

[113] Note the bronze (Greek) upper legs and iron (Roman) lower legs of the image (see Dan. 2:32, 33); the iron (Roman) teeth and bronze (Greek) nails of the beast (see Dan. 7:19); "number 1 of them" (see Dan. 8:9) refers to the first of the 4 horns and its associated compass direction, i.e., the western Greeks of Italy; the goat-faced king refers to Rome's Greek face (see Dan. 8:23).

In 13:3 is seen the (apparent) death of the papacy with the slaughtering of the seventh head, the head of the fourth beast of Daniel 7:7–8. Thus, the papacy experiences a counterfeit of Jesus' death as described in Revelation 5:6. This *apparent* slaughter occurred on February 10, 1798, when General Berthier entered Rome, demanded the resignation of Pope Pius VI, and, this not being tendered, took him captive on the 20th. While Pius VI died on August 29, 1799, the succession of popes has continued, and the papacy has slowly but surely been regaining its temporal authority, particularly under the reign of popular John Paul II (1978–2005) and his successors, Benedict XVI (2005–2013) and Francis (2013–present). Vatican City is the smallest independent state in the world and the only religious body to be a state, with ambassadors from all over the world, making all the more remarkable its extensive power. The papacy will continue to wield world-wide power until its final destruction at Jesus' return (see Rev. 19:20).

Let us note other connections with Revelation 4 and 5. The sea beast of 13:2 (a composite of the beasts from the sea in Daniel 7:3–8) is a parody of the 4 living creatures in Revelation 4 and 5. Second, John sees the Lamb standing before the throne as though slaughtered, after which He is given power, His throne, and great authority (see Rev. 5:12, 13; 11:15–17). Conversely, the Roman dragon gives the papacy his power, throne, and great authority *prior* to the papacy's slaughter.

When the papacy is fully revived, the entire world will marvel, worshipping the papal beast. Of course, worshipping Satan's agent amounts to worshipping Satan himself. What does pagan worship of the beast and Satan look like? Here is a sampling:

1. Worship of saints and relics.
2. Baptism as the lesser mystery or initiatory rite.
3. Use of a white robe during the initiatory rite.[114]

---

[114] White robes suggest purity, but not when wet. "The robes should be made of substantial material, of some dark color that water will not injure, and they should be weighted at the bottom. Let them be neat, well-shaped garments" (White, *6T*, p. 98).

4. Status as a catechumen until admitted to the greater mystery, the Lord's Supper.
5. Worshipping toward the east.
6. Observance of the *dies solis*, or "Sunday," as the sacred day.
7. Reassigning the pagan Easter (Ishtar's re-birth) to Jesus' resurrection and Christmas (the pagan birth of the sun) to the birth of Jesus as the Sun of Righteousness.

In verse 5, attention returns to the 42 months allotted the papacy during the Dark Ages. Who gave the papacy its blasphemous mouth? The dragon did, of course. What exactly is blasphemy? The Bible gives numerous examples of blasphemy:

1. Claiming to be the Son of God (see John 10:33, 36; Mark 14:61–64).
2. Claiming the power to forgive sins (see Matt. 9:2, 3; Luke 5:21).
3. Dealing unfaithfully with God (see Ezek. 20:27).
4. Anger and envy against or mistreating God's people (see Ezek. 35:11–13; Isa. 52:5).
5. Not loving our neighbors as ourselves in showing favor to some (see James 2:1–9).
6. Not honoring one's master (see 1 Tim. 6:1).
7. Not loving one's husband and children, being a good homemaker, or submitting to one's husband (see Titus 2:4, 5).

Does the papacy blaspheme in any or all of these areas? Consider the following:

1. "The Pope is of so great dignity and so exalted that he is not a mere man, but as it were God, and the vicar of God" (Ferraris, *Prompta Bibliotheca*, vol. 6, article "Papa," p. 17).

2. One of the 7 sacraments Catholics receive is penance—
   forgiveness of sins via the priest.

3. "If you love me, keep My commandments" (John 14:15). In
   this, the papacy is unfaithful: "The Pope can modify divine
   law, since his power is not of man but of God, and he acts
   as vicegerent of God upon earth with most ample power
   of binding and loosing his sheep" (Ferraris, *Prompta Bibliotheca*, vol. 6, article "Papa," p. 19).

4. She martyred tens of millions during the Dark Ages.

5. History is replete with popes courting the favor of emperors
   to their advantage.

6. She claims supremacy, bound by no one, hence she certainly
   gives no honor to any master.

7. The papacy holds that the Roman Catholic Church is the
   true church, Christ's bride. In attempting to take Christ's
   place as High Priest and leading her daughter churches
   into such corruption that God calls them harlots (see Rev.
   17:5), she demonstrates no love for Jesus or these daughter
   churches; she does not manage her household and is in no
   wise submitted to her pretended husband, Jesus.

Further, the papacy blasphemes God's tent (the heavenly sanctuary)
by corrupting His people, those who pitch their tents in heaven. How is
this? Christ's work in the heavenly sanctuary is the very work He does in
developing His character in the hearts of those who exercise faith in Him,
but the papacy has counterfeited the heavenly sanctuary with an earthly
substitute.

It was given authority to wage war against truth and God's people
for 42 prophetic months, or the 1,260 years of the Dark Ages, AD 538–
1798. While it was permitted to conquer them, this was ordained by
God, reminding us that *He* is in control, for unto Him belong "times and
appointed times" (Dan. 2:21).

The close of 13:7 foretells a time when the papacy will be "given authority over every tribe, people, tongue, and nation." Babylon commanded false religious worship of all "peoples, nations, and tongues" (Dan. 3:4), with no mention of tribes. When the mortal wound of verse 3 is fully healed, end-time Babylon seeks to fulfill Satan's ultimate goal: worship from *everyone*—which includes other churches.

Foreseeing all of this, it is no mere coincidence that God addresses His last-day message to "every nation, tribe, tongue, and people" (Rev. 14:6), calling people out of the false churches into His remnant church (see 18:1–4). As with Babylon in Daniel 3, false worship in the last days will be enforced on penalty of death (see 13:15), but Christ will develop His image in His people so that they will "not love their life, even unto death." (12:11).

When fully revived, "all those who dwell upon the earth will worship" the papacy. Those who dwell upon the earth are those "whose name is not written in the scroll of life of the Lamb slaughtered from the foundation of the world," i.e., those who refuse to submit their lives to Christ's full control. This is a fearful position in which to be, for only those whose names are written in the scroll of life will have a place in His kingdom. The faithful remnant instead pitch their tents in heaven, sitting in the heavenly realms (see Eph. 2:6).

In spite of the fierce persecution soon to be unleashed by the papacy, 13:10 makes clear that its doom is just as certain as that of Satan. All who kill will be killed. In 1798, the papacy experienced a first death from which it was revived; when Jesus returns, the papacy is cast in the lake of fire, its second, permanent death (see Rev. 19:20; 20:14).

The Lamb/Dragon Beast

John now sees another beast coming up out of the earth. A study of verses 11–17 reveals that it is this new beast that causes those who dwell upon the earth to worship the revived papal beast. We conclude that this new beast arises prior to the time of the papal beast's full restoration. More precisely, it is rising to power at the time of the (nearly) mortal wound.

This new beast is a curious creature. On the one hand, it has 2 horns like a lamb, reminiscent of Jesus as the Lamb slaughtered from the foundation of the world. It also hearkens back to the ram of Daniel 8:3–4. This ram represented Medo-Persia, in particular king Cyrus whom God recognized as His anointed (see Isa. 45:1), the one who was to issue the decree for the Jews to return home to rebuild God's house at the close of the 70-year Babylonian captivity (see Isa. 44:28; Ezra 1:1–4). On the other hand, this second beast speaks as a dragon, which we identified as Satan working through his agencies. Anciently, that agency was Egypt's Pharaoh (see Ezek. 29:3); in the days of Jesus, it was pagan Rome (see Rev. 12:4); during the Dark Ages, it was the papacy (see v. 16); in the end time, it is the accomplice of papal Rome (see v. 17).

The beast's horns resemble those of a lamb, not a full-grown ram, so we deduce that this beast *starts out* like Jesus (i.e., Christian in character), but over time develops the character of the dragon (Satan and his agents). It exercises the same authority as the end-time papacy does, even making an image to and of the papacy. Since Jesus is the "stamp of His [the Father's] underlying nature" (Heb. 1:3), this image of the beast is a perfect likeness of the papacy's character. How is it like the papacy? It *requires* worship of the papacy (see v. 12). God woos us (see Hosea 2:14), whereas Satan tries to force the will. The papacy seeks to "compel them to come in" (Luke 14:23), equating "compel" with "coerce."

The land beast arose around 1798, gained in power, is still powerful today, and will persecute God's people right up to the second coming. It arose in a relatively unpopulated area, indicated by its rise from the earth, distinct from the populous sea region (i.e., the Mediterranean) from which arose the kingdoms comprising the leopard beast. This beast has 2 sources of power, indicated by its 2 horns. This beast becomes just like the papacy— a blend of church and state—so the 2 horns in its early state represent the *separation* of these 2 powers—civil and religious. The absence of crowns upon its horns suggests that in its lamb-like stage, the beast had no monarch at the head of its civil or religious systems, i.e., no king and no pope. In its formative years, this country was a bastion of religious liberty.

The analysis so far positively identifies this beast as the United States of America. In its early history, America served as a refuge for those Europeans who were persecuted for their Protestant views, so this beast is more especially *Protestantism rooted in America*. Note the rapid development of the United States in the years leading up to 1798 and beyond:

Table 9: Key Dates in U. S. History Leading Up to 1798

DATE	EVENT
July 4, 1776	Declaration of Independence signed
March 1, 1781	Articles of Confederation ratified
May 25–September 17, 1787	Constitution drafted
March 4, 1789	Constitution becomes effective
April 30, 1789	George Washington inaugurated president
December 15, 1791	Bill of Rights ratified
April 30, 1803	Louisiana Purchase Treaty signed in Paris

The land beast eventually speaks like a dragon. What does it mean for a beast (a nation or its king) to "speak"? When a king speaks, whether verbally or in writing, laws are enacted. Pharaoh spoke the word, and Joseph became second in command over Egypt (see Gen. 41:40–44); Nebuchadnezzar spoke a decree commanding people not to speak against the God of Shadrach, Meshach, and Abednego (see Dan. 3:29); Darius' seal brought into effect a 30-day moratorium upon praying to anybody but himself (see 6:8, 9); in the name of King Ahasuerus, the decree went forth to destroy the Jews (see Esther 3:12, 13). Hence, the beast from the earth speaks by enacting civil laws that compel worship of the papal beast. In paying homage to the papacy, apostate Protestantism makes an image *to* the beast; in assuming the papacy's coercive character, it makes an image *of* the beast.

Revelation 13 bears an eerie similarity to the story of Moses and Aaron. Aaron "shall speak for you to the people. He will be your mouth, while you will be as God for him" (Exod. 4:16). Aaron was Moses' spokesman (the land beast exercises all the authority of the first beast on its behalf), while Aaron was to regard Moses as God's representative (the land beast requires all to worship the papacy as though it were God). "Aaron your brother will be your prophet" (7:1), just as the land beast is styled "the false prophet" (Rev. 19:20). The land beast makes an image of the first beast, while Aaron made a calf, an object of Egyptian sun worship (see Exod. 32:24). The land beast performs great signs, just as Aaron was commanded to perform signs with each new plague (see 7:10, 20; 8:6, etc.).

The authority granted the land beast is great indeed, for it will bring fire down from heaven. This will be pointed to as crowning evidence that this second beast is truly God's prophet. Elijah called down fire from heaven as punitive judgment upon the representatives of wicked King Ahaziah (see 2 Kings 1:10, 12). Hence, when the land beast calls for divine judgment upon those who honor God's holy Sabbath in defiance of the command to honor Sunday, and Satan supplies the needed miracle, it will be seen as the crowning evidence of God's displeasure with Sabbath worship and endorsement of Sunday worship. People the world over will be convinced that apostate Protestantism in the United States, in its call for Sunday worship, is God's true prophetic voice, and no doubt those who honor His holy Sabbath will be executed as false confessors, holding to an idol Sabbath. Such would do well to recall Elijah's previous fire-from-heaven experience: the sun-worshipping prophets of Baal were executed (see 1 Kings 18:38–40).

How does apostate Protestantism give breath to the image of the beast? When God breathed the breath of life into Adam, he became a living being (see Gen. 2:7). When the image speaks, apostate Protestantism causes the U.S. government to enact laws concerning Sunday worship. Giving life to this law means that it is enforced with a real penalty— in this case, death.

In pagan Rome, there were a number of persecutions against Christians, notably Diocletian's 10-year persecution (see Rev. 2:10). Often, death could be avoided, not by denouncing God and embracing idolatry wholeheartedly, but simply by the merest pretense, the slightest show of deference to the gods or the emperor (often considered the supreme god, the sun god).

> Still others were disposed to be favorable to the Christians, to sympathize with them in their difficult positions, and to temper as far as possible the severity of the laws against them. And when the Christians were prosecuted before their tribunals, they would make personal appeals to induce them to make some concession, however slight, that would justify the governor in certifying that they had conformed to the law, so that he might release them,—not only from that particular accusation, but from any other that might be made. Such governors would plead with the Christians to this effect, "I do not wish to see you suffer; I know you have done no real harm, but there stands the law. I am here as the representative of the empire to see that the laws are enforced. I have no personal interest whatever in this matter; therefore I ask you for my own sake that you will do some honor to the gods, however slight, whereby I may be relieved from executing this penalty and causing you to suffer. All that is required is that you shall worship the gods. Now your God is one of the gods; therefore what harm is there in obeying the law which commands to worship the gods without reference to any particular one? Why not say, 'The Emperor our lord,' and sprinkle a bit of incense toward his image? Merely do either of these two simple things, then I can certify that you have conformed to the law, and release you from this and all future prosecutions of the kind." (Jones, *The Two Republics*, pp. 157, 158)

Of course, such treachery before God is to forfeit the crown—eternal life (see Rev. 2:10). Those who have permitted Jesus to give them His faith will "not love their life, even unto death" (Rev. 12:11). Hence the faithful remnant will not compromise in the slightest detail or give the slightest impression that they approve of papal sun worship, but will remain steadfast to their Maker and Savior.

The death penalty and economic sanctions of verses 15 and 17 are to get everyone to take the mark of the beast. The Greek word χαραγμα ("mark") refers to a likeness made by a stamp, just as Jesus is the "stamp of His [the Father's] underlying nature" (Heb 1:3). Those who yield to pressure and accept the mark give evidence that their character is *identical* to that of the papacy, and by extension, Satan himself. By contrast, the seal of the living God indicates one's character is unchangeably like His is.

What is meant by giving oneself this mark upon the right hand or forehead? This alludes to Deuteronomy 6:8, in which the words of God are to be bound "as a sign upon your hand, and be as bands between one's eyes." The broader context of Deuteronomy 5:29–6:9 makes clear that these words are the commandments, statutes, and judgments of *Yahweh*. In fact, Jesus declares that the admonition "Thou shalt love the LORD thy God with all thine heart, and with all thy soul, and with all thy might" (6:5) is the first and greatest commandment (see Matt. 22:36–38), a summary of the first table of the Decalogue. Hence, the mark of the beast is a direct attack on the first four of the 10 Commandments.

Full conformity to God requires that our actions (indicated by the hand) *and motives* (His Word between our eyes in the frontal lobe, the moral decision center of the brain) be right. However, the mark of the beast can be *either* place, not necessarily both. Whether one truly believes the end time-deception or simply gives an outward show of worship to avoid economic penalties and death, this lack of complete fidelity to God marks one's character, making Satan sure of his prey.

It is through the exercise of the will contrary to God's will that people give themselves the mark of the beast. No matter how strong the pressure is to conform, it is ultimately a choice of *yielding* to God or sin (see Rom. 6:16). If we prefer our own lives over fidelity to God, Jesus says we forfeit eternal life (see Matt. 16:25).

The mark is received specifically upon one's *right* hand. The right hand is the one God uses to make His own unchanging oaths (see Isa. 62:8; Rev 10:5), and He also uses it to indicate the place of honor (see Ps. 110:1; Matt. 25:34). Hence, to mark oneself on the *right* hand shows one has pledged full allegiance and honor to Satan—that person has sold his or her soul to the devil.

What *is* the mark of the beast? We just saw that it is a rejection of the first table of the 10 Commandments, the first 4 commandments. It also identifies someone who values self-preservation over faithfulness to God. In verse 17, we find the real crux of the matter: apostate Protestantism will force passage of a bill forbidding *buying and selling* for those who refuse the mark. This is no arbitrary penalty. Reference to Nehemiah 13:15–22, especially verses 15 and 16, shows this to be the end-time perversion of God's prohibition against buying or selling on *His holy seventh-day Sabbath*. Satan wants no one to observe the Sabbath, for it is the memorial of God as Creator and Savior. We learned from Revelation 7 that the Sabbath is the seal of the living God; it should come as no surprise that the mark of the beast revolves around Sunday worship.

One can obtain the mark of the beast only when all of the following conditions are met: Sunday observance is mandated by law, and Sabbath observance is forbidden; one has had the chance to fully understand all of God's directions concerning His seventh-day Sabbath; one then willfully disregards His commands regarding His seventh-day Sabbath.

The *Textus Receptus* of verse 17 clearly distinguishes between the mark, name, and number of the beast by separating each of these items from the next with the word "or." The Majority text and critical text lack the word "or" between "the mark" and "the name of the beast." While the Majority Text editors supply a comma, thus distinguishing the mark from the name of the beast, the editors of the critical text do not, leading most translations to translate verse 17 as "the mark: the name of the beast or the number of its name." Which reading is correct? In Revelation 7, the *seal* (faithful Sabbath observance, signifying God's ownership of, and pledge to marry, the one sealed) was placed upon the forehead of the 144,000; in Revelation 14:1, the 144,000 have the *name* (i.e., the character) of the Lamb and the Father in their foreheads. Since the Sabbath commandment explicitly contains the name of God, there is no inconsistency in thus equating the seal of the living God and His name.

With the counterfeit, the mark of the beast corresponds to willful rejection of the Sabbath and at least nominal observance of Sunday (the idol Sabbath), while the name of the beast represents the character of Satan. The second commandment forbidding idolatry is the counterpart to the fourth commandment enjoining Sabbath worship. Close comparison of these two commandments reveals a notable distinction: *God's name is lacking* in the second commandment. Unlike God's seal and name, this suggests that the mark of the beast and its name are in fact to be distinguished. In confirmation of this understanding, the oldest extant manuscript containing Revelation 13, the P47 Chester Beatty Papyrus III from the late 200's, clearly distinguishes the three items with two instances of "or." Because it predates any other manuscript, it is the preferred reading; for further detail, the interested reader is referred to chapter four of Edwin de Kock's work, *The Truth About 666 and the Story of the Great Apostasy*.

Wisdom Riddle: The Number 666

Those who receive the seal of the living God are referred to as the 144,000. In turn, the number 144,000 points back to the covenant promise of deliverance from Egypt, for the 400 years of bondage work out to 144,000 days. Those who reject the Sabbath in favor of Sunday when the controversy reaches maximum intensity receive the mark of the beast, associated with the number 666. We conclude that the number 666 indicates something about a *refusal* of the covenant deliverance from spiritual Egypt. This is all the more reasonable, given other allusions to the exodus in Revelation 13: the dragon (Pharaoh, Ezek. 29:3); the land beast with the authority of the sea beast (Aaron speaking for Moses, Exod. 4:16); performing great signs (Aaron performed signs, 7:10); making an image of the beast (Aaron fashioning the golden calf, 32:24).

To compute this number 666 and see its relation to Egypt and Babylon, we explore complementary avenues: the historicist and scriptural. Both indict the same corrupt institution, the papacy, focusing attention on the head of that system, the pope himself.

Deciphering 666: The Historicist Avenue

The beast of Revelation 13:1–10 is the papacy. Scripture equates kingdoms with their kings (see Dan. 2:38, 39; 8:21, 22), so the "man" of Revelation 13:18 is clearly the pope. The pope has a number of names that apply to his position, so the historicist student must examine these names for the one that corresponds to the number 666. This involves gematria, which assigns numerical values to the letters of the appropriate alphabetic system. The language of Rome is Latin (see John 19:20), so we use Roman numerals for the pope's Latin title *Vicarius Filii Dei*,[115] meaning "Vicar of the Son of God." This title harmonizes perfectly with earlier quotes in which the papacy unabashedly claims to not only *represent* God on earth, but in fact, to *be* God on earth. Table 10 shows that the pope's title does work out to 666:

Table 10: Gematria Applied to *Vicarius Filii Dei*

ROMAN NUMERALS	GEMATRIA APPLIED	NUMERIC VALUE
M	1,000	
D	500	
C	100	
L	50	
X	10	
V and U[116]	5	
I	1	
All other letters	0	
Vicarius	5+1+100+0+0+1+5+0	112
Filii	0+1+50+1+1	53
Dei	500+0+1	501
Vicarius Filii Dei	112+53+501	666

---

[115] It is not the purpose here to give a thorough justification for this title. The interested reader is referred to Jerry A. Stevens' thorough but succinct work, *Vicarius Filii Dei—Connecting Links Between Revelation 13:16–18, the Infamous Number 666, and the Papal Headdress*, and Edwin de Kock's magnum opus, *The Truth About 666 and the Story of the Great Apostasy*.

[116] Latin uses the letters "V" and "U" interchangeably. Emperor Constantine's Latin designation, *Constantinus*, is sometimes written *Constantinvs*. The English speaker will notice that the letter "w" is called "double U," though in print it is clearly a "double V." In fact, in Spanish, it is called *doble V*.

Deciphering 666: The Scriptural Avenue

Another tack is to let Scripture define the number 666. The number 666 appears in only three other texts. In Ezra 2:13, it states that the number of sons of Adonikam is 666; we cannot deduce anything from this, however, for Nehemiah 7:18 reports his children as 667. The other texts, 1 Kings 10:14 and 2 Chronicles 9:13, refer to how many talents of gold King Solomon received in a year, establishing no discernible connection with the papacy.

Recall that verse 18 admonishes us to *compute* the number of the beast. To this end, instead of seeking the number 666 in Scripture, it is more reasonable to seek out the number(s) Scripture associates with Babylon and its king, as well as Egypt and Pharaoh, and see if these numbers total 666.

First, recognize that man was made perfect on day 6 of creation—this is the number God associates with humanity, a little lower than His own number 7.

Next, Babylon used a sexagesimal system, i.e., base 60, rather than the base 10 familiar to us. We are indebted to Babylon for our 60 seconds per minute, 60 minutes per hour, and $60 \times 6 = 360$ degrees in a circle. With this in mind, we recall that Babylonian King Nebuchadnezzar's image was 60 cubits high by 6 cubits wide. This height-to-width ratio of 10 is best appreciated when we recall that Daniel and his friends were found to be "10 hands above all the magicians and astrologers" in Nebuchadnezzar's kingdom. The image's dimensions suggest that Nebuchadnezzar's Babylon (60 cubits) was to be 10 times superior to any rival kingdom ruled by another man (6 cubits). Hence, the Babylonian image combines Babylon's number and man's number, contributing $60 + 6 = 66$ of the requisite 666. Bear in mind that Babylon's image was to be *worshipped falsely on pain of death*.

As for Egypt, Pharaoh refused to let the Israelites go into the wilderness to worship as *Yahweh* directed, accusing Moses and Aaron of causing them to "keep Sabbath from their labors" (Exod. 5:5), i.e., cease from their labor by keeping the Sabbath.[117] Following his release of Israel, Pharaoh hardened his heart once and for all against the Holy Spirit, choosing to retain them as slave labor, pursuing them with 600 choice chariots (see Exod. 14:7).[118] Hence, Egypt contributes the remaining 600 of the 666. Bear in mind that Pharaoh's 600 choice chariots are tied to his attempt to *prohibit true worship*.

Thus, the number 666 ties the papal sea beast and apostate Protestant land beast to each other, as well as to the ancient kings of Babylon and Egypt. The 66 identifies the papacy as the king of spiritual Babylon, complete with image, in its quest to *receive false Sunday worship*. The 600 shows apostate Protestantism in the United States to be the king of spiritual Egypt, seeking to *prevent true Sabbath worship* by enacting economic sanctions and a death decree against Sabbath-keepers. These are the same two kings of the south and north in Daniel 11:40 that together war against God's people during the time of the end.

The foregoing analysis of 666 identifies the plans of the papacy to supplant true worship with false, in complete harmony with the historicist understanding of *Vicarius Filii Dei*.

The Lamb and the 144,000: Firstfruits of Barley Harvest

Table 11 highlights the sharp contrast between the close of Revelation 13 and the opening of 14:1–5:

---

[117] "Moses had shown his people that obedience to God was the first condition of deliverance; and the efforts made to restore the observance of the Sabbath had come to the notice of their oppressors" (White, *PP*, p. 258).

[118] Further, the cost of Egyptian chariots was 600 silver pieces (see 1 Kings 10:29).

Table 11: Contrast Between Revelation 13:11–18 and 14:1–5

REVELATION 13:11–18	REVELATION 14:1–5
Second beast has 2 horns like a lamb.	The Lamb is Jesus.
The wicked have the number 666.	The righteous have the number 144,000.
Mark received on right hand or forehead.	Lamb and Father's name (equal to seal, see Rev. 7:3, 4) received in forehead.
All who dwell on earth (small, great, rich, poor, free, slave) receive mark.	144,000 (from all tribes of Israel, see Rev. 7:4–8) are sealed without blemish.
All who dwell on earth worship image (fornication, see Rev. 14:8, 9).	144,000 not defiled with women, are virgins.
All who dwell on earth led by counterfeit miracles to worship falsely.	144,000 follow Lamb wherever He goes.
All who dwell on earth are deceived.	No lie in mouth of the 144,000.
All who dwell on earth observe Sunday.	144,000 are Sabbath-keepers.
666: Points to Egypt's and Babylon's death decrees concerning worship.	144,000: Number of days (400 years) Israel was in Egypt before exodus.

The 144,000 and those who dwell on the earth are polar opposites. Jesus counselled the church that the wheat and tares are to grow together until harvest, for in an attempt to root out undesirable tares, we might err and pull up precious wheat (see Matt. 13:24–30, 36–43). However, when the harvest becomes fully ripe, the distinction between both classes will become so great that there will be no resemblance.[119] Like Job before them, the 144,000 will be permitted to undergo the severest of trials to demonstrate to all intelligences that their characters are immovable—perfect. This will satisfy the concerns of heavenly angels about bringing sinners to heaven and win those who are in bondage to Babylon, yet honest in heart.

---

[119] "The tares closely resembled the wheat while the blades were green; but when the field was white for the harvest, the worthless weeds bore no likeness to the wheat that bowed under the weight of its full, ripe heads. Sinners who make a pretension of piety mingle for a time with the true followers of Christ, and the semblance of Christianity is calculated to deceive many; but in the harvest of the world there will be no likeness between good and evil. Then those who have joined the church, but who have not joined Christ, will be manifest" (White, *COL*, p. 74).

To fully appreciate the picture of the 144,000 in 14:1–5, we must understand the imagery involved. In Revelation 5:6, the Lamb was seen standing before the throne in the heavenly sanctuary (on Mount Zion, see Ps. 20:2) at the commencement of the end-time judgment, where He would continue to stand, pleading His blood throughout the day of atonement. In verse 1, the Lamb is seen once more, still standing on Mount Zion. The 144,000 are standing with Him, indicating that they have entered into covenant with the Lamb and are in full harmony with Him; their probation has closed. "You are standing today—all of you—before *Yahweh* your God ... that you may enter into the covenant of *Yahweh* your God and into the oath which *Yahweh* your God cut with you today, that He may raise you up today as His people, and He will be your God" (Deut. 29:10–13). That the Lamb is standing indicates that He is still interceding—not for the 144,000, but for the world's masses still living in darkness who have yet to hear the last message of mercy. This is Jesus' sixth stance in Revelation.

In contrast with the wicked who dwell on the earth at the close of Revelation 13, the 144,000 have the name of the Lamb and His Father in their foreheads. Comparison with 7:2–8 shows this name to be identical with the seal of the living God; hence, their character is opposite those marked in the forehead at the close of Revelation 13. Our study of chapter 7 showed this seal of the living God was evidence that they have faithfully kept His seventh-day Sabbath holy, despite intense pressure to keep Sunday.

They are shown upon Mount Zion, the heavenly abode of God, so some assume that this is an interlude—a glimpse of the redeemed in heaven. While the redeemed will enjoy the privilege of standing upon Zion one day, Revelation 14:1–5 connects seamlessly with chapter 13, showing God's faithful people as they are *in the culmination of the great controversy in the closing days of earth's history*.[120] The seal that they receive

---

[120] "The vision of the prophet pictures them as standing on Mount Zion, girt for holy service, clothed in white linen, which is the righteousness of the saints. But all who follow the Lamb in heaven must first have followed Him on earth" (White, *AA*, p. 591).

not only secures them an entrance to heaven; it prepares them to stand as God's witnesses, immovable in character.[121] Sealed, they go forth to earth's multitudes sharing the 3 angels' messages of verses 6–12 so that they, too, may choose to have Jesus purify them fully before His return.

These people have been filled with the Holy Spirit. This may be demonstrated a number of ways. First, they have God's name, but Paul says, "You were made righteous in the name of the Lord Jesus, by the Spirit of our God" (1 Cor. 6:11). Second, they are sealed, and it is the Holy Spirit who seals us (see Eph. 1:13; 4:30). Third, the harp-like voice in verse 2 evidences the presence of the Holy Spirit: Elisha requested a harp player, and when he played, the hand of *Yahweh* came upon him, and he prophesied, i.e., the Holy Spirit prophesied through him (see 2 Kings 3:15); Saul prophesied in the presence of harps (see 1 Sam. 10:5, 6); David played the harp, which drove away evil spirits (see 1 Sam. 16:16, 23).

Joel refers to this end-time outpouring of the Holy Spirit as the latter rain (see Joel 2:23, 28, 29), the spring rain that occurs at barley harvest time. While the early (fall) rain initiates crop growth, it is the latter (spring) rain that causes trees to bear fruit (see Deut. 11:14; Jer. 5:24; Joel 2:23; James 5:7). The latter rain is withheld while we are in a state of rebellion; when we are totally surrendered to His will, the latter rain comes, enabling us bear fruit to His glory *apart from circumstances*.

This connection between the 144,000 and the latter rain prepares us to understand the harvest imagery of verses 1–5. This passage is the antitype of Israel's spring pilgrim feast, the Feast of Unleavened Bread (see Lev. 23:5–14). During this feast, there was a special ceremony the day following Sabbath in which the firstfruits of barley harvest were presented. On that day, a lamb was sacrificed, and an omer ("sheaf," KJV) of the firstfruits was brought to be waved before *Yahweh*. In Revelation 14:1–5, we

---

[121] "Just as soon as the people of God are sealed in their foreheads,—it is not any seal or mark that can be seen, but a settling into the truth, both intellectually and spiritually, so they cannot be moved,—just as soon as God's people are sealed and prepared for the shaking, it will come" (White, *1MR*, pp. 249, 250).

have the sacrificial Lamb, and the 144,000 are the firstfruits that Jesus, as High Priest, waves before the throne.

The description of the 144,000 as an omer provides further evidence that they are strict Sabbath-keepers. The word "omer" first appears in Exodus 16:32, in which *Yahweh* commands Moses to preserve an omer of manna as a memorial of His care for Israel after bringing them out of Egypt. Here, God gave Israel explicit direction concerning the collection of manna, highlighting the Sabbath as the day upon which Israel was to collect no manna. On the Sabbath, the people were to cease from their activity and focus exclusively upon God, so He mercifully provided them a double-portion of manna on the preparation day (Friday). The chapter closes with the curious statement, "The omer is the tenth part of the ephah" (Exod. 16:36). This tenth part of an ephah of manna was to be a special reminder to the people of *Yahweh's* Sabbath, a tenth part of His 10 Commandments.

During the Feast of Unleavened Bread, the firstfruits were offered the day after the Sabbath. As High Priest, Jesus presents the 144,000 before His Father right *after* they have been sealed with the sign of the everlasting covenant—the Sabbath (see Exod. 31:16, 17; Isa. 56:6).

Next, John hears a voice like many waters and great thundering, alluding to Psalm 29:3–4. Psalm 29 opens with a command for the sons of God to give *Yahweh* glory, strength, and His name's glory, as well as to worship Him in holy adornment. According to verse 9, they do so in His temple (on Zion). We conclude that the 144,000 are giving God true worship in His temple Zion as they manifest His glory, His holy character, before a world given over almost entirely to sin, selfishness, and Satan.

While Psalm 29 describes the voice of *Yahweh* as many waters and great thundering, the oneness of the Lamb and His people in Revelation 14:1–5 suggests that the voice from heaven is that of *both Yahweh* and His people. In support of this, note that the voice is like harpists (plural) harping, and *they* sing a new song. In 5:9–10, the elders and 4 living creatures sang the new song, and the Majority text suggests the holy people join in. Table 12 summarizes the Old Testament usage of the "new song":

Table 12: The "New Song" in the Old Testament

REFERENCE	SUMMARY
Psalm 33	*Yahweh* is Maker and Judge. All the earth is to fear Him.
Psalm 40	Song of deliverance and living righteously. Leads others to trust *Yahweh*.
Psalm 96	Song of salvation. Declare His glory among the nations. *Yahweh* is Creator and Judge.
Psalm 98	Song of *Yahweh's* salvation and righteousness. *Yahweh* is coming to judge the world.
Psalm 144	Song of salvation and rescue. Contrasts the unfaithful with *Yahweh*.
Psalm 149	*Yahweh* is Maker. Gives the humble salvation. Permits holy people to execute judgment.
Isaiah 42	*Yahweh* will bring judgment and light to the Gentiles.

The foregoing passages confirm that 14:1–5 pictures the 144,000 *before* they are in heaven. This new song is sung in view of this fallen world before Jesus comes, proclaiming that He gives victory—perfect victory—over sin:

> What we make of ourselves in probationary time, that we must remain to all eternity. Death brings dissolution to the body, but makes no change in the character. The coming of Christ does not change our characters; it only fixes them forever beyond all change. (White, *5T*, p. 466)

> And they sing "a new song" before the throne, a song which no man can learn save the hundred and forty and four thousand. It is the song of Moses and the Lamb—a song of deliverance. None but the hundred and forty-four thousand can learn that song; for it is the song of their experience—an experience such as no other company have ever had. (White, *GC*, pp. 648, 649)

Naysayers decry such victory prior to the second coming, noting that there has never before been a group of people that has experienced victory over sin. True, but how many naysayers lived to argue with Noah about his message of an unprecedented flood? Those who live to see Jesus come *must* have this experience before His return.

Their pure character explains their description as "virgins." They are separate from the idolatrous image worship (same as fornication, see Exod. 20:4–6) of those who dwell upon the earth in Revelation 13. In Scripture, women represent churches, and Isaiah 4:1–6 makes plain that those in Zion have escaped the corrupt teachings and practices of the fallen church bodies (compare Rev. 17:1–6). This is not to say that the 144,000 have never *previously* sinned; rather, they have accepted Christ's imputed righteousness, which cleanses their past, and learned in His school to *die daily to self* and hunger and thirst after righteousness, so they have been filled with His imparted righteousness (see Matt. 5:6). By His grace, they attain to the point where they will never again yield to sin, no matter how strong Satan's temptations are. They have prepared themselves to be His bride without spot or blemish (see Eph. 5:27) and are ready for the heavenly Bridegroom to come for them (see Rev. 19:7, 8; Matt. 25:6, 10).

Their absolute purity of character is further emphasized by their mouths being free of any lie. Jesus called Nathanael a true Israelite, for there was no deception in his mouth (see John 1:47), and the one who does not stumble in word is a perfect man (see James 3:1–12). Speaking of the remnant of Israel, *Yahweh* promises, "they will not do iniquity, not speak a lie, nor will there be found in their mouth a deceitful tongue" (Zeph. 3:13). "Blessed is the man to whom *Yahweh* does not impute iniquity, in whose spirit is no deceit" (Ps. 32:2).

The Greek word αμωμος ("without blemish") is consistently used by the Septuagint when referring to sacrifices that are *tamim* (Hebrew for "perfect"). Hence, the 144,000 have developed a perfect character by learning to die daily, their lives a living sacrifice (see 1 Cor. 15:31; Rom. 12:1, 2). By experience, they have learned to say with Paul, "I am crucified with Christ: nevertheless I live; yet not I, but Christ liveth in me: and the life which I now live in the flesh I live by the faith of the Son of God, who loved me, and gave himself for me." (Gal. 2:20, KJV).

Proclamation of 3 Angels' Messages: Ripening Earth for Harvest

John's attention is drawn to 3 angels, each having a message to prepare people for the return of Jesus. "[John] records the closing messages which are to ripen the harvest of the earth, either as sheaves for the heavenly garner or as fagots for the fires of destruction" (White, *GC*, pp. 341, 342). The content of their messages matches that of the "new song" of the 144,000: they declare *Yahweh* as Creator, lead others to put their absolute trust in Him, bear tidings of His salvation, proclaim that He is coming to judge the world in righteousness, and state plainly that He will be victor over His enemies. How is it that no one else can sing this song if all can plainly read it in verse 6–12? To *read* the lyrics is not to sing the song; one sings passionately about what one has *lived*. Those who sing the message of the 3 angels are those who have allowed themselves to be completely *transformed* by this message into Jesus' likeness.

John sees an angel flying in mid-heaven, hearkening back to the eagle of Revelation 8:13, which announced the woes of the 3 angels, the last 3 of the 7 trumpets. Those 3 angels each had a woe anticipating the end-time judgment; *these* 3 angels have a message to prepare the world to stand during the 7 last plagues *following* the end-time judgment.

This angel has the everlasting gospel to proclaim to those sitting upon the earth. While there is much contained in the message of the 3 angels, the essence of it is the everlasting gospel. Many people think they know and believe the gospel, but is it the "everlasting" gospel? One would expect "covenant" to follow "everlasting." The phrase "everlasting gospel" blends the concepts of "everlasting covenant" and "gospel," indicating that the true gospel *is* the message of the everlasting covenant. The everlasting covenant made with Abram is the gospel message of righteousness by faith. By exercising faith in Him who has pledged His very existence (see Heb. 6:17; 7:22; 9:15–17), we can be made righteous creatures, restored to the image in which humanity was originally made (see Gen. 1:26, 27).

This message goes to those sitting ("dwelling," *Textus Receptus*) upon the earth. Those seated upon the earth are those who do not recognize that the *judgment* is now seated (see Dan. 7:9, 10) and are in no wise prepared to *stand* during the judgment hour. Instead of pitching their tents in *heaven* during their earthly sojourn, they are content to sit (make their home) on this sin-stained *earth*, rather than prepare to one day sit with Jesus on His throne (see Rev. 3:21).

To fully appreciate the first angel's message, it is helpful to recognize its source. The content mirrors that of Psalm 96 and its parallel passage, 1 Chronicles 16:23–33. This psalm was given by David to Asaph for the purpose of thanking *Yahweh* (see 1 Chron. 16:7). He was joyful that the ark had been reinstated in the tent David had pitched for it. Likewise, the first angel's message is to arouse those seated upon the earth, focusing their attention on the ark of the judgment in the heavenly tent (sanctuary). Table 13 enumerates the parallels between the first angel's message and Psalm 96:

Table 13: Comparison of First Angel's Message and Psalm 96

FIRST ANGEL'S MESSAGE (REVELATION 14:6, 7)	PSALM 96
v. 3: 144,000 sing a new song.	v. 1: All the earth invited to sing a new song.
v. 6: Proclaim the everlasting gospel.	v. 2: Bear tidings of His salvation daily.
v. 6: To every nation, tribe, tongue, and people.	vs. 3, 7, 10: among the nations ... peoples ... tribes ... nations.
v. 6: Fear the Lord.	vs, 4, 9: *Yahweh* is great ... to be feared above all gods. Tremble before His face.
v. 6: Give Him glory.	vs. 3: Recount His glory!
v. 6: The hour of his judgment has come.	vs. 10, 13: He will judge peoples with uprightness, world in righteousness.
v. 7: Worship him.	vs. 9: Worship *Yahweh* with the adornment of holiness.
v. 7: Who made heaven, earth, sea, and water springs.	vs. 5, 11: *Yahweh* made the heavens. Let heavens, earth, and sea rejoice.

The first angel refers to judgment without mentioning the heavenly sanctuary. On the other hand, Psalm 96 says, "Strength and beauty are in His sanctuary" and refers to judgment in verses 10 and 13. Thus, by allusion to Psalm 96, the first angel's message is designed to point those sitting upon the earth to what is *going on in the heavenly sanctuary*, i.e., the end-time work of judgment. If they are willing, they may be transformed into God's likeness (see 2 Cor. 3:18), ready to meet Jesus as a bride adorned for her Bridegroom when He returns (see Isa. 61:10).

The first angel informs the world that the One to judge them is their Creator. The command to worship Him who "made heaven, the earth, the sea" is lifted directly from the fourth commandment: "Remember the Sabbath day to keep it holy. ... *Yahweh* made the heavens, the earth, the sea, and everything therein" (Exod. 20:8–11). The everlasting gospel leads one to acknowledge *Yahweh* as Creator and keep holy His Sabbath. Evolution, Darwinism, natural selection, and a causeless Big Bang are all rejected by those preparing to be part of the bride that meets Jesus at His return.

What about the reference to "the water springs?" On the one hand, this reminds us of when God opened the springs of the great deep in awful judgment on impenitent humanity in Noah's day (see Gen. 7:11; 8:2), typifying the end-time judgment. On the other hand, water springs also refer to God's blessings from which we are to drink freely (see Rev. 7:17). This latter understanding is a judgment as well, *one in favor of those who submit to Jesus' lordship*. Both understandings point to God as supreme Judge. "Choose you this day whom ye will serve" (Josh. 24:15), "whether sin unto death, or obedience unto righteousness" (Rom. 6:16).

The second angel's message is very brief, pointing the finger squarely at the end-time apostasy, Babylon the great. The first message points out the arrival of God's end-time judgment, admonishing all to worship him as Creator, obedience to which *leads* to a positive verdict—eternal life. Babylon's fallen state identifies her as the object of *condemnation* for *rejecting* Him as Creator, preferring instead her idols.

Babylon's "fallen" condition identifies her idolatry. In Daniel 3, all were commanded to "fall down" before Nebuchadnezzar's golden image and worship. Papal Babylon calls for everyone to worship its idols, notably the idol sabbath, Sunday. "Fallen" also signals judgment, as in the story of wicked Haman. His wife and counselors told him, "If Mordecai, before whom you have begun to fall, is of the seed of Jews, you will not prevail against him; rather, you shall surely fall before him." Sure enough, Haman was hanged that very day upon the gallows intended for Mordecai (See Esther 6:13; 7:10). Similarly, when the voice from the heavens "fell," the 7-times judgment passed over Nebuchadnezzar (see Dan. 4:31). The papacy's doom is certain.

The reference to fornication confirms idolatry as the chief, aggravating sin of Babylon. The second commandment promises that those who surrender fully to *Yahweh* will not make any images, prostrate themselves in worship of them, or serve them, for God is "jealous" of our allegiance (see Exod. 20:4–6). God is jealous for His bride's purity, and Babylon's idolatry arouses His jealousy, for she has intoxicated all the nations—she has *seduced* them.

The fall and judgment of Babylon is prophesied in Jeremiah 50 and 51. Babylon is so far sunk in sin that her condition is incurable: "We attempted to heal her, yet she would not be healed. Forsake her, let us go each to his own land, for her judgment has reached unto heaven" (51:9). This is why the Holy Spirit empowers the 144,000 to give the message, "Come out of her, My people, lest you share in her sins, lest you receive of her plagues" (Rev. 18:4). All who would be saved must come out of the darkness and into His marvelous light (see 1 Peter 2:9).

The third angel completes the message. The first angel announces that judgment has arrived and calls for worship of the Creator, which necessitates keeping holy his Sabbath. The second angel points to the irreparably fallen condition of Babylon. The third angel spells out the dire consequences for those who reject the first angel's call for true worship, choosing instead to remain in Babylon.

The third angel makes clear that anyone who worships the beast and his image takes the mark upon his forehead or hand. Our study of Revelation 13 showed that the image *to* the beast was a move to glorify the papacy via Sunday worship. The image *of* the beast was apostate Protestantism's enforcement of this false Sunday worship via the papacy's historical tactic, i.e., employing the strong arm of the state. Whether one chooses to believe the lie that worship of the beast is correct (to take the mark in the forehead), or one simply goes along with an outward show of worship to preserve one's own life (to take the mark in the hand), one has submitted to the beast and hence rejected God and the salvation He offers via His everlasting covenant. All who choose to be intoxicated by Babylon's intolerance for obedience will ultimately drink of *God's* intolerance for sin.

The death sentence in God's cup is torment via "fire and brimstone before the holy angels and before the Lamb." We saw that the Lamb and all the angels were gathered before the throne in the courtroom of judgment (see Rev. 5:6, 11). The wicked are destroyed by fire and brimstone before the great white throne in Revelation 20. This judgment mirrors that which befell Sodom and Gomorrah (see Gen. 19:24, 25). Those cities have not continued burning; they were destroyed, turned to ashes, with nothing but smoke arising afterward. Such will be the fate of the wicked in the great day of accounts (see Gen. 19:28, 29; 2 Peter 2:6; Mal. 4:1, 3).

This may *seem* to contradict the assertion in Revelation 14:11 that "the smoke of their torment ascends forever and ever." At first glance, this might seem to confirm the papacy's pagan teaching of eternal torment in hell. To get at the truth, we turn to the source of verse 11: Isaiah 34, which refers to the end-time destruction of God's enemies, labeled symbolically as Edom: "Then shall her [Edom, cf. vs. 5, 6] torrents turn into pitch, and her dust into brimstone; her land shall become burning pitch. By night and by day, she shall not be quenched. Her smoke shall ascend forever. From generation to generation, she shall lie waste. Forever and ever, no one will pass through her" (Isa. 34:9, 10). Far from a perpetual fire that torments sinners forever, the nations are described as a barren wasteland, with no one passing through and nothing but smoke continuing to rise from the burnt remains. The remainder of Isaiah 34 speaks of unclean birds, thorns, and wild animals living among the rubble—impossible if the fires continued for eternity.

Jude 7 speaks of Sodom and Gomorrah as "undergoing the penalty of eternal fire." However, the parallel passage in 2 Peter 2:6 says Sodom and Gomorrah were turned into ashes. They were destroyed in Genesis 19:29. Hence, the fire is eternal not in *duration*, but in its destructive *effect*.

The popular picture of a hell that burns for the ceaseless ages of eternity necessitates that the wicked must *never* die—the very lie the serpent spoke to Eve (see Gen. 3:4). How can they live forever when only those who conquer sin and keep His commandments have access to the tree of life, which is in paradise? (see Gen. 3:22; Rev. 2:7; 22:14). It was this pagan belief in the immortality of the soul that the great reformer Martin Luther classed among the most "monstrous fables that form part of the Roman dunghill of decretals" (Petavel, *The Problem of Immortality*, p. 255).

An incredible irony in the fate of the wicked is that "they have no cessation, day nor night." The word αναπαυσις ("cessation") comes from the same root as the verb καταπαυω, used to describe God ceasing on the seventh-day Sabbath from His creative activity of the prior 6 days (Gen 2:2, 3, LXX). Those who do not honor *Yahweh* as their Creator by ceasing from worldly cares during His seventh-day Sabbath are in the end unable to partake of *any* such cessation or rest.

The third angel's message concludes on a brighter note, commenting on the endurance of the end-time remnant, in spite of all the persecution calculated to sway them from their allegiance to *Yahweh*. "Let patience [or endurance] have her perfect work, that ye may be perfect and entire, wanting nothing" (James 1:4, KJV). Those who endure every trial will experience the fulfillment of the everlasting covenant.

The present translation refers to "those who keep God's commandments and Jesus' faith." The traditional KJV reading is "they that keep the commandments of God, and the faith of Jesus." It is plain that "the commandments of God" are "God's commandments." How about "the faith of Jesus"—is it the same as "Jesus' faith?" The Hebrew of Habakkuk

2:4 reads, "The righteous shall live by his faith." However, the LXX reads, "the righteous shall live by the faith of Me," i.e., "the righteous shall live by My faith." Jesus says the Scriptures "testify about Me" (John 5:39), so "My faith" in Habakkuk 2:4 (LXX) is Jesus' faith.

In keeping God's 10 Commandments, the faithful remnant people are keeping the words of the everlasting covenant (see Exod. 34:28; Deut. 4:13; 1 Kings 8:9, 21). At the same time, "without faith, it is impossible to please" God (Heb. 11:6). By the exercise of a living faith—Jesus' faith—the holy people keep God's 10 Commandments without the slightest transgression. They have become truly righteous. Thus, Revelation 14:12 is a marvelously compact assertion of righteousness by faith.

In verse 13 is a wonderful assurance to all who should die, having assimilated these truths in their life experience. The message of the 3 angels is designed to prepare a people for translation—to meet their Lord having never faced the sleep of the first death. However, before the time that the remnant of the woman's seed comes into full unity of the faith, presenting a perfectly united message to the world, there will be *individuals* who *are* entirely transformed by the message. Before the time comes that the bride as a whole is ready (see Rev. 19:7), such who die are not to be regarded as lacking that faith that the 144,000 will demonstrate. Their salvation is secure, and they will arise to meet their Lord face to face (see 1 John 3:2, 3). "All who have died in the faith of the third angel's message come forth from the tomb glorified, to hear God's covenant of peace with those who have kept His law" (White, *GC*, p. 637).

Son of Man Reaps Earth's Wheat Harvest

Following the proclamation of the 3 angels, John sees Jesus in the likeness of the Son of man. This designation for Jesus points us back to Daniel 7:13–14, in which He comes with the clouds of heaven to the opening of the end-time judgment in 1844. At His ascension, Jesus took His seat at the Father's side, awaiting His kingdom (see Rev. 3:21). Throughout the judgment, He stood before the Father in the Holy of Holies (see 5:6), ministering His blood and making the final atonement. Now that He is seated once again, it is clear that His kingdom is finally made up, and Jesus may begin to reign as King *de facto*. The 144,000 have faithfully proclaimed the 3 angels' messages, and everyone on earth has made up their mind for or against the true worship of God. Probation is now closed for everyone—forever.

The waving of the omer in 14:1–5 marked the *beginning* of the *spring barley harvest*, while verses 14–16 correspond to the *close* of the *summer wheat harvest*, for the angel from the temple describes earth's harvest as "dry," an agricultural term signifying grain ready for harvest. In type, the start of wheat harvest was marked by the Feast of Weeks, which began 7 weeks after the waving of the barley omer (see Lev. 23:15, 16; Deut. 16:9, 10). Does this imply a 7-week period for preaching the 3 angels' messages of Revelation 14:6–12 from the time probation closes for the 144,000 until probation finally closes for the rest of earth's population? No, for 10:6 stated that all prophetic periods stopped with the *beginning* of the judgment in 1844. We are not to set dates for any of the closing events.

Jesus is wearing a golden crown (compare "diadems" in 19:12). The gold crown of verse 14 matches that which Mordecai wears in Esther 8:15 (LXX). In the story of Esther, a death decree went forth throughout the empire against God's people, but the king allowed Mordecai to seal another decree, granting the Jews the right to defend themselves. Though the day of both decrees was yet future, there was great rejoicing as Mordecai went forth, for deliverance at that point was certain. This parallels with Revelation: though God's people are to be put to death (see Rev. 13:15), their deliverance is sure (though future), for they are sealed. They hail Jesus as triumphant (see 14:1–5), for when the day for the final showdown arrives, God's people will be rescued and His enemies will be killed (see Rev. 16:12–21; 19:11–21).

What exactly is the harvest? Jesus states, "Now the enemy who sowed them [the tares] is the devil, while the harvest is the end of the age" (Matt. 13:39). What "age" is this? "The tares and the wheat are to grow together until the harvest; and the harvest is the end of probationary time" (White, *COL*, p. 72). Clearly, the "end of the age" is the "end of probationary time."

Is the end of probationary time precisely coincident with the second coming? According to Revelation 15 and 16, the 7 last plagues must fall upon the impenitent following the close of probation, demonstrating to all that their hearts are beyond the Holy Spirit's call to repent (see 16:9, 11, 21). All the angels are with Jesus at His second coming (see Matt. 25:31), but observe that the angel who speaks to Him in verse 15 has just come out of the heavenly temple. Before the plagues fall, Jesus "casts" His sickle over the earth in verse 16, marking the close of probation for everyone (compare Rev. 2:22; 8:5; 12:9; 14:19; 18:21) and the sealing of the righteous. *Following* His casting of the sickle and the subsequent demonstration of the character of the wicked during the 7 last plagues, Jesus arrives; *then* His angels *gather* the precious wheat (see Matt. 24:30, 31).

The picture in 14:14 is what Jesus looks like as He prepares to *leave* the Holy of Holies. He will *remain* seated on this cloud until He is first glimpsed by the righteous at the second coming, after which He rides forth as described in 19:11:

> Soon there appears in the east a small black cloud, about half the size of a man's hand. It is the cloud which surrounds the Saviour and which seems in the distance to be shrouded in darkness. The people of God know this to be the sign of the Son of man. In solemn silence they gaze upon it as it draws nearer the earth, becoming lighter and more glorious, until it is a great white cloud, its base a glory like consuming fire, and above it the rainbow of the covenant. Jesus rides forth as a mighty conqueror. (White, *GC*, pp. 640, 641)

Trampling the Winepress

Thus far, Revelation 14 has been based on the Hebrew agricultural calendar: the antitypical waving of the omer of barley harvest (vs. 1–5), the ripening of earth for harvest via the 3 angels' messages (vs. 6–12), and the antitypical feast of weeks, marking the end of wheat harvest (vs. 14–16). As we might expect, chapter 14 finishes with the final feast of the Hebrew calendar, the Feast of Ingathering (also known as the Feast of Booths or Tabernacles).

Following wheat harvest, fruit must be picked *before* celebrating the Feast of Ingathering (see Exod. 23:16; Deut. 16:13). The fruit (grapes) are declared ripe in verse 18, meaning the character of the wicked is fully developed, and there is no more chance that any of them will repent. These wicked grapes are cast into the winepress, corresponding to the outpouring of the 7 last plagues of Revelation 16. The winepress is trampled outside the city (God's faithful people), meaning that these 7 last plagues fall only on the wicked, just as the last 7 of the plagues in Moses' day fell only on Pharaoh's Egyptians (see Exod. 8:22, 23). The blood reaches unto the bridles of the horses when Jesus comes, for in 19:11–15, Jesus and the hosts of heaven come seated upon white horses, and He Himself tramples the winepress. We conclude that the antitypical feast of ingathering is coincident with the second coming.

In verse 17, we meet with an Angel who has a sickle to gather fruit, which the text distinguishes from the sickle used by the Son of man for the wheat. However, this Angel is still Jesus, for He is the One who tramples the winepress (see 19:15). Then in verse 18, another angel comes forth, one who has "authority επι του πυρος," which all translations render as "authority over fire." Such a translation assumes that the word πυρος is the genitive case (possessive case in English grammar) of the noun πυρ ("fire"). This translation is perfectly valid, yet it misses an extremely important point.

In the phrase επι του πυρος, each word is in the genitive case (possessive case in English grammar). This is certain because the definite article του ("the") is unquestionably genitive, and Greek grammar expects επι and πυρος to match the case of the article. However, a knowledge of Greek vocabulary and the overall agricultural imagery of Revelation 14 reveals another meaning for πυρος that cannot be dismissed. Unlike the New Testament, which uses σιτος for "wheat," the Septuagint *always* translates "wheat" with πυρος.[122] If "wheat" is intended in verse 18, one might object that πυρος should appear with its genitive spelling πυρου, but this would have masked the reference to "fire." The clearest and most compact way to communicate both ideas—"fire" and "wheat"—simultaneously is with the word πυρος.

Why should verse 18 blend the ideas of "fire" and "wheat"? Unlike God, who reads the heart *directly*, angels and people alike need *evidence* to be convinced of what is in a person's heart. For their benefit, God must use πυρ ("fire") to *test* everyone's character (see Mal. 3:3; 1 Cor. 3:10–15; 1 Peter 1:7) *prior* to the final πυρος ("harvest").

The Angel casts His sickle into the earth, signifying the close of probation (see Rev. 2:22; 8:5; 12:9; 14:16; 18:21), and casts the vine into the winepress, marking the onset of the plagues. Verse 20 marks the second coming, when Jesus *tramples* the winepress (compare 19:15). His bride is now forever secure from the hands of the wicked.

---

[122] See LSJ and GSG, s.v. πυρος.

PART 4B: THE KEY POINTS

REVELATION 12–14: JESUS IN THIS PASSAGE

Jesus is the Male born of the woman, then caught up to God and His throne. As Michael, Jesus cast Satan out of heaven. He is the Lamb slaughtered from the foundation of the world who stands on Mount Zion with the 144,000. As the Son of man, He sits on the cloud to reap the earth for the antitypical wheat harvest. As the Angel with the second sickle, He casts the vine into the winepress, which He in turn tramples at the second coming.

REVELATION 14:1: JESUS STANDS FOR HIS BRIDE

When the end-time day of atonement begins, Jesus stands upon sea and earth—the very places whence the end-time beasts of Revelation 13 arise—showing His sovereignty over earthly affairs. In Revelation 14:1, the Lamb stands upon Mount Zion with the firstfruits of barley harvest, the 144,000. The work of atonement complete in their lives, they are prepared to give the 3 angels' messages to the world.

REVELATION 12–14: THE WEDDING THEME

The pure woman of Revelation 12 is Jesus' bride. God is preparing her to become one flesh with Him, so that like Jesus, she will not love her life, even unto death. The remnant of her seed is the end-time church entrusted with the wedding invitation. As the end-time struggle of Revelation 13 comes to a head, she finally stands with Jesus, having His name written on her forehead—the Bridegroom's character sealed in her mind. At last she is empowered to give the end-time wedding invitation, the 3 angels' messages, to the world.

REVELATION 12–14: THE SEAL OF GOD AND MARK OF THE BEAST

Sabbath observance does not confer the seal of the living God upon anyone. The seal will be placed upon those who are *fully* given over to God and His service. Likewise, those who now (or in centuries past) worship on Sunday in integrity of heart, have in no sense received the mark of the beast. That said, when the conflict of Revelation 13 is fully developed and everyone comes to clearly understand all aspects of true versus false worship, then people *will* receive the mark of the beast if they continue in error. The decisive factor is one's character. The litmus test that will reveal to whom each person has given allegiance is the choice one makes, when faced with death, regarding God's seventh-day Sabbath and the papacy's idol sabbath.

REVELATION 12–14: THE END-TIME REMNANT CHURCH

Our study of Revelation 12 concluded with reference to the end-time remnant church. Since God desires all to be part of his end-time church, the following are marks to help identify this movement:

1. It upholds the Bible alone as the rule of faith and the standard for all living (see Isa. 8:20). It rejects the erroneous "quadrilateral" (Scripture, tradition, reason, and experience) for theological and doctrinal understanding.
2. It articulates the sanctuary message of Daniel and Revelation, a message of righteousness by faith in Jesus' work of

atonement—both His atoning sacrifice upon the cross and the application of His blood during the end-time day of atonement in the heavenly sanctuary. During the end-time day of atonement, He creates in us a clean heart, perfectly reproducing His life within us. God does not merely *account* us righteous beings; He truly *makes* us righteous beings in this life (see Ps. 51:10; 103:12).

3. It upholds all 10 of God's Commandments without emendation, including the Sabbath (see Rev. 12:17; Exod. 20:8–11).

4. It upholds the Sabbath as God's seal, the sign of His everlasting covenant, His pledge to marry His people (see Exod. 31:16, 17; Isa. 54:5; 56:6; Rev. 7:2, 3).

5. It proclaims the advent near without setting dates. God will return once His people reflect His character fully. We may hasten His coming by allowing Jesus to live an obedient life in us (see Matt. 25:13; 1 John 3:1–3; 2 Peter 1:4; 3:11, 12).

6. It teaches that at death, one sleeps without thinking, and without praising *Yahweh*. God alone is immortal; at His return, He grants the righteous immortality (see John 11:11–14; Eccl. 9:5; Ps. 6:5; 115:17; 146:4; 1 Tim. 1:17; 6:16; 1 Cor. 15:51–55).

7. It teaches that the wicked do not burn forever in hell. Forfeiting immortality by choosing wickedness, with no access to the tree of life, they are consumed in the lake of fire and cease to be (see Rom. 6:12, 16; Rev. 2:7; 20:9; 21:8).

8. It teaches that our bodies are the temple of the Holy Spirit (see 1 Cor. 3:16, 17; 6:19, 20). Unclean animals are not food (see Lev. 11). We are to get regular rest, be temperate in all things, and drink ample water (see Ps. 127:2; Prov. 3:24; 23:2; Isa. 55:1). Kindness and generosity to others promote our own well-being (see Isa. 58:6–8).

9. It recognizes that the prophetic gift is to remain until Christ's church is in complete unity and has grown up into the fullness

of His character (see Eph. 4:11–13). It is blessed with the testimony of Jesus, the spirit of prophecy (see Rev. 12:17; 19:10), in the person of Ellen G. White, whose writings provide enormous insight into Scripture, practical counsel on right and wrong and day-to-day Christian living, and much comfort. Her writings are not an extension of Scripture, nor do they supersede Scripture; they are God's inspired commentary, whose sole purpose is to drive each of us to a deeper study of Scripture and implement its teachings in the life.

10. It proclaims the 3 angels' messages of Revelation 14:6–12 to prepare the world to stand for Jesus in the end-time judgment.

11. It teaches that Jesus is coming for His bride, who is holy and without spot, wrinkle, or blemish (see Eph. 5:27). His bride is His church (see Eph. 5:32). There are many churches, but only one remnant church that keeps the commandments of God and has the testimony of Jesus Christ (see Rev. 12:17; 17:5). It is the privilege and duty of members of the remnant church to support the mission of God's Seventh-day Adventist church with their tithes and offerings (see Mal. 3:8–12). Entrance into the church is by a public acknowledgment of one's faith via the act of baptism, full immersion in water (see John 3:23; Matt. 3:16; Acts 8:39).

REVELATION 12–14: DECISION QUESTIONS

Jesus is the faithful Bridegroom, developing His character in His bride-to-be. As the faithful Bridegroom, He protects His bride at every advance step, defending her against the attacks of the serpent and end-time papal and Protestant beasts. He cares for her in the wilderness and will soon rejoice with her as she stands with Him on Mount Zion, fully reflecting His character. Do you choose to submit to Him now, that you may become faithful and one day stand with Him as His bride, without blemish?

It is clear from Revelation 12 that the Seventh-day Adventist Church is the remnant church of Bible prophecy, His bride-to-be during the judgment hour. Do you choose to become part of Jesus' corporate bride? If so, contact your local Seventh-day Adventist Church so that you may begin Bible studies. This will permit you to locate biblical answers to your questions and settle into the truth. To locate the nearest church, use the Yellow Pages or search online (e.g., https://1ref.us/13h).

By God's grace, do you choose to stand faithful to your Bridegroom, Jesus (who is certainly faithful to His bride), during the closing scenes of the great controversy, loving not your life unto death, even in the face of the death decree of Revelation 13:15?

Do you choose to be among the harvest that Jesus is coming to reap? If so, say yes to His wedding invitation right now, and share the invitation with others. Then you, along with others won through your efforts, may soon go to be with the Bridegroom when He returns at the close of the judgment-hour wedding.

4A':
WEDDING OVER

REVELATION 15: JESUS
NO LONGER INTERCEDES

15 ¹Then I saw another sign in heaven, great and marvelous: 7 angels holding 7 plagues—the *last* [7]—because with them, God's intolerance [for sin]¹²³ is complete.

Conquerors Stand and Sing on Sea of Glass

²Then I saw something like a sea of glass mixed with fire, and the conquerors of the beast, of its image, and of the number of its name standing upon the sea of glass, holding the harps of God. ³They were singing the song of Moses, the servant of God, and the song of the Lamb, saying, "Great and marvelous are Your works, *Yahweh*, God of hosts,¹²⁴ righteous and true are Your ways, King of the nations. ⁴Who would not fear You, Lord, and glorify Your name? For [You] alone are holy. 'All the nations will come and worship before You,'¹²⁵ because Your righteous ways have been manifested."

Probation Closes

⁵Afterward I looked, and in heaven the temple of the tent of the testimony was open. ⁶Then the 7 angels who were holding the 7 plagues emerged

---

¹²³ See footnote 98.
¹²⁴ Greek, "Lord God Almighty."
¹²⁵ Psalm 86:9.

from the temple; they were wearing clean, radiant linen and were bound about their chests with golden sashes. [7]Then 1 of the 4 living creatures gave the 7 angels 7 golden bowls full of the intolerance [for sin][126] of God who lives forever and ever. [8]Then the temple was filled with smoke due to God's glory and due to His power; nobody was able to enter the temple until the 7 plagues of the 7 angels were complete.

COMMENTARY

The table of contents of the present work shows the structure for Revelation. It shows that Revelation 8:2–6 (probation open) matches up with chapter 15 (probation closed). Revelation 8:7–11:19 (the 7 trumpets) leads up to the *start* of the end-time judgment, while Revelation 16 (the 7 plagues) immediately follows the *close* of probation.

The chapter opens with "another sign in heaven, great and marvelous." This points back to the great signs in Revelation 12:1 and 3: a woman representing God's faithful people throughout history (Israel and the church) and a great, fiery dragon seeking to devour the woman's seed, Jesus. The present scene is not merely "great," but "marvelous." Whereas Revelation 12 began to lay out the great controversy between Christ and Satan, the 7 plague-filled bowls of chapter 15 contain the fullness of God's intolerance for sin; they will forever lay to rest any notion that He tolerates or excuses sin.

Conquerors Stand and Sing on Sea of Glass

In 15:2 are those who have conquered in the struggle with the beast, its image, and the number of its name. Accordingly, they may now inherit the covenant promises "to the one who conquers" outlined in the letters to the 7 churches of Revelation 2 and 3.

---

[126] See footnote 98.

These people have the harps of God, just like the 144,000 of 14:2. However, chapter 15 takes place at the close of probation for all mankind; hence, those with harps in verse 2 are *all* of the living righteous when probation closes: the 144,000 of the barley harvest and those of the later wheat harvest. Their harps indicate they are filled with God's Spirit (see 2 Kings 3:15; 1 Sam. 10:5, 6; 16:16, 23), fully prepared to face the most terrible crisis ever to befall mankind.

In the days of ancient Israel, the last 7 of the 10 plagues fell on Egypt, but not on the Israelites, though they were still physically in Egypt. Only after the seventh plague fell did God deliver Israel out of Egypt. Likewise, the 7 last plagues must fall on spiritual Egypt, but not on spiritual Israel, though they are still physically among spiritual Egypt (Psalm 91:10–11 promises that no plague will touch the righteous, for angels are commissioned to protect them). Once the seventh plague falls, there is deliverance at the second coming.

The conquerors are standing "επι the sea of glass." Those familiar with Greek are faced with the question as to whether the righteous are standing "at" or "upon" the sea of glass. The Greek preposition επι can be understood either way, context being the determining factor. Comparison with Exodus 14:2 shows that the sons of Israel, prior to crossing the Red Sea, were standing "επι the sea." In that context, it is plain that they were "at," not "upon," the sea. However, the comparison is not quite appropriate, for in that verse, the plagues had *already* fallen; in Revelation 15, the plagues are *about* to fall.

With that said, how do we determine whether it is "at" or "upon" in verse 2? We consider clues from Revelation itself. In 4:5–6, the 7 Spirits of God and the sea of glass are "before the throne." In 5:6, the Lamb with the 7 Spirits of God stands between the throne and the elders who encircle it at some distance. Comparison of these texts shows that the Lamb is standing in the very area where the sea of glass is, hence *upon* the sea of glass (Jesus also appears upon the waters of the Nile in Daniel 12:6–7 and walks on water in John 6:19). In Revelation 14:1–3, the 144,000 hold harps as they stand *with the Lamb before the throne*. We conclude that the conquerors who are holding harps in Revelation 15:2 stand in the same spot as do the Lamb and the 144,000—before the throne "upon" the sea.

What does it mean that the sea is "of glass, mixed with fire"? Before his fall, Lucifer walked among the stones of fire on Mount Zion (see Ezek. 28:14, 16). As a covering cherub, he was one of the seraphs, or living creatures, hence he walked in the immediate presence of God's throne, which is of sapphire stone (see Ezek. 1:26). When God delivered unto Moses the 10 Commandments upon stone, there was "under His feet something like a paved work of sapphire stones, like the heavens itself in purity" (Exod. 24:10). This refers to the base of God's throne. The sea of glass mixed with fire is a vivid description of the pavement of sapphire stones that extends about God's throne.

Why are the people in Revelation 15 pictured standing upon the pavement of sapphire stones? Jesus' work of judgment during the wedding has enabled His bride to uphold the 10 Commandments (written in sapphire stone, see Exod. 24:10, 12) perfectly. Having endured the process of purification, they are fitted to sit on thrones (in the same spot as God's own throne, hence the sea of glass, see Rev. 3:21) in judgment of the wicked during the 1,000 years following the second coming (see 20:4–6).

Does Revelation 15 picture the righteous literally in heaven at this point? This cannot be, for they are taken to heaven at Jesus' return, and the second coming occurs at the conclusion of the plagues, which are yet to fall. They stand before the throne because their lives have come to be a perfect reflection of the Bridegroom, Jesus, who also stands before the throne. The song they sing hearkens back to the song of deliverance sung by the Israelites upon crossing the Red Sea (see Exod. 15). They sing because they have been delivered from the power of sin. Since no group in history has had this experience, only they can sing this song (see Rev. 14:3). There is an irony in their song, for they describe God's works as "great and marvelous," the very words used of the plagues in verse 1. All have a choice: acknowledge how great and marvelous are His ways, or experience how great and marvelous are His judgments unmixed with mercy upon the impenitent!

Why is the song "the song of the Lamb?" Just as Moses led the Israelites in their deliverance from Egypt right up to the promised land of Canaan, so it is the Lamb (Jesus) who has granted these people their victory over sin. He is pictured as singing *with* His bride in Revelation 14:1–5. After all, He too conquered sin while in the flesh (see Rev. 3:21). The words "All the nations will come and worship before You" are a quotation from David's prayer in Psalm 86:9 (LXX). Psalm 86 is David's acknowledgment of his utter dependence on God. In short, the allusion to this psalm informs us that the righteous in Revelation 15 have come to have the same experience as did Jesus, the true David: one of complete surrender. As a result, they cannot stop singing His praises and honoring His name.

In stating that "all the nations" will come and worship, some might understand this to mean universal salvation, whereby God does not destroy the wicked. This is plainly contradicted by the outpouring of the 7 last plagues in the very next chapter, as well as the final destruction of the wicked in the lake of fire in Revelation 20. By comparison with Isaiah 66:18–24, it is evident that it is all the *saved* of the nations who come to worship, while "their corpses" in Isaiah 66:24 confirms the destruction of the wicked. We might add that verse 23 notes that all flesh will worship *Yahweh* each Sabbath in the new earth; hence, the song of Revelation 15:3–4 affirms the permanence of the Sabbath.

Probation Closes

The open temple of the tent of the testimony hearkens back to the open temple in Revelation 11:19, when the pre-advent judgment *commenced*. With the onset of the 7 plagues, judgment is over, and no one may enter the temple. Why is the temple open? Recall from Jesus' message to the angel of Philadelphia that only Jesus can open and close the door to the Most Holy Place. Once the atonement was complete on the annual Day of Atonement, the high priest *came forth*. Jesus has to come back to earth to rescue His bride and place full responsibility for the purged sins upon Satan, represented by the live goat (see Lev. 16:20–22; Rev. 20:1–3).

With Jesus outside the Holy of Holies, He no longer intercedes for mankind. This will provide the crowning evidence that His bride is ready: when she continues to not sin during earth's darkest hour, it will show that atonement is indeed complete. She is now one with her Bridegroom, no longer indulging sin.

The 7 angels with the 7 bowls emerge from the temple with their dress just like that of Jesus in Revelation 1: white linen with gold sashes about the chest. For Jesus, this dress signifies His office as High Priest during the antitypical day of atonement. Their same dress shows them to be His *agents* to pour out His sevenfold judgment upon those who have fully rejected His character-purifying work during the closing hours of the end-time judgment (see Lev. 26:27, 28).

A living creature gives the angels 7 golden bowls full of God's intolerance for sin. In Revelation 5:8, each of the 4 living creatures and 24 elders had golden bowls full of incense, identified as the prayers of the holy people. These prayers were disclosed in Revelation 6:9–10 as pleas for vindication of their blood, (apparently) shed in vain. The bowls now contain God's final answer to the martyrs' pleas: His intolerance for sin, unmingled with mercy (see Rev. 14:10), is to be poured on the impenitent.

To appreciate 15:8, we consider where Scripture records such occurrences of God's glory. At the dedication of the wilderness sanctuary, a cloud covered it as *Yahweh's* glory filled it, preventing Moses, Israel's intercessor with *Yahweh* (see Exod. 20:19; 34:34), from entering therein (see 40:34, 35). When Solomon dedicated the temple, a cloud of *Yahweh's* glory filled it, so the priests could not continue ministering (see 1 Kings 8:10, 11). Moses' inability to enter the sanctuary typifies that time when Jesus will no longer act as Intercessor between God and man. The inability of priests (plural) to enter Solomon's temple typifies the futility of God's faithful people during the plagues to intercede on behalf of a world lost in sin.

At both of these dedications, sanctuaries uncontaminated by sin were dedicated. At the time of verse 8, the heavenly temple is fully restored, cleansed of all the defiling sins of believers. Of course, concurrent with this, the bodily temples of fully surrendered believers (see 1 Cor. 3:16, 17; 6:19, 20) have been fully cleansed from all defiling sins. In this sense, Revelation 15:8 can be seen as a dedication of 1) Jesus' bride, now fit for heaven, and 2) the heavenly temple itself, now prepared to receive His bride, who will sit on His throne judging the cases of the wicked for 1,000 years (see 20:4, 6). Jesus has completed atonement for His bride and sanctuary, and He is nearly ready for the grand consummation!

REVELATION 16:
THE 7 LAST PLAGUES

16¹Then I heard a great voice from the temple saying to the 7 angels, "Go! Pour the 7 bowls of God's intolerance [for sin]¹²⁷ into the earth."

Plagues 1–6

²So the first departed, and poured his bowl into the earth; a terribly bad sore developed upon the people which had the mark of the beast and worshiped its image.

³Then the second angel poured his bowl into the sea; it became blood like that of a dead man, and every living being in the sea died.

⁴Then the third poured his bowl into the rivers and into the water springs, and they became blood. ⁵Then I heard the angel of the waters saying, "You are righteous, He who is and He who was, He who is of perfect character,¹²⁸ for You rendered these [judgments]. ⁶Since they poured out blood of holy people and prophets, so You gave them blood to drink. They are deserving." ⁷Then I heard the altar¹²⁹ saying, "Indeed, *Yahweh*, God of hosts,¹³⁰ true and righteous are Your judgments!"

---

¹²⁷ See footnote 98.

¹²⁸ Greek οσιος ("holy, devout, pious"). The source is Psalm 145:17, in which οσιος translates *chasid* (God's character).

¹²⁹ BYZ and NTG read, "altar." TR reads, "Then I heard another [voice] from the altar."

¹³⁰ Greek, "Lord God Almighty."

⁸Then the fourth angel poured his bowl upon the sun; it was permitted to scorch people with fire. ⁹People were scorched with searing heat, yet the people blasphemed the name of God who has authority over these plagues, and would not repent to give Him glory.

¹⁰Then the fifth poured his bowl upon the beast's throne; its kingdom became darkened, and they were gnawing their tongues due to the pain. ¹¹They blasphemed the God of heaven due to their pains and their sores, yet they would not repent of their deeds.

¹²Then the sixth poured his bowl upon the great river Euphrates; its water was dried up, so that the way for the kings from the sunrise might be prepared.

¹³Then I saw 3 unclean spirits like frogs [coming] from the dragon's mouth, from the beast's mouth, and from the false prophet's mouth, ¹⁴for they are spirits of demons performing signs, which go forth to the kings of the entire world, to gather them for the war of that great day of God of hosts.[131]

¹⁵"Behold—I am coming like a thief! Blessed is he who watches and guards his garments, that he not walk about naked and they see his shame." ¹⁶Then He[132] gathered them into the place which in Hebrew is called Har Megiddon.[133]

The Seventh Plague: Pre-advent Judgment Concludes

¹⁷Then the seventh poured his bowl upon the air, and a loud voice went forth from heaven's temple, from the throne, saying, "It is over!" ¹⁸Then there were lightning flashes, thunderclaps, voices, and a great earthquake, such as has not been since men have been upon the earth—so massive an earthquake, so great. ¹⁹The great city became [split] into 3 parts, and the cities of the nations fell. Babylon the great was remembered before

---

[131] Greek, "God Almighty."

[132] The Greek can be read "He [God]" or "they [the unclean spirits]." See commentary for why "He" is preferred.

[133] Greek, "Armagedon" (BYZ and NTG); "Armageddon" (TR).

God, to give her the cup of the wine of the retribution[134] stemming from His intolerance [for sin].[135] **20**Every island flew away; mountains were not found. **21**A great hail, like a talent [in weight], was falling from heaven upon men; men blasphemed God due to the plague of hail, for this plague is exceedingly great.

COMMENTARY

The plagues begin to be poured out in 16:1. The Greek for "pour" first appears in Genesis 9:6, in which God directs Noah and his family that if anyone "pours out" the blood of his fellow man, his own blood will be "poured out." The 7 last plagues are a perfect example of the principle of *lex talionis*: "the punishment must fit the crime" in kind and degree (see Lev. 24:19, 20; Deut. 19:18–21).

Plagues 1–6

The first plague answers to the sixth plague upon Egypt (see Exod. 9:8–12). It also brings to mind the severe trial with which Satan was permitted to afflict Job. In fact, Job 2:7 (LXX) uses the same Greek words translated as "terribly" and "sore" in the present translation. In Job's case, God *permits* Satan to strike Job for the purpose of demonstrating Job's immovable, righteous character. In the case of the last 7 plagues, God *Himself* pours out His intolerance for sin to demonstrate that the hearts of the wicked are immovable in their allegiance to Satan.

It is to be noted that this plague afflicts those who have the mark of the beast (those who keep Sunday, though they fully understand the claims of the fourth commandment enjoining worship on the seventh-day Sabbath) and worship the beast's image (in violation of the second commandment).

---

[134] See footnote 46.
[135] See footnote 98.

The chapter on covenant curses and blessings opens with a prohibition against image worship and the command for Sabbath worship (see Lev. 26:1, 2). As the plagues begin to fall upon the irrevocably wicked, it is no surprise that both these commandments are especially highlighted.

To fully appreciate the second plague, one needs to recognize its connection with the first of the Egyptian plagues. In Exodus 7:20–25, the Nile turns to blood, and the fish die. The apparent difficulty is that in Revelation 16:3, it is the *sea* that turns to blood. In fact, there is no contradiction. Pharaoh is called the great dragon who lies in the midst of the Nile River and its tributaries (see Ezek. 29:3). Elsewhere, the dragon (identified as Leviathan and the serpent, i.e., Satan), inhabits the *sea* (see Isa. 27:1; Job 41:31). This interchange is understandable, given that the Nile empties into the Mediterranean Sea.

The idea seems to be that God, via the plagues, is systematically targeting aspects of the end-time apostasy so that He can ultimately deliver His people. During the second plague, He targets the great water source of spiritual Egypt, the Nile, and during the sixth plague is seen the fulfillment of Isaiah 11:15–16 regarding the drying up of the great Babylonian water source, the Euphrates River, so that His people can be delivered. To be sure, the Nile and the Mediterranean Sea within which it ultimately empties may indeed turn to blood, and the fish therein may die. However, just as the drying up of the Euphrates River under the sixth plague symbolizes support for spiritual Babylon drying up (see comments on verse 12), we cannot afford to miss the *symbolism* of the second plague: those who have remained in spiritual Egypt (apostate Protestantism) will find in the end that the "water" it offers is death.

The Bible refers to running water as "living water" (see Lev. 14:5; John 4:10, 11; 7:38). Likewise, when the Bible says, "the life of the flesh is in the blood" (Lev. 17:11), it is referring to healthy blood circulating throughout the body. The blood Jesus shed on the cross is life to those who accept His work of atonement (see Matt. 26:28; Heb. 9:22), letting it course through them; for those who reject the ministration of His blood during the end-time day of atonement, the water in the sea becomes stagnant "blood, like that of a dead man," killing everyone therein.

The third plague is very similar, turning the smaller bodies of water, the "rivers and water springs," into blood. Again, this points back to the first Egyptian plague, in which the Nile's tributaries and all of Egypt's lesser water bodies became blood, and the Egyptians could no longer drink the water (see Exod. 7:19–21).

Once the second plague has done its job on apostate Protestantism in America, the third plague is a natural follow-up: all streams of Protestantism throughout the world, fueled by Protestantism in America, receive of God's plagues. Recall that the first angel's message of Revelation 14:7 refers to God as the Maker of heaven, earth, and sea (pointing to Sabbath worship), *as well as the water springs* (referring to the worldwide flood). Having rejected the proclamation of the 3 angels' messages, particularly the first angel's call to Sabbath worship, apostate Protestantism now experiences a worldwide judgment.

The foregoing understanding is supported by verses 5–7. The angel of the waters points to the shed "blood of holy people and prophets" as the reason they are now given blood to drink. Indeed, under the combined influence of the beasts of Revelation 13 (Roman Catholicism and apostate Protestantism), people are threatened with death if they persist in Sabbath worship, refusing Sunday worship. The wicked "deserve" this judgment. The word "deserving" refers to a balancing of both sides of a scale,[136] most appropriate for Revelation's focus on Jesus' work of judgment in the heavenly sanctuary.

To complete the irony, recall that Jesus said that unless one drinks the blood of the Son of man, he has no life in himself (see John 6:53). Having rejected the atoning work of the Son of man during the antitypical day of atonement, the wicked are now forced to drink the blood of judgment that He provides them, *devoid of the power of living water*. The irony is perfectly, yet tragically, bitter.

God's judgment is affirmed from the altar. This hearkens back to the fifth seal, when the voices of martyrs cried out for vindication from the altar. The 7 trumpets serve as God's answer to this plea, with the seventh

---

[136] See ANLEX and LSJ, s.v. αξιος.

trumpet culminating in the 7 last plagues. The collective voice of all martyrs through history express satisfaction that God has indeed acted justly—their blood was not shed in vain. He and His ways are unquestionably right, so their lives of service are now vindicated.

As the central plague, the fourth plague is extremely important and telling. The book of Revelation has centered around the issue of worship, culminating in a litmus test: the loyal remnant people learn to sacredly keep the Sabbath, while those who dwell upon the earth observe Sunday, the *dies solis* observed by pagans throughout earth's history. God now permits their darling idol to strike them. They should implore *Yahweh* to deliver them; but, having refused the first angel's message to "Fear *Yahweh*, and give Him glory" as Creator by keeping holy His Sabbath, they choose instead to blaspheme the name of God. They show their hearts to be completely hardened. Further probation would avail nothing.

The fifth plague answers to the ninth of the Egyptian plagues. All of Egypt was dark and immobilized, "but for all the sons of Israel, there was light in their dwellings" (Exod. 10:23). Allowing type to inform our understanding of antitype, the remnant is not affected by the darkness. In fact, the darkness is limited to the *beast's throne*. God's throne is where He sits as Judge; in darkening the enemy's throne (i.e., the seat of the papacy, Vatican City enclaved within Rome), He makes manifest that the papacy's effort to unseat Jesus as supreme Judge is futile.

By contrast, Daniel 12:3 reports that "the wise will blaze forth, like the brilliance of the firmament; those instrumental in leading many to become righteous as the stars ever onward." This prophecy finds fulfillment both literally and spiritually under the fifth plague: the literal darkness serves to highlight the radiant, Christ-like character of the righteous, who also literally light up as did Moses and Stephen of old (see Exod. 34:33–35; Acts 6:15). As in the previous plague, the wicked do not repent. The very reason God permits trials is to *lead us to true repentance*, which is *reformation*. If their hearts were open at all, the enormity of these plagues would lead them to plead with God for deliverance; instead, the plagues simply confirm the wicked in their course. God has done all He can. Their hearts are closed, so there remains nothing but for the plagues to run their course so that the onlooking universe may be fully convinced of their incurable condition. The wicked blaspheme God on account of their pains and sores, unlike righteous Job, who under similar affliction "did not sin with his lips" (Job 2:10).

The sixth plague hearkens back to the overthrow of Babylon by Cyrus, king of Persia. "Thus says *Yahweh* to His anointed, to Cyrus, whose right hand I have strengthened to subdue nations before him as I unhinge loins of kings, to open double doors before him so that gates will not be shut. I will go before you, and level the mountains, shatter the bronze doors, and cut through iron bars" (Isa. 45:1, 2).

Cyrus took Babylon by diverting the Euphrates River (which ran through Babylon), exposing the open doors prophesied in the previous passage. Scripture records that King Belshazzar did tremble as prophesied (see Dan. 5:6). Just as the water of the Euphrates was the life source running through ancient Babylon, so the water running through spiritual Babylon is its support. Water represents people (see Isa. 57:20; Rev. 14:2; 17:15), so the drying up of the water indicates that those who have gone along with Babylon's lies up to this point now turn away. They recognize that her path is leading to destruction and those with the seal of the living God have been right all along. Sadly, they do not turn to righteousness, for they have forever stamped their characters with the mark of the beast.

The drying up of the river prepares the way for the kings from the sunrise. John the Baptist quoted Malachi 3:1 and Isaiah 40:3 as he preached the baptism of *repentance* as a means of preparing the way for the Lord. This repentance made the path straight (see Mark 1:1–5). In the years leading up to October 22, 1844, those who preached the message of the advent near preceded Jesus' arrival in the Holy of Holies to begin His final, day-of-atonement ministry. While they misunderstood what was meant by Jesus coming to cleanse the sanctuary, their preaching had the desired effect of *preparing* a people to meet the Lord: they repented, making full confession of (and when merited, restitution for) sin.

In Scripture, entry into the promised land is preceded by rivers drying up: the Hebrews crossed over Jordan on dry land into the earthly promised land, and Elijah crossed over Jordan on dry land immediately prior to his translation to heaven (see Josh. 3:13–17; 2 Kings 2:8–11). Before the plagues fell, the righteous made full repentance and were sealed, hence when the Euphrates dries up, it is the sign that they are about to go home.

The "kings from the sunrise" stand in contrast to the "kings of the entire world," just as "those who pitch their tents in heaven" stand in contrast to "those who dwell upon the earth." These kings are not the Father and Jesus, angels, or any earthly kings; rather, they are those who have humbly submitted to the message of righteousness by faith, thereby becoming conquerors over sin. In fulfillment of Jesus' promise to Laodicea, they are the kings who will sit upon His throne during the 1,000 years (see Rev. 3:21; 20:4, 6).

Frogs come from the mouths of the dragon, beast, and false prophet. Recall that the dragon points ultimately to Satan, as well as his agents: "Kings and rulers and governors have placed upon themselves the brand of antichrist, and are represented as the dragon who goes to make war with the saints—with those who keep the commandments of God and who have the faith of Jesus" (White, *TM*, p. 39). Thus, the threefold union comprises the worldly rulers, papacy, and apostate Protestantism in the United States.

These frog-like spirits are explained with reference to the lone occurrence of frogs in Scripture: the second of the Egyptian plagues (see Exod. 8:1–15; Ps. 78:45; 105:30). Pharaoh's enchanters brought forth frogs by employing "sorceries" (Exod. 8:7, LXX) in imitation of divine power. God successfully marshalled His people with the proclamations of 3 angels (which pointed people to Scripture, not miracles) as the reason to 1) worship God as Creator by honoring His seventh-day Sabbath and recognize Him as Judge, 2) announce Babylon is fallen, for she has intoxicated (deceived) all nations by her false teaching, and 3) reject beast and image worship as incurring the wrath of God.

On the other hand, Satan will seek to deceive by dazzling the senses with the most sensational signs ever witnessed—strong, almost overmastering displays put on by spirits of demons—to promulgate a counterfeit threefold message to try to hold his crumbling empire together. These frog-like spirits aim to convince the entire world to 1) worship God by keeping Sunday, 2) proscribe Sabbath-keepers as those in error, and 3) believe God blesses those who worship the beast and his image:

> The *spirits of devils* will go forth to the *kings of the earth and to the whole world*, to fasten them in deception, and urge them on to unite with Satan in his last struggle against the government of heaven. By these agencies, rulers and subjects will be alike deceived. Persons will arise pretending to be Christ Himself, and claiming the title and worship which belong to the world's Redeemer. They will perform wonderful miracles of healing and will profess to have revelations from heaven contradicting the testimony of the Scriptures.
>
> As the crowning act in the great drama of deception, Satan himself will personate Christ. The church has long professed to look to the Saviour's advent as the consummation of her hopes. Now the great deceiver will make it appear that Christ has come. In different parts of the earth, Satan will manifest himself among men as a majestic being of dazzling brightness, resembling the description of the Son of God given by John in the Revelation. Revelation 1:13–15. The glory that surrounds him is unsurpassed by anything that mortal eyes have yet beheld. The shout of triumph rings out upon the air: "Christ has come! Christ has come!" The people prostrate themselves in adoration before him, while he lifts up his hands and pronounces a blessing upon them, as Christ blessed His disciples when He was upon the earth. His voice is soft and subdued, yet full of melody. In gentle, compassionate tones he presents some of the same gracious,

heavenly truths which the Saviour uttered; he heals the diseases of the people, and then, in his assumed character of Christ, he claims to have *changed the Sabbath to Sunday, and commands all to hallow the day which he has blessed.* He declares that *those who persist in keeping holy the seventh day are blaspheming his name by refusing to listen to his angels* sent to them with light and truth. This is the strong, almost overmastering delusion. Like the Samaritans who were deceived by Simon Magus, the multitudes, from the least to the greatest, give heed to these *sorceries*, saying: This is "the great power of God." Acts 8:10.

But the people of God will not be misled. The teachings of this false christ are not in accordance with the Scriptures. *His blessing is pronounced upon the worshipers of the beast and his image*, the very class upon whom the Bible declares that God's unmingled wrath shall be poured out. (White, *GC*, pp. 624, 625, emphasis added)

These evil spirits gather the kings of the entire world in desperate response to the preparation of the way of the kings of the east. Satan and his angels recognize the fulfillment of prophecy as the plagues fall, realizing that without a successful last stand, Jesus will come very soon, take His righteous people with Him, and the battle for control of this world will be forever lost. However hopeless the plight of the faithful remnant may look in comparison with the wicked hordes composing earth's kingdoms, it is the wicked who are now doomed. Note that in describing Egypt's 10 plagues, Psalm 78:45 states that the frogs of old corrupted (most translations render this even stronger: "destroyed") the Egyptians, not the Israelites.

At this point, God intrudes His voice, issuing a solemn alarm to the reader: those who are not deceived in the end are those who are *now watching* for the return of the Judge, the Son of man, just as He warned the angel of the church of Sardis (see Rev. 3:3). By His grace, we are to keep our garments of character spotless. Like Adam and Eve before the fall, His glory is to cover our nakedness, that there be no shame (see Gen. 2:25; Ps. 104:1, 2).

Through his deceptions, Satan marshals his forces for the final showdown, but the God of hosts takes control of events in Revelation 16:16, gathering everyone to Har Megiddon. Many today, particularly those of an evangelical persuasion, speculate as to a possible Middle East location for Har Megiddon. However, Revelation 1:1 told us that the book is symbolic, so Har Megiddon is not to be understood literally.

To understand what is here signified by Har Megiddon, the Scriptures speak for themselves. The Bible refers to Megiddo as a *valley*, while the phrase Har Megiddon signifies "mountain of Megiddon." Since Revelation 16:16 employs the spelling "Megiddon," not "Megiddo," we will focus our attention on the lone instance outside Revelation where this spelling is employed: Zechariah 12:11.

In Zechariah 12–14 is found a description of the end-time remnant's complete surrender to Jesus, the gathering of the nations against Jerusalem, the descent of New Jerusalem to earth following the 1,000 years, and the destruction of the wicked by fire. In 12:9, *Yahweh* announces His intent to destroy all the unconverted nations who come against Jerusalem (the remnant of end-time believers). Those composing the remnant bewail, not the siege, but their sins, which they understand contributed to the death of Jesus:

> As Satan influenced Esau to march against Jacob, so he will stir up the wicked to destroy God's people in the time of trouble. ...
>
> ... the anguish which they suffer is not a dread of persecution for the truth's sake; they fear that every sin has not been repented of, and that through some fault in themselves they will fail to realize the fulfillment of the Saviour's promise: I "will keep thee from the hour of temptation, which shall come upon all the world." Revelation 3:10. If they could have the assurance of pardon they

would not shrink from torture or death; but should they prove unworthy, and lose their lives because of their own defects of character, then God's holy name would be reproached. (White, *GC*, pp. 618, 619)

The mourning over sin is so great that it is likened to the "wailing of Hadad-Rimmon in the valley of Megiddon" (see Zech. 12:11). This refers to the great wailing made on behalf of King Josiah, the reformer king who died in the valley of Megiddo when he went to fight against Pharaoh Necho, in spite of God's warning through Necho himself to the contrary (see 2 Chron. 35:20–25).

Why does Revelation 16:16 refer to Megiddon as a mountain, rather than a valley? The key is to recognize that God represents the people who comprise His kingdom as a mountain, as with the stone that becomes a mountain in Daniel 2:35 (see also Revelation 14:1). In Obadiah, there are two mountains: Mount Zion is God's people, and Mount Esau represents the rebels who follow Satan, who is rallying his forces to finally quash the remnant before Jesus returns. The battle of Har Megiddon is the final battle between the two great mountains, as it were.

One last comment is in order. The text indicates that "He," i.e., God himself, gathers the wicked world to Har Megiddon. Many translations render it "they," referring to the spirits of verse 13, based on a peculiarity of Greek grammar in which grammatically neuter plural nouns such as "spirits" take a singular verb rather than the expected plural verb. Since grammar alone is indecisive on this point, we must let the Bible explain itself by examining related passages of Scripture.

In Ezekiel 38:16, we read that in the latter days, Gog comes against God's people, but more than this, *Yahweh brings Gog against His own people*. In verse 22, it says God will enter into judgment with Gog with hailstones (the seventh plague of Rev. 16:21), as well as fire and brimstone (which ignite the lake of fire following the 1,000 years; see Rev. 20:9, 10). Thus, He gathers everyone for the conflict with Gog, which includes the battle of Har Megiddon. Since Megiddo(n) is a valley, this explains why it is also said that God calls everyone to the "valley of decision" (the valley of Megiddo) where He will judge all nations who have surrounded His precious bride (see Joel 3:12, 14).

The Seventh Plague: Pre-advent Judgment Concludes

The seventh plague is the culminating judgment prior to Jesus' return. The declaration "It is over!" indicates no further judgment is necessary to manifest the impenitent hardness of the hearts of the wicked.

The seventh plague is poured upon the air. This refers back to Psalm 18:11 (LXX), in which God's secret place is described as "storm clouds of air." Psalm 18 is a psalm of judgment, picturing both destruction of the wicked (verses 40–42) and deliverance for God's people (verses 48–50). This informs the reader that the seventh plague is not simply the cataclysmic demise of the wicked; it signals deliverance for God's people who were gathered unto Har Megiddon during the sixth plague.

The lightning flashes, thunderings, voices, and earthquake point back to Sinai as recorded in Exodus 19:16 and 18. At the culmination of God's pre-advent judgment, these signs confirm His 10 Commandment law as the basis of the judgment (see Eccl. 12:13, 14). The massive earthquake, "such as has not been since men have been upon the earth," is described as was the hail in the seventh plague upon Egypt (see Exod. 9:18, 24). Likewise, Daniel 12:1 describes the time of distress as "such as has not been since becoming a nation until that time." History's greatest accumulation of wickedness is judged by the greatest earthquake.

The great city, Babylon, now splits into 3 parts, as the union of dragon, beast, and false prophet has led nowhere but destruction. Only God's city, Jerusalem, His faithful remnant bride, remains standing. The cup he makes Babylon drink fulfills the prophecy of the third angel's message (see Rev. 14:10).

The islands and mountains that disappear confirm that the seventh plague occurs at the close of the sixth seal (compare Rev. 6:14). Why would islands disappear? Islands in the Bible are the location of the unconverted nations (see Gen. 10:5; Isa. 66:19; Zeph. 2:11). Likewise, mountains represent earthly kingdoms. The disappearance of the islands and mountains confirms that the wicked are being blotted from the face of the earth.

God foretold His use of hail in the time of distress, the final war (see Job 38:22, 23). In Revelation 16:21, it is described as a talent in weight, the talent being the largest weight associated with the sanctuary, 60 times larger than the next weight, the mina. By contrast, in Exodus 16, God rained down manna upon His people as a blessing, and in verse 14, the manna is described as "a small, flaky substance, small like the frost on the ground." Of course, the manna served as a test of fidelity regarding His seventh-day Sabbath, and an omer (one tenth of an ephah) was preserved as a memorial of that one tenth of the commandments (see Exod. 16:32–36).

Note the irony: God rained down a small, flaky substance as a blessing for His people (which would memorialize His Sabbath)—*before* He proclaimed the 10 Commandments (the basis of judgment) at Sinai. On the other hand, as the consummate, punitive judgment upon those who have refused to keep His Sabbath holy, God rains down enormous hail upon everyone who has stayed in Babylon—*after* proclaiming the 3 angels' messages of judgment.[137]

---

[137] To fully appreciate the hail, recall that Babylon used a sexagesimal number system, or base 60 (see remarks on Revelation 13:18). The talent is 60 times greater in weight than the next smaller unit of sanctuary weight, the mina. Hence, the hail of the seventh plague is of the perfect weight to punish Babylonians.

PART 4A': THE KEY POINTS

REVELATION 15–16: JESUS

When probation closes, the saved sing the song of the Lamb. Jesus orders the 7 last plagues to be poured out on the impenitent. He admonishes us to watch and keep our garments of character *now*. He gathers all to Har Megiddon and declares, "It is over!" at the onset of the seventh plague.

REVELATION 15–16: THE WEDDING THEME

The 7 last plagues mark the time when probation has forever closed and the wedding has concluded. A sober reading of Revelation 15 and 16 should lead each of us to consider our love for Jesus. Are we prepared to spend *eternity* in *full* submission to Him as His God-fearing wife?

REVELATION 15–16: DECISION QUESTION

Jesus' wedding invitation is extended to all, but there is coming a time when the door to the marriage closes, beyond which no one may find admittance (see Matt. 25:10–13).

Do you find yourself unwilling to undergo the persecution soon to break out upon those who are entirely faithful to Jesus? Are you lothe to give up some cherished idol? If you answered yes to either of these questions, ask yourself if it is worth it. Surely you do not want to be among those upon whom the plagues fall, those who refuse to repent and who blaspheme God until the very end. You don't want to be among those who seek to put Jesus' bride to death at the battle of Har Megiddon, do you?

Have you answered Jesus' wedding invitation? If you have said yes to Jesus in the past, are you remaining faithful to Him during this tarrying time? Don't grow lukewarm. Please renew your commitment to surrender everything to Him, trusting that He will rescue His bride, and cherish you for all eternity. Please don't be indecisive—will you choose Jesus as your Bridegroom today?

4B':
SON OF MAN COMES FOR HIS BRIDE AND DRAGON DESTROYED

REVELATION 17–19: FINAL CONFLICT AND SON OF MAN COMES

The Whore

17 ¹Then came 1 of the 7 angels which have the 7 bowls; he spoke with me, saying, "Come, I will show you the judgment of the great whore who is seated upon the many waters, ²with whom the kings of the earth committed fornication, and those dwelling upon the earth were made drunk by the wine of her fornication."

³So he carried me into the wilderness in the Spirit, and I saw a woman sitting upon a scarlet beast full of blasphemous names, having 7 heads and 10 horns.

⁴Now the woman was clothed with purple and scarlet, adorned with gold, precious stone, and pearls, holding a golden cup in her hand, full of abominations and unclean things of her fornication. ⁵Upon her forehead a name [was] written: Mystery, Babylon the great, the mother of the whores and the abominations of the earth. ⁶I saw the woman, drunk due to the blood of the holy people—due to the blood of those testifying[138] of Jesus. I was greatly astonished when I saw her.

---

[138] Greek μαρτυς ("martyr," "one who testifies"). "Martyr" has come to mean "one who dies for those beliefs of which he testifies." Those in verse 6 were "martyred," but translating it as "those who testify of Jesus" makes a clearer connection with Revelation 12:17.

The Scarlet Beast

[7]Then the angel said to me, "Why were you astonished? I will tell you the mystery of the woman and the beast that carries her, the one that has the 7 heads and the 10 horns. [8]The beast which you saw was, is not, and is about to come up from the abyss, then go unto destruction. But those who dwell upon the earth, whose names are not written upon the scroll of life from the foundation of the world, will marvel as they see that the beast was, is not, yet will come.

The Wisdom Riddle

[9]"Here is the mind that has wisdom: the 7 heads are 7 mountains whereupon the woman sits. [10]They are also 7 kings: the 5 fell, the 1 is, and the other has not yet come. When he *does* come, it is necessary he remain a little while. [11]The beast which was and is not, it is also an eighth, yet is of the 7 and is going unto destruction. [12]The 10 horns which you saw are 10 kings who have not yet received a kingdom, but receive authority as kings 1 hour with the beast. [13]These have 1 purpose: their power and authority they give to the beast. [14]These will wage war with the Lamb."

Those with the Lamb

"The Lamb will conquer them, for He is Lord of lords and King of kings, and those with Him are called, chosen, and faithful."

Result of the 3 Angels' Messages

First Angel's Message Echoed: Whore Who Sits is Judged

[15]Then he told me, "The waters which you saw, where the whore sits, are peoples, multitudes, nations, and tongues. [16]The 10 horns which you saw, and the beast—these will hate the whore. They will make her desolate and make her naked. They will consume her flesh and burn her up with fire.

¹⁷For God has put it into their hearts to carry out His purpose, acting with 1 purpose, in giving their kingdom to the beast, until the words of God are fulfilled. ¹⁸The woman which you saw is the great city which holds dominion over the kings of the earth."

Second Angel's Message Illuminates the Earth

18 ¹Afterward, I saw another angel coming down from heaven, having great authority, and the earth was illuminated by his glory. ²He cried out in a strong voice, "Babylon the great has fallen, and become a dwelling for demons, a prison for every unclean spirit and a prison for every unclean and hateful bird, ³for due to the wine of intolerance [for obedience]¹³⁹ of her fornication, all the nations are fallen, the kings of the earth have committed fornication with her, and the merchants of the earth became rich due to the extent of her arrogant self-indulgence."

Third and First Angels' Messages Echoed

⁴Then I heard another voice from heaven saying, "Come out of her, My people, that you not join in her sins, nor receive of her plagues, ⁵for her sins have joined together on up to heaven, and God has remembered her unrighteous deeds. ⁶Render unto her as she also rendered: give double portions unto her according to her deeds; in the cup which she mixed, mix for her a double portion. ⁷As much as she glorified herself and acted arrogantly, to that degree give her torment and mourning, for in her heart she says, 'I sit as queen! I am not a widow, and there is *no* chance I will see mourning.' ⁸For this reason, her plagues will come in 1 day: deadly disease, mourning, and famine, and with fire she will be burned up, for strong is *Yahweh* God¹⁴⁰ who has judged her.

⁹"The kings of the earth, those who have committed fornication and lived arrogantly with her, will weep and beat their breasts over her when

---

¹³⁹ See footnote 98.
¹⁴⁰ Greek, "The Lord God."

they see the smoke of her burning, [10]standing far away, for fear of her torment, saying, 'Woe, woe, the great city Babylon, the strong city, for in 1 hour, your judgment came!'

[11]"The merchants of the earth will weep and mourn over her, for their wares no one buys any longer: [12]wares of gold and silver; precious stone and pearl; fine linen, purple, silk, and scarlet; every type of citron wood; every utensil of ivory and every utensil of most precious wood; bronze, iron, and marble; [13]cinnamon, incense, perfume, and frankincense; wine and olive oil; fine wheat flour and wheat; sheep and cattle; horses and chariots; bodies and lives of men. [14]The ripe summer fruit of your life's desire has passed away from you, all your fineries and sparkling things are lost to you; most assuredly, you will not find these things any longer. [15]The merchants of these things, those enriched by her, will stand far away for fear of her torment, weeping and mourning, [16]saying, 'Woe, woe, the great city, clothed in fine linen, purple, and scarlet, adorned with gold, precious stone, and pearls,[17]for in 1 hour such great wealth was desolated!'

"Every helmsman and everyone who sails somewhere, both sailors and as many as trade by sea, stood far away, [18]crying out as they see the smoke of her burning, saying, 'Who is like the great city?' [19]They threw dust upon their heads, crying out while weeping and mourning, saying 'Woe, woe, the great city, by whom all those who have ships on the sea got rich by her precious articles, for in 1 hour she was desolated!'

[20]"Rejoice over her, heaven and holy people, apostles and prophets, for God has exacted your judgment from her."

[21]Then 1 strong angel picked up a stone like a great millstone, and cast it into the sea, saying, "With such violence Babylon the great city will be cast away; she will *not* be found anymore. [22]Most assuredly, the voice of harpists, musicians, flutists, and trumpeters will not be heard in you anymore; most assuredly, any craftsman of any trade will not be found in you anymore; most assuredly, the voice of a millstone will not be heard in you anymore; [23]most assuredly, a lamp's light will not shine in you anymore; most assuredly, the voice of bridegroom and bride will not be heard in you anymore, for your merchants were the rulers of the earth, for by your

sorcery, all the nations were led astray. **24**In her, the blood of prophets and holy people was found, all of those who were slaughtered upon the earth."

19

1Afterward, I heard something like a loud voice of a vast multitude in heaven, saying, "Hallelu-*Yah*! The salvation, power, and glory of our God, **2**for His judgments are true and righteous, since He judged the great whore who was completely corrupting the earth by her fornication, and vindicated the blood of His servants [shed] by her hand." **3**A second time it said, "Hallelu-*Yah*! Her smoke ascends forever and ever!" **4**Then the 24 elders and the 4 living creatures fell down; they prostrated themselves in worship of God who is seated upon the throne, saying, "Amen! Hallelu-*Yah*!"

5Then a voice from the throne came forth, saying, "Praise our God, all you His servants, you who fear Him, small and great." **6**Then I heard something like a voice of a vast multitude, like a voice of many waters, like a voice of strong thunderclaps, saying, "Hallelu-*Yah*! For *Yahweh*, our God of hosts,[141] has begun to reign. **7**Let us rejoice, exult, and give glory to Him, for the wedding of the Lamb has come—and His wife has prepared herself!" **8**It was granted her that she wear fine linen, radiant and clean, for the fine linen is the righteous ways of the holy people.

9Then he said to me, "Write, 'Blessed are those who are called unto the wedding supper of the Lamb.'" Then he said to me, "These words of God are true." **10**Then I fell before his feet to worship him, but he said to me, "See that you don't do that! I am your fellow servant, and of your brethren who have the testimony of Jesus. Worship God, for the testimony of Jesus is the spirit of prophecy."

Son of Man Comes for His Bride

11Then I saw the heaven opened, and behold, a white horse, and the One sitting upon it, called Faithful and True; in righteousness He judges and

---

[141] Greek, "Lord our God, the Almighty."

wages war. [12]Now, His eyes were a fiery flame, and upon His head were many diadems. He had names written, even a name written which no one knows but Himself. [13]He was clothed with a garment immersed in blood. He is called by His name: The Word of God. [14]The armies, those in heaven, were following Him upon white horses, wearing clean, white, fine linen. [15]From His mouth a sharp double-edged sword was proceeding, that by it He might strike the nations; He will shepherd them with an iron rod, and He will tread the winepress of the God of hosts'[142] retribution[143] for [His] intolerance [for sin].[144] [16]He has upon His garment and upon His thigh a name written: King of kings and Lord of lords.

Wicked Killed

[17]Then I saw an Angel **standing** in the sun; He cried out in a loud voice, saying to all the birds flying in mid-heaven, "Come! Gather together unto the great supper of God, [18]that you may eat the flesh of kings, the flesh of principal military figures, the flesh of the strong, the flesh of horses and those seated upon them—the flesh of everyone, free as well as slave, both small as well as great."

[19]Then I saw the beast, the kings of the earth, and their armies gathered together to wage war with the One sitting upon the horse and with His army. [20]The beast was seized, and with him the false prophet who had performed signs before him, by which he led astray those who had taken the mark of the beast and those worshipping his image; these 2 were cast alive into the lake of fire burning with brimstone. [21]Then the rest were killed by the sword of the One sitting upon the horse, which [sword] came out of His mouth; all the birds were gorged with their flesh.

---

[142] Greek, "God Almighty."
[143] See footnote 46.
[144] See footnote 98.

COMMENTARY

The Whore

The angel declares that he will show John the judgment of the great whore, indicating that the vision has now returned to a point *prior* to the pouring out of the plagues.

John is first taken into the wilderness to see the great whore. In Revelation 12, God's people were represented as a woman caused to fly into the wilderness for 1,260 years. In chapter 2, the papacy's 1,260-year reign corresponded to the time of the church of Thyatira, when a false woman (church), Jezebel, was permitted to begin corrupting God's people. We saw fulfillment among the Waldenses as they began attending mass, going to confession, and having their children baptized by Roman Catholic priests. The great whore in the wilderness in chapter 17 is none other than this Jezebel—the papal church. The great whore is already drunk "due to the blood of those testifying of Jesus," suggesting that this is toward the close of the 1,260 years of papal supremacy, after the papacy has slaughtered tens of millions of faithful martyrs.

Why is the papal whore seated on many waters? According to Psalm 29:2–3, *Yahweh* is upon many waters, signifying that *He* is in control and therefore due glory and worship. Further, waters represent wicked people (see Isa. 57:20). Hence, the whore seated on many waters portrays the papacy seeking to be in control, receiving the worship of all the wicked.

She is seated upon a scarlet beast. Its 7 heads and 10 horns remind us of the papal sea beast of Revelation 13:1–10. It is full of blasphemous names, again pointing to the papal beast whose mouth speaks blasphemous things. However, the scarlet beast lacks crowns upon its 10 horns, and the sea beast was nowhere said to be scarlet. And of course, it would be most confusing to picture the great whore sitting upon the sea beast— what would it mean for the papacy to sit upon itself? We deduce that the scarlet beast is very *similar* to the papal sea beast, but it is an entity *distinct* from the papacy.

The papal whore has in her hand a golden cup. In Jeremiah 51:7, we read that "Babylon is a golden cup in the hand of *Yahweh*, intoxicating the entire earth; the nations have drunk of her wine, therefore the nations are senseless." The Babylonian whore intoxicates the nations, but in Revelation 17, *she* holds the cup, as though she is in the place of God. In reality, she is doomed, for all who drink of her cup will have to drink of the wine of God's intolerance for sin, mixed undiluted in the cup of His retribution (see Rev. 14:8–11).

This whore, Jezebel, is a counterfeit of the High Priest, Jesus Christ. To see this clearly, Table 14 compares the whore's attire with that of the high priest of ancient Israel:

Table 14: Comparison of High Priest and Great Whore

REFERENCE	DESCRIPTION OF HIGH PRIEST	DESCRIPTION OF GREAT WHORE	REFERENCE
Exod. 28:5	Clothed in gold, blue, purple, scarlet, and fine linen	Clothed in purple and scarlet	Rev. 17:4
Exod. 28:6–36	Adorned with gold	Adorned with gold	Rev. 17:4
Exod. 28:17–21	Precious stones of breastplate	Precious stones	Rev. 17:4
Exod. 28:36–38	Name on forehead: "Holiness for *Yahweh*"	Name on forehead: "Mystery … abominations of the earth"	Rev. 17:5
Exod. 28:38	Sons of (father) Israel	Daughter whores of mother Babylon	Rev. 17:5

The purple and scarlet confirm papal Rome as the institution seeking to counterfeit Jesus' office of High Priest and Judge. On high days of papal Rome's religious calendar, one may see a sea of high-ranking bishops and cardinals dressed in purple and scarlet. Gold and precious stones (jewels) adorn the headdresses, rings, vestments, staffs, crucifixes, etc. of Rome's highest-ranking leadership.

Papal Rome is certainly a counterfeit of Jesus, claiming to be His vicar on earth; even claiming to be God Himself on earth. Ever since Lucifer's disaffection in heaven, it has been his object to unseat Jesus as High Priest and Judge, assuming this office for himself (see Isa. 14:13, 14). The papacy is Satan's earthly agency to secure this coveted position.

Another significant observation is in order regarding the dress of the whore. The high priest had garments unique to his office (see Exod. 28). He was to be a son in the lineage of Aaron (see Deut. 10:6; Neh. 10:38), hence, only a *man*. It follows that the high priestly garments were necessarily specific to the male. Therefore, in presuming to usurp the role of high priest, the papal whore is pictured as a *transvestite*, which Deuteronomy 22:5 states, in the strongest language possible, is an *abomination* to *Yahweh*: "A man's article is not to be upon a woman, neither is a man to put on a woman's garment, for everyone who does these things is an abomination to *Yahweh* your God."

The transvestitism of the whore is not merely a curiosity. The true remnant church humbly and willingly submits to Jesus, and the woman of Revelation 12 was pictured clothed with the sun (representative of Christ's throne; see Ps. 89:36), indicating that His rule and judgments envelop every aspect of her life. By contrast, the whore disrespects her so-called Husband by usurping His position, depicted as her wearing the garments of His office. Her transvestitism reveals her bold, ungodly character. Truly, "the dress and its arrangement upon the person is generally found to be the index of the man or the woman" (White, *CG*, p. 413).

The papal whore's transvestitism goes right along with her pagan sun worship. Paganism is, in essence, the worship of nature in one form or another. The most incredible feature of nature is its ability to reproduce, and pagan worship routinely involved the worship of divinity in both male and female aspects, characterized by the filthiest rites involving this mysterious gift. Consider the following descriptions:

> As the sun was the great god, the supreme lord, and as he exerted his most glorious powers in reproduction, it was held to be the most acceptable worship for his devotees so to employ themselves and their powers. Consequently prostitution was the one chief characteristic of sun worship wherever found. As the

association of a female without reference to relationship was the only requirement necessary to worship, the result was the perfect confusion of all relationships among the worshipers, even to the mutual interchange of garments between the sexes. In the eighteenth chapter of Leviticus there is a faithful record of such a result among the sun worshipers of the land of Canaan whom the Lord caused to be blotted from the earth. The prohibition in Deuteronomy xxii, 5—"The woman shall not wear that which pertaineth unto a man, neither shall a man put on a woman's garment"—was aimed directly at this practice in sun worship. ...

The universality of the worship of the sun in Hercules has been already shown. Of the manner in which his worship was conducted, we have the following account:—"It seems to have been marked by an almost delirious sensuality. Married and unmarried females prostituted themselves at the festival of the gods. The two sexes changed their respective characters; and tradition reported that Hercules himself had given an example of this, when, assuming the vestments and occupation of a female, he subjected himself to the service of the voluptuous Omphale. The Lydian Hercules was named Sandon, after the robe dyed with sandyx, in which Omphale had arrayed him, and which the females of the country imitated in celebrating his licentious worship." [*The Classical Dictionary*, s.v. "Hercules"] ...

The name under which the sun was worshiped at Emesa, where Bassianus was high-priest, was Elagabalus. His accession to the office of emperor he attributed to the favor of this sun-god. Therefore as emperor he assumed the name of Elagabalus as greater and more honorable than any that might be derived from any other source, and by this name alone is he known in history. (Jones, *The Two Republics*, pp. 187–190, 198)

The Sun was worshipped at Emesa under the name of Elagabalus, and under the form of a black conical stone, which, as it was universally believed, had fallen from heaven on that sacred place. To this protecting deity, Antoninus, not without some reason, ascribed his elevation to the throne. The display of superstitious gratitude was the only serious business of his reign. The triumph of the God of Emesa over all the religions of the earth, was the great object of his zeal and vanity: and the appellation of Elagabalus (for he presumed as pontiff and favourite to adopt that sacred name) was dearer to him than all the titles of Imperial greatness. In a solemn procession through the streets of Rome, the way was strewed with gold dust; the black stone, set in precious gems, was placed on a chariot drawn by six milk-white horses richly caparisoned. The pious emperor held the reins, and, supported by his ministers, moved slowly backwards, that he might perpetually enjoy the felicity of the divine presence. In a magnificent temple raised on the Palatine Mount, the sacrifices of the god of Elagabalus were celebrated with every circumstance of cost and solemnity. The richest wines, the most extraordinary victims, and the rarest aromatics, were profusely consumed on his altar. Around the altar a chorus of Syrian damsels performed their lascivious dances to the sound of barbarian music, whilst the gravest personages of the state and army, clothed in long Phoenician tunics, officiated in the meanest functions, with affected zeal and secret indignation. (Gibbon, *Decline and Fall*, vol. 1, ch. 6, p. 186)

It was in perfect harmony with the rites of sun worship everywhere that all the laws of nature and decency should be violated and subverted by Elagabalus; that he should have a long train of concubines, and a rapid succession of wives; that a vestal virgin should be taken by force from her sacred retreat to feed his passion; and that he should put on the dress, and play the part, of a woman, while he publicly assigned to another the title and the place of husband to himself. All these things belonged with the worship of the sun, and all this Elagabalus did, not as emperor, but as imperial high-priest and representative of the sun.

As emperor and high-priest of the sun, it was his chief purpose,
and "it was openly asserted, that the worship of the sun, under
his name of Elagabalus, was to supercede all other worship."
(Jones, *The Two Republics*, p. 199, closing quotation from
Milman's *History of Christianity*, book ii, chap. viii, par. 22)

The foregoing historical accounts of sun worship confirm the aptness
of the papal whore's representation as a cross-dressing high priestess of
sun worship.

In defiance of Deuteronomy 22:5, Satan attempted to introduce
cross-dressing with women's rights activists Amelia Bloomer (after whom
"bloomers" are named) and Elizabeth Cady Stanton in the later 1800s.
This departure from cultural norms was not well-received in relatively
Christian America. Decades later, Satan made another foray with cross-
dressing Hollywood actresses Katharine Hepburn and Marlene Dietrich.
With the onset of World War II, women went to work in droves in
America's factories to fill the vacancies left by men serving in the military.
This adoption of men's jobs afforded a plausible excuse to adopt mens-
wear in the workplace. When men returned from war, though, the custom
had become so entrenched that there was no turning back. Nowadays,
cross-dressing for women is well-nigh universal in westernized countries.

Those in westernized countries would do well to ponder with grave
sobriety the indisputable link between cross-dressing and sun worship.
Just so long as we cling to this custom, we are being groomed to adopt
sun worship when mandated by law. Those who refuse to give up every
feature of sun worship as God graciously reveals it to them will eventually
be eternally lost:

There is an increasing tendency to have women in their dress
and appearance as near like the other sex as possible, and to
fashion their dress very much like that of men, but God pronounces it abomination. "In like manner also, that women
adorn themselves in modest apparel, with shamefacedness and
sobriety." (1 Timothy 2:9).

Those who feel called out to join the movement in favor of woman's rights and the so-called dress reform might as well sever all connection with the third angel's message. The spirit which attends the one cannot be in harmony with the other. The Scriptures are plain upon the relations and rights of men and women. Spiritualists have, to quite an extent, adopted this singular mode of dress. ... Let them [Seventh-day Adventists] adopt this costume, and their influence is dead. The people would place them on a level with spiritualists and would refuse to listen to them.

With the so-called dress reform there goes a spirit of levity and boldness just in keeping with the dress. Modesty and reserve seem to depart from many as they adopt that style of dress. I was shown that God would have us take a course consistent and explainable. Let the sisters adopt the American costume and they would destroy their own influence and that of their husbands. They would become a byword and a derision. Our Saviour says: "Ye are the light of the world." "Let your light so shine before men, that they may see your good works, and glorify your Father which is in heaven." There is a great work for us to do in the world, and God would not have us take a course to lessen or destroy our influence with the world. (White, *1T*, pp. 421, 422)

In describing the end-time papacy, God chose to use the symbolism of a transvestite woman. This should be a wake-up call to all who believe that women may wear women's *or* men's clothing without a blush. Its well-nigh universal acceptance is no argument in favor of its acceptability to God. His word plainly forbids it, and He specifically says *not* to look to the heathen nations around us to mold or justify our practices, for we will be ensnared (see Deut. 12:30; 18:9). God calls for a decided reform in dress before His people are prepared for translation. Any changes in dress we adopt are to show us to be *reformers*, not *conformed to* this world (see Rom. 12:1, 2):

> Many dress like the world, to have an influence. But here they
> make a sad and fatal mistake. If they would have a true and
> saving influence, let them live out their profession, show their
> faith by their righteous works, and make the distinction great
> between the Christian and the world. ... Then a holy influence
> will be shed upon all, and all will take knowledge of them that
> they have been with Jesus. Unbelievers will see that the truth
> we profess has a holy influence and that faith in Christ's coming
> affects the character of the man or woman. If any wish to have
> their influence tell in favor of the truth, let them live it out and
> thus imitate the humble Pattern. (White, *1T*, p. 132)

The whore has a name upon her forehead. Just as the seal of the living God and the name of God are placed upon the forehead (see Rev. 7:2, 3; 14:1), so the mark and name of the beast are placed upon the forehead (see Rev. 13:17). The seal of the living God is the Sabbath, and for those who enter fully into the Sabbath experience, it is the means of Jesus fulfilling His everlasting covenant in the life of the believer—the great mystery of godliness. The name the great whore has upon her forehead indicates just what Sunday worship is—an abomination in the sight of God. When the state legislates Sunday observance, those who persist in sun worship once they come to understand the issues will receive the mark of the beast and be lost.

The ruinous character of this apostate Christianity comes to the fore in 17:6, for this whore is intoxicated by all the blood of Christ's martyrs, which she has shed throughout the centuries.

The Scarlet Beast

The angel assures John that he will tell him the mystery of the woman *and* the beast that carries her. The beast is described as that which "was, is not and is about to come up from the abyss." Again, the angel speaks of the beast that "was, is not, yet will come." Thus, the scarlet beast is a parody of

Jesus, who in Revelation 1:8 is introduced as "He who is, He who was, and He who is coming." This is underscored by reference to the phrase "scroll of life from the foundation of the world," which appeared in augmented form in Revelation 13:8 in reference to the Lamb who was slaughtered from the foundation of the world, i.e., Jesus.

The reference to the "foundation of the world" suggests a connection between the scarlet beast and the papal sea beast of Revelation 13:1–10. However, the reference to coming up from the abyss points us to Revelation 11:7, in which atheistic France is described as coming up from the abyss at the end of the eighteenth century. Of course, the United States came up from the earth *at the very same time* (see 13:11), and its rise coincided with the infliction of the deadly wound upon the papacy in 1798.

The Wisdom Riddle

Is the scarlet beast the United States? To answer, we will consider things from several perspectives. First, the wisdom riddle in 17:9 hearkens back to the wisdom riddle in 13:18, following the description of the United States land beast. That riddle dealt with the number 666, which we saw to refer to both Egypt and Babylon.

The angel refers to the scarlet beast's 7 heads, which are 7 mountains. Mountains, in turn, represent kings/kingdoms in Scripture, as the angel himself notes in 17:10. We identified the 7 heads of the beasts in Daniel 7:1–8 as Babylon, Medo-Persia, the 4 heads of Hellas (Antigonids, Seleucids, Ptolemies, and the pagan Greco-Roman empire that grew out of Magna Grecia and Sicily), and finally papal Rome. We equated these 7 heads with those of the sea beast in Revelation 13, for that beast is plainly a composite of the 4 beasts of Daniel 7.

Are the 7 heads in Revelation 17 identical with those of Daniel 7 and Revelation 13? In chapter three of *7 Heads and 10 Horns in Daniel and Revelation*, de Kock evaluates nine competing interpretations for the 7 heads, handily dismissing each one. Then in chapter four, he eloquently argues that the 7 heads are in fact the same as in Daniel 7. The similarity between the scarlet beast and the sea beast would suggest that the 7 heads are the same, but we consider the angel's remarks in 17:10 as the final authority: "the 5 fell, the 1 is, and the other has not yet come." Indeed, from John's frame of reference, 5 heads had fallen (Babylon, Medo-Persia, the Antigonids, the Seleucids, and the Ptolemies), 1 was currently in existence (the pagan Greco-Roman empire), and the other had not yet come (the papacy was still future).[145] The 7 heads are the same as those of the sea beast.

In verse 11, the angel notes that the scarlet "beast which was and is not, it is also an eighth" king. De Kock argues that this eighth beast is Satan himself, noting that the scarlet beast and the red dragon (Satan) of Revelation 12 both have 7 heads and 10 horns. Further the scarlet beast arises from the abyss and goes to destruction, similar to Satan in Revelation 20:1–10. The author of the present work disagrees, but the interested reader is invited to prayerfully study his interpretation (de Kock, *7 Heads and 10 Horns in Daniel and Revelation*, pp. 81–98) and compare with the following presentation to determine what best fits the prophetic data.

The 7 heads represented a chronological progression of empires, so this eighth king arises *after* the seventh king. While the papacy does continue until the second coming, it is also true that it received a mortal wound in 1798, marking the end of its 1,260-year reign. It is after this time that the scarlet beast arises. Revelation has identified one beast—the land beast, the United States—as arising following the papacy.

In Daniel 11:43, it is noted that the king of the north (the papacy) rules over the gold, silver, and all the articles of high esteem of Egypt (apostate Protestantism in the United States). In other words, the union of papacy and Protestantism is unequal, with the papacy in control. This is reflected in Revelation 17:3, with the papal whore sitting upon the scarlet beast. The papacy rules over the scarlet beast.

We have already noted that the Jezebel who infected the true church of Thyatira was the papal whore. Israel's king Ahab took heathen Jezebel

---

[145] For this insight, the author is indebted to Edwin de Kock's *7 Heads and 10 Horns in Daniel and the Revelation*.

as his wife (see 1 Kings 16:31–33). She was the daughter of Ethbaal ("with Baal"), king of Tyre and Sidon and high priest of Baal. Through her influence, Ahab built an altar for Baal, as well as an object to worship Asherah. Since Jezebel was from Tyre, it is appropriate that the fall of the papacy in Revelation 18 fulfills the fall of Tyre described in Ezekiel 26–28, as the numerous references to merchants, seamen, and articles for sale make clear. Just as Jezebel was the controlling power in her husband's life, leading Ahab to worship as she did, so the whore sits atop the beast, as though *she* were king, and the beast were her throne. Finally, observe that Ahab was king of the 10 tribes of Israel, south of Tyre and Sidon, just as apostate Protestantism in the United States is the king of the south, and the papacy is the king of the north. Thus, the scarlet beast with its 10 horns represents apostate Protestantism in the United States.

There is one more feature that permits us to positively identify the beast of Revelation 17: its *scarlet color*. At the simplest level, this confirms its sinful character, for Isaiah 1:18 refers to our "sins like scarlet." However, this does not help us determine *which* sinful entity is in view. We may also note that its color matches that of the dragon of Revelation 12, hence it shares the satanic character of the 7 heads through which Satan worked in former centuries. And of course, the land beast of Revelation 13 speaks as a dragon.

The most convincing approach is to consider the first instance of scarlet in Scripture—the birth of twins Perez and Zerah recorded in Genesis 38. In verse 18, Jacob's son Judah goes into a woman he believes to be a harlot. In verse 24, Jacob learns that his daughter-in-law Tamar has behaved like a harlot and become pregnant by fornication. Angry, Judah orders her to be burned. In verses 27–30 is recorded Tamar's delivery. She had twins. When one stuck his hand out, the midwife tied a scarlet thread about it to note he was first. However, the hand withdrew, and Perez ("breach") came out, with the result that scarlet-bound Zerah ("brightness of sunrise") came out second.

This story, with its details of fornication and the order to burn Tamar, clearly provides the background for Revelation 17. From Genesis 38, we infer that the scarlet color of the beast in Revelation 17 points to it as the *twin* of another beast—apparently born first yet ultimately second in sequence. The land beast rose to power after the papacy received its deadly wound. Initially, though, the land beast was like a lamb, Christian in character. During the end time, the papacy emerges with renewed strength, and the land beast (apostate Protestantism in the United States) makes an *image of the papal beast*, becoming like it in character—a twin, we might say—legislating false sun worship on pain of death for those who disobey. When the United States enforces Sunday worship by law, pretending to be the Savior of the world, it will have fully developed the image of the papacy. This is the scarlet beast of Revelation 17, the beast upon which the whorish papacy rides. As prophesied in verse 11, this scarlet beast goes unto destruction when the false prophet (apostate Protestantism in the United States) is cast into the lake of fire (see Rev. 19:20).

The angel notes that the 10 horns upon the scarlet beast are 10 kings that have not yet received a kingdom. The papal sea beast of Revelation 13:1–10 had crowns upon its 10 heads, referring to the kings of Europe during the 1,260 years. The scarlet beast has no crowns upon its heads, for *these* 10 horns receive authority for 1 hour with the scarlet beast, i.e., in the very end of all things, once the United States wields the power of the state to exalt the papacy. We will not know the exact identity of these 10 kings until this part of the prophecy comes to pass, but we do know from verse 13 that they combine their forces, unitedly backing the scarlet beast in its efforts to enforce Sunday worship and destroy the faithful remnant. The irony of this church-state union is that the 10 horns unite to exterminate the end-time remnant who, by Jesus' faith, keep God's 10 Commandments!

Those with the Lamb

Those who follow the Lamb are called, chosen, and faithful, despite persecution by the 10 kings. This brief section matches with Revelation 14:1–5, which describes the 144,000 standing with the Lamb on Mount Zion amid the firestorm of persecution described at the close of chapter 13. The Lamb conquers these 10 kings as Lord of lords and King of kings at the second coming (see Rev. 19:16). This is the fulfillment of Daniel 2:44, which states that "in the days of those kings [the 10 toes of the Daniel 2 image], the God of the heavens will establish a kingdom which will never be destroyed."

Result of the 3 Angels' Messages

First Angel's Message Echoed: Whore Who Sits Is Judged

The whore sits upon many waters. According to Psalm 18:16–17, *Yahweh* delivers people from their enemies, called many waters. Hence, the whore is *keeping* people in sin, *forcing* them to remain enemies of God, while God longs to *free* them from sin.

According to verse 12, the 10 kings reign for 1 hour with the whore, while in verse 16, they turn on her, in fulfillment of God's purpose to judge her. This hour is to be identified with "the hour of his [God's] judgment" that has come in Revelation 14:7, part of the first angel's message. While the first angel's message is addressed to every "nation, tribe, tongue, and people," the whore is sitting upon "peoples, multitudes, nations, and tongues." Observe that "tribes" have been replaced by "multitudes." This is because the 12 tribes that compose the 144,000 of 7:1–8 have taken their stand and are faithful to Jesus as noted in 17:14. They go forth, declaring with great power the 3 angels' messages of 14:6–12, preparing the earth for the harvest of many more souls. The whore is sitting upon these multitudes, attempting to prevent them from hearing and being transformed by the 3 angels' messages. The first angel's message announced the *commencement* of the judgment hour; Revelation 17:15–17 points to its *close*.

Why do the kings ultimately turn on the whore? This is the natural result of inappropriate sexual desire, as seen in the case of Amnon, who raped his sister Tamar when she refused him (see 2 Sam. 13:14, 15),[146] as well as Judah, who thought to burn the woman into whom he had gone, also named Tamar. Initially, these 10 kings support papal supremacy, but when probation closes, it becomes apparent that her ways are the ways of death, and their initial "love" for her turns into vengeful hatred that is just as strong.

---

[146] As with all typology, there are limits to applicability. In this case, Tamar was virtuous, not a whore.

The whore is burned up. The daughter of any priest who indulged in fornication was to be burned to death (see Lev. 21:9). God calls His church His daughter.[147] The papal church is plainly guilty of idolatry (which Scripture calls fornication), and in usurping Jesus' position as High Priest, it is clear that her greatest idol is herself. Destruction by fire is the perfect punishment for the papal whore.

The papal whore is called the mother of whores in 17:5, and her daughters make up apostate Protestantism. The kings of the earth have fornicated with both. This is important, for Leviticus 20:14 states that if a man takes both a woman and her mother, the trio is to be burned with fire. According to Revelation 19:19–21, when the 10 kings, the papal beast (the whore), and the false prophet (the scarlet beast, identical to the image beast) gather to destroy God's people, the beast and false prophet are thrown into the lake of fire at the second coming. The 10 horns are part of the scarlet beast, so they too are burned with fire, fulfilling Leviticus 20:14.

The chapter concludes with the observation that the papal whore holds dominion over the kings of the earth. Like Jezebel of old, she exercises her power to corrupt kings with pagan idolatry.

Second Angel's Message Illuminates the Earth

Chapter 18 opens with the earth illuminated by the glory of an angel. This fulfills *Yahweh's* promise that all the earth will be filled with His glory (see Num. 14:21). When *Yahweh* made that promise, the spies had returned from Canaan, and because they saw giants, they disbelieved God's promise that they could take the land. *Yahweh* declared that the faithless people would *not* enter Canaan, while Caleb, because he had a different spirit in him and followed *Yahweh* fully, would enter Canaan, along with Joshua and those under age 20.

Hence, the angel's glorious illumination of the earth in Revelation 18 signals that the entrance into the heavenly Promised Land is at hand for those who accept the 3 angels' messages and follow God *fully* from

---

[147] See, for example, Jer. 6:2, 23; 8:19; Lam. 1:6; 2:13; Mic. 4:10, 13; Zech. 2:10; 9:9.

this point forward. Those who doubt will be forever debarred from the Promised Land.

The beginning of Revelation 18 is a repeat of the second angel's message of Revelation 14. Babylon is again charged with being fallen and having intoxicated the nations due to the wine of her intolerance for obedience—her persistent idolatry. This time there is the much stronger charge that she is inhabited by *demons*. There is no reformation possible for the fallen church; she is given fully over to the control of Satan when the proclamation of Revelation 18 goes forth. Those who choose to remain with their idols in end-time spiritual Babylon will do so with full understanding of the end-time message and hence commit the unpardonable sin. Such people forever harden their hearts to the Holy Spirit, choosing instead to be fully possessed by Satan and his evil angels.

The reference to the kings of the earth and their fornication with Babylon refers to the formation of church-state unions, contrary to Scripture. Even in the days of Israel's theocracy, church and state were kept distinct, with the king governing civil affairs and the priests and Levites tending to religious affairs. When the king attempted to intervene in religious affairs, this was regarded as a most grievous sin. God rebuked King Jeroboam for his gross error of setting up 2 golden calves for worship at the very time that he was officiating at an idolatrous ritual, highlighting his crime of taking on priestly duties (see 1 Kings 13:1–10). King Uzziah sinned in similar fashion. After his initial successful reign, he presumed to enter the temple and burn incense at the altar. The priests rebuked him, and God struck him with leprosy, which remained the rest of his life, necessitating that his son reign in his stead (see 2 Chron. 26:16–23).

The reference to the merchants of the earth can be understood literally and spiritually, both supported with reference to Ezekiel 28. On the one hand, Tyre's earthly ruler amassed great wealth by "your great wisdom in your trading" (vs. 4, 5). Hence, corporations that go along with papal policy will thrive until God turns the tide. Going deeper to the spiritual root of the matter, verses 12–19 refer to the *king* of Tyre, he who was in Eden, the one cast out of the mountain of God because of his "great trading."

This refers to Lucifer, who peddled his own supposedly superior ideas of government among the angels of heaven. This created dissatisfaction and led to his expulsion from the mountain of God, along with a third of the angels. In this spiritual sense, the "merchants of the earth" are those who promulgate papal doctrine: the apostate religious leaders of the world. They thrive for a time, amassing great audiences and substantial incomes in their megachurches—until God turns the tide.

The reference to Babylon's "arrogant self-indulgence" (Greek στρηνος) refers to the only other instance of στρηνος in Scripture, 2 Kings 19:28, where it translates the Hebrew *sha'anan* ("arrogance"). It is used of the incredible "arrogance" of the King of Assyria when he boasted that King Hezekiah should not trust in *Yahweh*, for He could not deliver Jerusalem from the Assyrian king any better than could the false gods of the surrounding nations whom he had conquered. Thus, the charge against Babylon is that she has exalted herself above God.

Third and First Angels' Messages Echoed

Following Babylon's indictment as a dwelling for demons, the plea is made for everyone whom God still regards as "My people" to "come out of her." The extent of her crime is described as accumulating unto heaven, with the additional mention that "God has remembered her unrighteous deeds." This is not to suggest that her unrighteousness has just now come back to God's remembrance, for He never forgets anything. When He remembers something, it means He will act accordingly. As an example, God promised Abram that He would deliver His people after 400 years in Egypt; when the time was up, He remembered this covenant promise by granting deliverance through Moses (see Gen. 15:13, 14; Exod. 2:23–3:8). In like manner, God has not forgotten Babylon's exhaustless list of crimes, and He will assuredly fulfill His promise to pour upon her the 7 last plagues on the "1 day" He has appointed.

The wording "her sins have joined together on up to heaven" alludes to the building of the tower of Babel, which was to reach unto heaven (see Gen. 11:4). Moses stated that idolatry was absolutely prohibited, and for the one who chose to serve the idols of the nations, "all the curses of this covenant which are written in the scroll, this Torah, shall be joined unto him, and *Yahweh* will wipe out his name from under heaven" (Deut. 29:16–20, LXX). Similarly, King Jehoram "was joined to the sin of Jeroboam" (2 Kings 3:3), referring to the establishment of the 2 golden calves for worship. These texts inform our understanding of Revelation 18:5, pointing out Babylon's crime of idolatry and ultimate fate.

In verse 6, we meet with a challenging passage. Most translations, including that of the present commentary, indicate that Babylon is to be recompensed double for her deeds. This might seem problematic, since God is perfectly just. To pay her double might seem to contradict the command to "render unto her as she also rendered." The Greek words under consideration in this verse are the verb διπλοω and the corresponding adjective διπλους. The various lexica routinely assert that these words mean "double" or "twofold." What is the proper understanding of this verse?

Old Testament passages shed much-needed light. " 'Comfort, comfort My people,' says God. 'Priests, speak unto the heart of Jerusalem, comfort her, for her humiliation is fulfilled, her sin has been removed, for she received from *Yahweh's* hand διπλους her sins' " (Isa. 40:1, 2, LXX). How comforting would it be for Jerusalem to know that she had been punished twice as much as her sins warranted? This would only embitter her against God. The text suggests that she has received just exactly what she deserved. The idea of a one-for-one match between her sins and her punishment leads not to "double" retribution, but a retribution that perfectly "duplicates" her crimes.

Jeremiah speaks of the restoration of Israel in Jeremiah 16:14–21. Before her restoration, however, she needs to be purified from her idolatrous past, so we read, "I will repay διπλους their unrighteous acts and their sins" (v. 18). To repay double would discourage and embitter, but to repay one-for-one, or with a perfect duplicate of Israel's catalog of crimes, would satisfy the claims of justice perfectly.[148]

---

[148] For an analysis of this understanding of "duplicate" rather than "double" payback, see Meredith G. Kline, "Double Trouble," Meredith G. Kline, https://1ref.us/13l (accessed July 8, 2019).

Such an understanding of διπλους harmonizes with Jesus' own utterance of the so-called golden rule, "As ye would that men should do to you, do ye also to them likewise" (Luke 6:31, KJV). If we do *otherwise* than we wish others to do to us, we can only expect that they will do *likewise* unto us. In meting out justice, God certainly holds Himself to His own counsel.

Having garnered an understanding of διπλους from Scripture, we can recognize a harmony with other passages that relate to the destruction of end-time Babylon. "Wretched daughter, Babylon, happy is He who will recompense you your recompense *with which you recompensed us*" (Ps. 137:8, LXX). "It is vengeance from God: exact vengeance upon her [Babylon]—just as she did, do unto her!" (Jer. 50:15, LXX). When one brings charges against another that are shown to be false, such a one suffers the very penalty (a "duplicate") that *would have been inflicted* upon the exonerated defendant: "Life for life, eye for eye, tooth for tooth, hand for hand, foot for foot" (Deut. 19:21).

This "matching" or "duplicate" portion Babylon receives is especially ironic when we recall the papacy's claim to be the vicar of Christ, even God Himself on earth. As the firstborn (preeminent) Son, Jesus has a just claim to a double portion of the inheritance among His siblings (see Deut. 21:17). In her failed attempt to usurp Christ's position, Babylon winds up receiving her own "double" portion, just not that of the firstborn Son.

The whore's proclamation in verse 7 of her exalted status as queen comes from Isaiah 47:7–9:

> You said, "I will be queen forever onward!" You have not taken these things to heart, you have not considered its outcome. Now hear this, carnal-minded woman, you who sits in security, who says in her heart, "Me—and there is no one else besides! I will not sit as a widow, nor shall I know loss of children." These 2 things will come upon you instantly, in 1 day: complete loss of children and widowhood will come upon you in spite of the abundance of your sorceries, in spite of the great potency of your enchantments."

God has particular compassion for widows and those who further lose their children as their only means of support, admonishing the church to care for such (Jer. 49:11; Luke 7:11–17; 1 Tim. 5:4; James 1:27). The boast of the whore, then, is that she is not in any way powerless. In her exaltation against the kingdom of heaven, she thinks herself to be in complete control. In fact, her very self-confidence is the sure means of her destruction, for "before destruction [is] pride; before stumbling, an arrogant spirit" (Prov. 16:18). She will be burned up, and "there is no one to save you" (Isa. 47:15).

We now consider the reaction of various parties as they witness Babylon's dissolution. In Revelation 18:9, we meet the kings of the earth who fornicated with her. Like Esau, their regret is purely selfish (see Heb. 12:16, 17): they mourn that their source of self-advancement is no more and their own doom is certain.

At Mount Sinai, God appeared as a consuming fire, giving to those people who were to be a kingdom of priests the words that would form the basis of judgment for everyone who has ever lived (see Exod. 19:6; Eccl. 12:13, 14). Just as the Israelites "stood far away" while Mount Sinai was "smoking" (Exod. 20:18), so the kings of the earth stand far away as they watch the smoke ascending from the burning of Babylon, that "destroying mountain" (Jer. 51:24, 25).

Another class is brought to view: the "merchants of the earth." The laundry list of fine goods that follows might at first suggest that these are the very wealthy. To be sure, certain corporations and those who operate them will benefit materially by supporting the papal agenda, while those who abide by the biblical principle of separation of church and state will experience complete financial loss. However, we saw in Revelation 2:9 that those who were materially impoverished were in fact rich in character, due to their fidelity to God. Revelation is concerned with peoples' *characters*, not their material wealth.

Recall that Lucifer trafficked lies about God's character and government in Ezekiel 28:16. Like their forefather, Satan, the merchants of the earth are engaged primarily in trafficking *lies* rather than material goods. About what do the merchants lie? We deduce the answer by noting that the wares listed in verses 12 and 13 appear in two places: 1) Ezekiel 26–28, indicating that the great city Babylon is likened to Tyre, the ancient sea-faring merchant city, and 2) in connection with the earthly models of the heavenly sanctuary (the house of *Yahweh*, the king's house that Solomon built, and the wilderness sanctuary). Hence, the merchants' lies point people away from true salvation in the heavenly sanctuary to the Babylonian (papal), earthly counterfeit. Table 15 shows the key connections:

Table 15: How the Goods of Revelation 18:12–13 link Tyre and the Sanctuary

GOODS	REFERENCE	TYRE	SOLOMON'S HOUSES AND WILDERNESS SANCTUARY	REFERENCE
Gold and silver	Ezek. 28:4	Earthly king put in his treasuries.	King Solomon put in treasury of *Yahweh's* house.	1 Kings 7:51
	Ezek. 28:13	Gold covering for king (Lucifer).	Overlaid walls of houses.	1 Chron. 29:4
Precious stone and pearl	Ezek. 28:13	Every precious stone for king (Lucifer).	Precious stones for house of God.	1 Chron. 29:2
Fine linen, purple, silk, scarlet	2 Chron. 2:14	Huram skillful with these.	In vail before Most Holy Place.	2 Chron. 3:14
Citron wood, ivory, most precious wood	Ezek. 27:5, 6	Fir planks, cedar masts, oak oars.	House: cedar, fir, algum. Porch of judgment: cedar.	2 Chron. 2:8, 9; 1 Kings 7:7
	Ezek. 27:6	Ship planks inlaid with ivory.	Solomon's ivory throne of judgment.	1 Kings 10:18
Bronze, iron, marble	Ezek. 27:13	Traded for bronze from Yavan (Hellas).	Bronze, iron, marble for house of David's God.	1 Chron. 29:2
	Ezek. 27:12	Tarshish paid Tyre in iron.		

(*continued*)

Table 15: How the Goods of Revelation 18:12–13 link Tyre and the Sanctuary (*continued*)

GOODS	REFERENCE	TYRE	SOLOMON'S HOUSES AND WILDERNESS SANCTUARY	REFERENCE
Cinnamon, incense, perfume, frankincense	Ezek. 27:22	Sold principal spices.	Cinnamon used in holy anointing oil.	Exod. 30:23–25
			Incense for altar of incense.	Exod. 30:34–36
			Frankincense used in most holy incense.	Exod. 30:34–36
	Ezek. 27:17 (LXX)	Judah sold perfume to Tyre.	Holy anointing oil was a perfume.	Exod. 30:25
Wine and olive oil	Ezek. 27:18	Tyre sold wine to Damascus.	Both used in daily drink offerings.	Exod. 29:40
	Ezek. 27:17	Judah sold olive oil to Tyre.	Olive oil for menorah, matzah, holy anointing oil.	Exod. 27:20; 29:2; 30:24, 25
Fine wheat flour and wheat	2 Chron. 2:10	Solomon provided ground wheat.	Fine wheat flour for matzah; drink offering.	Exod. 29:2, 40
	Ezek. 27:17	Judah sold wheat to Tyre.	Wheat for support of priests.	Num. 18:12
Sheep and cattle	Ezek. 27:21	Arabia trafficked in lambs and rams.	Offered for *Yahweh*.	Lev. 1:2
			For dedication of house of *Yahweh*.	1 Kings 8:63
Horses and chariots	Ezek. 27:14, 20	Togarmah provided horses, Dedan outfitted Tyre's chariots.	Trust *Yahweh* instead of.	Ps. 20:7
			Solomon bought from Egypt.	1 Kings 10:28, 29
			Represent Egypt's might.	Exod. 14:9; 15:19
Bodies and lives of men	Ezek. 27:13	Yavan (Hellas) paid with lives of men.	People valued by sanctuary weight.	Lev. 27:2–8
			Character valued by sanctuary weight.	Dan 5:24–28

The connection between Tyre and the sanctuary is explicit in the story of Solomon building his temple. Beginning in 1 Kings 7:13, we read that he hired Hiram from Tyre to oversee the building effort. While he was immensely talented, there was no warrant for bringing in pagan assistance for this holy enterprise. Just as we are not to mix dissimilar seeds in agriculture (see Deut. 22:9), so Scripture forbids the mixing of the holy seed (God's people) with the pagan (see Ezra 9:2; 2 Cor. 6:14).

The sanctuary is a model of how salvation works in the lives of believers, and these merchants are lying about how people in the end time are saved. Their false teaching puts dependence on faulty humanity, as emphasized by the inclusion of "horses and chariots" in the list. These most definitely were not related to God's sanctuary; rather, the Israelites were expressly forbidden to put their trust in such earthly sources of strength, leaning instead on God alone (see Ps. 20:7; Exod. 15:19). Jesus drove out those who were turning God's house into a den of thieves (see Luke 19:45). When He comes the second time, He will miserably destroy such wicked shepherds of the flock (see Matt. 21:41).

The term "merchant" is apt for these dissolute religious teachers. It is common knowledge that a number of the religious leaders of popular Christianity enjoy enormous income and have a net worth of tens or even hundreds of millions of dollars.[149] Some are quite literally merchants, hawking one bestselling book after another on the talk show circuit, while "the Son of man hath not where to lay his head" (Luke 9:58).

Table 15 reveals that along with all the pagan nations with whom Tyre trafficked, *Judah* sold olive oil and wheat to Tyre, and King Solomon himself provided ground wheat for building services that Tyre provided for the house of *Yahweh* and the king's house. The spiritual counterpart to these goods relates to the priests: the olive oil and fine wheat flour were used when installing priests, and wheat was to support them. Spiritual Babylon and those with whom she traffics, including some but not all of spiritual Judah, deny that Christ's work in the heavenly Holy of Holies is

---

[149] See, for example, Karen Bennett, "The Shocking Net Worth of These 10 Richest Pastors Will Blow Your Mind," Showbiz Cheatsheet, https://1ref.us/13i (accessed July 19, 2019).

to reproduce His character of perfect righteousness in His people preparatory and prerequisite to His return. This is why Revelation 18:13 concludes by noting that these wicked merchants deal in the bodies and lives of men; they not only sell out the truth, but they barter others made in the image of God to secure their own earthly advantage.

Like Tyre of old, the religious merchants interact with every nation under the sun, influencing national governments to enact laws favorable to the propagation of Babylon and the extermination of the remnant. At the time pictured in Revelation 18, the multitudes are now fully awake. They recognize that they have been lied to and no longer buy into the lies. The merchants are exposed as the charlatans they are, and of course they are devastated by this turn of events. Their exposure not only ends their temporal pleasures, but makes them the focus of universal enmity.

Their cry in verse 16 hearkens back to the whore of Revelation, dressed in imitation of the high priest. In fact, their description focuses specifically on the colorful ephod and breastplate of judgment (see Exod. 28:5–30). Scripture reveals that the ephod was at times misused as a mark of a false priest and associated with idolatry (see Hos. 3:4, 5; Judges 8:27; 17:5; 18:14–20). The merchants' cry confirms that Babylon is indeed the high priest of idolatry. They are shocked that her great wealth is decimated.

A third class is brought to view, bewailing the downfall of the great city: the helmsmen and sailors. Tyre was an island, so it would seem natural that her trade was almost entirely by sea, hence her merchants conducted affairs by sea. The merchants of the preceding verses might be better understood as the ship owners, and the helmsmen and sailors are those who work *for* them. This includes the multitude of lesser religious leaders: the elders, pastors, priests, and evangelists of no particular prominence. Like their more well-known counterparts, they promulgate the lies of Babylon's false sanctuary:

1. When people die, their spirit lives on, just as in pagan Greek philosophy.
2. The Sabbath has been changed to the pagan *dies solis* (day of the sun).

3. Salvation depends on a mere verbal profession of faith in Jesus.

4. We may spend eternity with God without forsaking sin and being made holy by His grace.

In contrast with the pathetic cries of those who peddled Babylon's lies for a season, heaven calls upon the faithful ones to rejoice. At long last, they are vindicated! Though long mocked, and in the very closing days of earth's history, mercilessly tormented in a vain attempt to overthrow their steadfast faith, the answer to the cry of the martyrs under the fifth seal (see Rev. 6:9–11) is now fully realized. "God has exacted your judgment from her." Scripture declares that when a party brings demonstrably false charges against another, then the prosecuting party is to suffer the penalty of the charge that the defendant would have suffered had justice miscarried (see Deut. 19:15–21). Since Babylon has mistreated God's faithful throughout history, He Himself steps in, exacting their judgments from her. Praise God!

At this point, John's accompanying angel casts a stone into the sea, explaining that Babylon will disappear into oblivion. Just as Satan was cast from heaven to earth, so his agent Babylon is cast from earth into the sea. Use of the stone is terribly ironic. God's kingdom is represented by a stone, indicating its permanence (see Dan. 2:44, 45) because it is founded on the 10 Commandments, cut out of the sapphire base of God's throne (see Exod. 24:10, 12; Ezek. 1:26). Babylon sinks as a stone to the depths of the sea to take up its abode with all the sins forsaken by those who compose God's stone kingdom (see Mic. 7:19). Since Revelation ties Babylon and Egypt together, it is worth noting that Pharaoh and his soldiers were cast into the sea like a stone (see Neh. 9:11).

The reference to musicians not being heard in Babylon points back to the fall of earthly Tyre, in which songs and harp-playing were prophesied to be heard no more (see Ezek. 26:13). This is particularly ironic, given that the one prophesied to invade Tyre was Nebuchadnezzar (see v. 7), who in Daniel 3 summoned all to bow down before his golden image *once all manner of music was heard*. That music was calculated to confuse the senses and encourage false worship. Babylon now forever loses this charm.

Why will craftsmen not be found in her anymore? The proper understanding comes from the observation that God is the true Craftsman (see Prov. 8:30; Heb. 11:10) who calls others to devote their talents to building His wilderness sanctuary and earthly temple (see Exod. 31:1–11; 1 Chron. 22:15; 28:21). He condemns the work of the craftsman who devotes his skill to making carved or cast images (see Deut. 27:15). There will be no more idolaters when Babylon falls.

One might wonder about the reference to a millstone. In Isaiah 47:2, which prophesies Babylon's ultimate demise, her humiliation involves taking millstones to grind grain. Exodus 11:5 contrasts it with the office of Pharaoh, king of Egypt, hence it is the humblest of all occupations. Having rejected the light of God's Word until the very end, she will no more have the chance to acknowledge that "your word is a lamp for my feet, and a light for my path" (Ps. 119:105).

It was prophesied that during Judah's 70 years of Babylonian captivity, God would "destroy from them the voice of rejoicing and the voice of gladness, the voice of bridegroom and the voice of bride, the voice of millstones and the light of a lamp" (see Jer. 25:10). At the close of probation, the tables turn as heaven rejoices that the Lamb's bride is now ready, and both go forth triumphantly (see Rev. 19:7, 8; Joel 2:16). This true union complete, "the voice of bridegroom and bride will not be heard" in Babylon anymore.

The chapter ends with a reminder that Babylon's merchants were the rulers of the earth. The false religious leaders, along with the state leaders whom they convince to enact laws to force people into Babylon's ranks, have deceived billions of people on earth with φαρμακεια ("sorcery"). Babylon has effectively *drugged* everybody. Her system is incapable of saving anyone, so her adherents must be bewitched.

"In her, the blood of prophets and holy people was found, all of those who were slaughtered upon the earth." Babylon is a murderer, just like her true father has been from the beginning (see John 8:44). The Lamb is slaughtered in the person of His faithful followers.

This should tell everyone to steer clear of all of Babylon's lies, and from the corrupt system itself—the papacy and her daughters, the apostate

Protestant churches. All other religions, those that do not profess to worship the one God of the Bible or presently acknowledge Jesus as Lord, will soon come under Babylon's spell and worship as she dictates. There is only one remnant church: the Seventh-day Adventist church. However imperfect her individual members may be at the moment, the time is hastening on when those who are willing will be fully purified by the master Refiner, reflecting Jesus alone. The tares among her ranks will be shaken out, to be burned at Jesus' second coming.

After viewing the demise of the great whore, John's attention is once more directed heavenward. He hears what seems to be the loud voice of a vast multitude praising *Yahweh,* in awe of His salvation, power, and glory. This hearkens back to Revelation 12:10, in which a loud voice is heard extolling salvation, power, the kingdom of God, and the authority of His Anointed, following Satan's final expulsion from heaven when Jesus offered His atoning self-sacrifice at the cross.

Just as Jesus has vindicated the blood of all those who have fallen in His service, so the righteous character of those in the very end serves to vindicate *Him.* This does not mean that by some merit of their own they put Jesus in the best light, but rather, in making a full surrender to Him, Jesus is able to fulfill His everlasting covenant in their lives so that they reflect nothing *but* Him. "He is able also to save them to the uttermost that come unto God by him" (Heb. 7:25, KJV).

At the commencement of the pre-advent judgment, when the 4 living creatures would praise *Yahweh*, the 24 elders would prostrate themselves in worship before Him (see Rev. 4:9, 10). At the conclusion of the pre-advent judgment, the 24 elders and 4 living creatures both fall prostrate before God, exclaiming "Hallelu-*Yah!*"

In the first angel's message, everyone is called upon to fear the Lord and worship Him because the appointed hour for the *commencement* of the investigative judgment has arrived. Here in Revelation 19:5, a call is made for all those who fear Him to "praise our God" at the *conclusion* of the investigative judgment just prior to the second coming in verse 11.

Notice also that the call to praise God goes to "small and great." In 11:18, it was said that the time had come to give God's servants, "small and great," their reward, that time being the judgment from 1844 until the second coming. At the peak of the end-time conflict between the Lamb's remnant and Babylon's wicked multitudes, the lamb-like beast sought to force everyone, "small and great," to worship the papal sea beast (see 13:16).

At the start of the judgment in Revelation 11:17, *Yahweh* God of hosts *began* to reign, in the sense that the subjects of His kingdom began to be made up. At the completion of His kingdom in 19:6, *Yahweh* God of hosts *begins* to reign *de facto*.

In Revelation 14:2, the 144,000 have a voice like "many waters" (like Jesus in 1:15) and "strong thunderclaps" (pointing back to the giving of God's law in Exodus 20:18). The vast multitude is described in nearly identical terms in Revelation 19:6. Recall that the 144,000 of 14:1–5 are the firstfruits of earth's end-time harvest, the *first* to experience the close of their probation as judgment passes to the living. On the other hand, the vast multitude includes the 144,000 *as well as* those who respond to their final proclamation of the 3 angels' messages. Their description in these passages is nearly identical for the simple reason that the end result is the same for both groups: they both have undergone a *complete* transformation of character and come to understand by experience what *total* surrender to Jesus means.

The imagery introduced in 19:7 is that of a wedding that "has come" (meaning the ceremony has just *concluded*), just as the statement "the hour of His judgment has come" (Rev. 14:7) marked the *beginning* of the judgment. Of course, in Scripture, the end-time judgment and marriage are in fact synonymous. For those not familiar with this, reference to Jesus' parables of the 10 virgins (see Matt. 25:1–13) and king's wedding banquet (see 22:1–14) are especially helpful. The latter parable combines the wedding imagery and investigative judgment themes. In verse 11, the king goes in to see the guests, and his *investigation* reveals that one of the guests was not wearing his wedding garment. Like all guests, he had been provided the garment as a gift (Christ's righteousness freely given; see Isa. 61:10; Gal. 3:27), but he had not bothered to put it on and was therefore not prepared.

When the end-time judgment commenced in 1844, there began coming up in review the names of all who have ever professed Christ as their Savior from the power of sin. Their faithfulness during the period of their "courtship" (that portion of their lives following acceptance of Jesus' proposal) was judged. Those found unfaithful had their names removed from the book of life, their life records testifying that they had left Jesus standing at the altar. Those who proved faithful are those of whom it is said, "His wife has prepared herself." Such people proved themselves worthy of Jesus, being *fully* submitted to their Fiancé (see Eph. 5:22–24). Hence, their character became *fully* transformed by Jesus, "not having stain, wrinkle, or any such thing," being instead "holy and without blemish" (v. 27). His bride is said to be clothed in "fine linen, radiant and clean," identified as "the righteous ways of the holy people," i.e., the manifestation of Jesus' character.

John is now directed to write that all who are called unto the wedding supper of the Lamb are blessed, with the assurance that "these words of God are true." Revelation focuses on the great controversy over worship of the Creator versus idol worship, so it is shocking that John falls before the angel to worship him. In comments on Revelation 10:10 and 13:1, we noted that John's actions typify those of the end-time remnant. If the beloved apostle, to whom God committed the writing of Revelation, could fall down to worship an angel, how much more susceptible are we to false worship, weakened by another 2,000 years of sin?

The angel promptly reproves John, reminding him that he, too, is but a servant of Jesus, not worthy of any worship. He counts himself a brother of those who "have the testimony of Jesus," using the same phrase that described the end-time remnant in Revelation 12:17. The remainder of 19:10 defines the testimony of Jesus as "the spirit of prophecy." In other words, the angel refers to himself as one of God's prophets. If it seems odd to consider an angel a prophet, recall that Moses identified even *Jesus* as a prophet (see Deut. 18:18), and Jesus called *Himself* a prophet (see Matt. 13:57). All difficulties vanish when we recognize that a prophet is simply one who utters the inspired words God gives him or her.

The word "spirit" here has a double-meaning. As in English, it can have the meaning inherent in the phrase, "the spirit of the law," referring to the intent of the law. Thus, the intent or purpose of all prophecy is to instruct about and/or point to Jesus. At the same time, the spirit that produces all true prophecy is indeed the Holy Spirit, who testifies of Jesus: "When the Advocate comes, whom I will send unto you from the Father— the Spirit of truth, He who comes from the Father—He will testify of me" (John 15:26).

The end-time remnant has the testimony of Jesus, hence the spirit of prophecy. Does this mean that every member of record in the Seventh-day Adventist church is a prophet? Hardly. In fact, as a survey of Scripture makes clear, many professed believers will be shaken or sifted out, for the tares must grow alongside the wheat until the harvest is ready (see Matt. 13:30). Analogy with the Exodus movement suggests that just as the prophet Moses was appointed of God to lead His people out of Egypt to the Promised Land (though he died prior to entry), so the end-time remnant can be expected to have a prophet to lead them out of (spiritual) end-time Egypt into the true Promised Land (heaven). Since the Seventh-day Adventist Church was established in 1863, any prophet raised up in the beginning would, like Moses, have passed off the scene by now. The Seventh-day Adventist Church has steadfastly maintained that this gift of prophecy to God's end-time church was fulfilled in the life of Ellen G. White (1827–1915).

Can there be such a modern-day prophet? The plethora of false prophets blanketing the covers of grocery store tabloids gives the skeptic plenty of reason to cavil. Nevertheless, the activity of the devil in raising up so many false prophets is a fulfillment of Jesus' warning in Matthew 24:23–27. In fact, there is a concerted effort to raise so much confusion that the lone voice of a *true* prophet in the wilderness, calling God's people back to faithfulness, will be drowned out. Since Scripture calls everyone to be faithful Bereans, "examining the Scriptures, whether these things might be so" (Acts 17:11) and directs us to "quench not the Spirit, despise not prophesies, but test all things; hold fast that which is good" (1 Thess. 5:19–21), the way to test whether Ellen White was indeed a prophet is relatively simple: read her voluminous writings, praying for the guidance of the Holy Spirit to see whether her writings are in *full* harmony with the Scriptures. If anything is not so, she is false. The writer of the present work is fully convinced that Ellen White's writings are indeed inspired of the Holy Spirit and will successfully lead anyone to a much deeper, more correct understanding of the Scriptures than they could possibly possess apart from this precious gift to the remnant church.

Since the 144,000 have no lie in their mouths (see Rev. 14:5), it follows that their utterances are perfectly pure, which can only be so if those words come from God. These faithful people, fully transformed by Jesus, are his end-time mouthpieces. They are the brethren who have the "spirit of prophecy," not only in the writings of Ellen White, but in their very being. This special group will indeed prophesy. This is *not* to claim that they will be predicting future events and working sensational miracles; far from it. They will be a simple, humble people, but their lives will proclaim nothing but Jesus, and their understanding and proclamation of Scripture will be pure, free from any and all error, heresy, and fanaticism. In this sense, the 144,000—those who by God's grace will live above the power of sin—will be prophets.

Son of Man Comes for His Bride

As Table 16 makes clear, the description of Jesus upon a white horse has numerous parallels with the seals, especially the horses and their riders in seals 1–4:

Table 16: Links Between the Horseman of Revelation 19:11–16 and the Seals of Revelation 6

REFERENCE	HORSEMAN OF REV 19:11–16	SEALS OF REVELATION 6	REFERENCE
Rev .19:11	Heaven opened.	#6: Heaven disappeared like a scroll being rolled up.	Rev. 6:14
Rev. 19:11	White horse.	#1: White horse.	Rev. 6:2
Rev. 19:11	The One sitting upon it called Faithful and True.	#5: "How long, *Adonai*, Holy and True?"	Rev. 6:10
Rev. 19:11	In righteousness He judges.	#3: Rider holds balance scale of judgment; not to price unrighteously.	Rev. 6:5, 6
Rev. 19:11	And wages war.	#4: Given authority to kill.	Rev. 6:8
Rev. 19:12	Eyes are a fiery flame.	#2: Fiery red horse.	Rev. 6:4
Rev. 19:12	Upon His head were many diadems.	#1: One sitting upon white horse given a crown.	Rev. 6:2
Rev. 19:12	A name written which no one knows but Himself.	#4: One sitting upon green horse has the name Death.	Rev. 6:8
Rev. 19:13	A garment immersed in blood.	#5: Martyrs' blood. Martyrs given white robes.	Rev. 6:10, 11
Rev. 19:13	His name: The Word of God.	#5: Martyrs slaughtered for the Word of God.	Rev. 6:9
Rev. 19:14	Heaven's armies following Him.	#4: Grave following him [Death].	Rev. 6:8
Rev. 19:14	Heaven's armies wear clean, white, fine linen.	#5: Martyrs each given a white robe.	Rev. 6:11
Rev. 19:15	Sharp double-edged sword to strike the nations.	#4: Death given authority to kill by sword.	Rev. 6:8
Rev. 19:15	Winepress of the God of hosts' retribution.	#3: Don't price wine unrighteously; #6: Lamb's retribution.	Rev. 6:6, 16
Rev. 19:16	A name written: King of kings and Lord of lords.	#4: One sitting upon green horse has the name Death.	Rev. 6:8

Glimpses of the second coming have been given previously under the sixth seal, as well as at the harvest of the earth and the gathering of the vine following the proclamation of the 3 angels' messages (see Rev. 6: 14–17; 14:14–20). In Revelation 19:11–21, the second coming is presented in bold relief.

The seals commenced with horsemen; the second coming opens with a description of the true Horseman. During the fifth seal, the martyrs cried out for judgment; the true Horseman has come as the One who judges in righteousness. The martyrs under the fifth seal were each given a white robe and told to wait for their judgment and vindication; now following the true Horseman are the faithful—the living and the resurrected righteous, including these faithful martyrs—wearing clean, white, fine linen. Note that they are "following Him," for they follow the Lamb wherever He goes (see Rev. 14:4). Under the sixth seal, the wicked cower because it is the day of the Lamb's retribution; the true Horseman treads the winepress of His retribution.

Jesus is the King of kings and Lord of lords, i.e., the supreme King and supreme Judge (in Malachi 3:1, Jesus is "the Lord" who commences the end-time judgment; hence, He is the Judge). This perfectly suits Him, for He is coming for His faithful bride, those who will reign with Him, judging for 1,000 years (see Rev. 20:4, 6).

Some may be surprised to read that the armies of heaven following Jesus were just identified as people rather than angels. It might seem natural to conclude that they are angels, as heaven is of course their abode. In fact, the armies of heaven include the angels, without question: "And 'the armies which were in heaven' (Revelation 19:11, 14) follow Him. With anthems of celestial melody the holy angels, a vast, unnumbered throng, attend Him on His way" (White, *GC*, p. 641). Nevertheless, the dress of these warriors points *primarily* to faithful believers. Observe that Jesus was seen wearing an ankle-length robe with a golden sash about His chest, and the angels were seen wearing clean, radiant linen, with a golden sash about their chests (see Rev. 1:13; 15:6). The armies of heaven, however, are described as wearing clean, white, fine linen, with no mention of sashes. The golden sash about Jesus' chest marks Him as the High Priest.

The golden sash about the angels marks them as priests who have participated in the investigative judgment since October 22, 1844, specifically in reviewing Jesus' decisions about those who have professed faith in Him. The lack of sashes about the armies of heaven indicates that this group is not made up of priests. *After* Jesus comes, they will judge as priests during the 1,000 years.

Wicked Killed

What can be meant by an Angel standing in the sun? This is in fact Jesus' seventh and final stance in the book of Revelation. Table 1 shows the chiastic arrangement of His stances throughout the book:

Table 17: Jesus' 7 Stances in Revelation

REFERENCE	SUMMARY
Rev. 3:20	Son of man is the **Angel** (compare Rev. 14:14, 17) **standing** at the door.
Rev. 5:6	**Lamb standing** before **throne.**
Rev. 8:3	**Angel standing** over the altar, **holding** a golden censer.
Rev. 10:5	**Angel standing** upon the sea and earth, swears prophetic time will be no more.
Rev. 10:8	**Angel standing** upon sea and earth, **holding** an open scroll.
Rev. 14:1	**Lamb standing** before **throne** (see verse 3).
Rev. 19:17	**Angel standing** in the sun.

In verse 17, Jesus appears "standing in the sun." Earlier, His "appearance was like the sun shining in its intensity" (see Rev. 1:16). God's throne is likened to the sun (see Ps. 89:36). In Psalm 19:4–5, God has pitched a tent in the heavens for the sun (think "throne"), likened to a groom coming out of his chamber. At the second coming, when Jesus the Bridegroom has finished the wedding judgment, He emerges from the Holy of Holies to receive His bride. Satan has a counterfeit for everything, and indeed, the worship of Satan always manifests itself in sun worship. It is very interesting to note that "the Egyptians, according to Plutarch, thought that

Hercules had his seat in the sun" (*Classical Dictionary*, s.v. "Hercules").[150] How fitting that in the great controversy with Satan over worship, Jesus would be manifest as the Victor while standing in the sun!

Jesus cries to the birds flying in mid-heaven, inviting them to eat the flesh of the wicked. According to Revelation 18:2, Babylon is the prison of every unclean bird, and now such birds are portrayed as feasting on the carcasses of the impenitent wicked. Why be eaten by birds? This particular judgment points out the idolatrous nature of the sin of all the wicked. This is apparent from 1 Kings 14:11, in which birds will eat those of the house of Jeroboam who die in the field outside the city. Jeroboam was notorious for his idolatry (see 1 Kings 12:32), with every succeeding king of Israel being said to walk in his ways. Those who follow the idolatrous papacy die outside the city at the second coming (see Rev. 14:20) and are thus eaten by the birds.

Now John witnesses the pre-millennial destruction of the wicked who provide the fare for the birds flying in mid-heaven. The beast (the papacy), the kings of the earth (the state powers that have lent their support to the papacy), and their armies are poised to take their final, doomed stand against Jesus and heaven's armies. The image of the beast (apostate Protestantism in the United States employing the strong arm of the state) is styled the false prophet, hearkening back to Aaron, who was to be a prophet for Moses (see Exod. 7:1) and whose signs were to convince the Israelites and Pharaoh of the true God (see Exod. 4:28–31; 7:10), yet caved into the Israelites' demand for false gods and had them worship the image of the golden calf (see 32:1–6).

Let us examine Jesus' call for the birds to eat the flesh of the wicked and the lake of fire. The 10 horns of the scarlet beast (the governments of the world that cooperate with the United States) turn on the papacy

---

[150] For those who read Hercules' exploits as a child, thinking they were harmless tales of adventure, let them be disabused of any such notion. In Greek mythology, Hercules is often interchanged with Adonis, Apollo, and Bacchus as the *sun god*. In all cultures throughout history, the sun god has a female consort with whom he engages in the filthiest licentious behavior. For a concise yet thorough survey of sun worship through history, see Jones, *The Two Republics*, pp. 183–202.

and "consume her flesh and burn her up with fire" (Rev. 17:16). Further, 18:2 equates the birds of Babylon with the unclean spirits (the demons) who possess those who follow her. Thus, not only do the governments turn on the papacy, but all of Babylon's followers turn on their leaders, thereby carrying out the destruction in verses 17–21. The following states things plainly:

> The people see that they have been deluded. They accuse one another of having led them to destruction; but all unite in heaping their bitterest condemnation upon the ministers. Unfaithful pastors have prophesied smooth things; they have led their hearers to make void the law of God and to persecute those who would keep it holy. Now, in their despair, these teachers confess before the world their work of deception. The multitudes are filled with fury. "We are lost!" they cry, "and you are the cause of our ruin;" and they turn upon the false shepherds. The very ones that once admired them most will pronounce the most dreadful curses upon them. The very hands that once crowned them with laurels will be raised for their destruction. The swords which were to slay God's people are now employed to destroy their enemies. Everywhere there is strife and bloodshed. (White, *GC*, pp. 655, 656)

The papacy and its image are thrown into the lake of fire burning with brimstone. According to Leviticus 21:9, the punishment for a priest's daughter who brings shame upon her father by committing fornication is to be burned with fire. The fire-and-brimstone imagery points back to the destruction of Sodom, noted for its gross license in sexual sin. The papacy and its image have encouraged idolatry (spiritual fornication), so God's appointed judgment is destruction by fire burning with brimstone.

The chapter closes with the demise of "the rest." This points back to "the rest" under the sixth trumpet who refused to repent of their idolatry, holding fast to every idol (see Rev. 9:20). Therefore, "the rest" in Revelation 19:21 have clung to their idols. They are slain by Jesus' sword, forever debarred from walking with their Creator in the Garden of Eden in the heavenly sanctuary.

REVELATION 20:1–10: DRAGON DESTROYED

Satan Sealed

20 ¹Then I saw an angel coming down from heaven, having the key of the abyss and a great chain [draped] over his hand. ²He laid fast hold of the dragon—the ancient serpent, who is [the] devil, that is, Satan, the one who has been leading the entire world astray—and bound him 1,000 years. ³He cast him into the abyss, then locked and sealed [it] over him, that he no longer lead the nations astray until the 1,000 years should be fulfilled; yet afterward, it is necessary he be loosed a short time.

The Righteous Judge for 1,000 Years

⁴Then I saw thrones, and they sat upon them, and judgment was entrusted with them: the lives of those who had been beheaded on account of the testimony of Jesus and for the Word of God, and those who did not worship the beast, nor its image, and did not take the mark upon their forehead nor their hand, lived and reigned with the Messiah the 1,000 years, ⁵while the rest of the dead did *not* live until the 1,000 years were fulfilled: this is the first resurrection. ⁶Blessed and holy is he who has part in the first resurrection; upon these, the second death has no authority, but they will be priests of God and the Messiah, and will reign with him 1,000 years.

Magog Gathered for Final Destruction

[7]When the 1,000 years are fulfilled, Satan will be loosed from his prison, [8]and he will come forth to lead astray the nations which are in the 4 corners of the earth, Gog and Magog, to gather them together for the war, of whom the number is as the sand of the sea. [9]They came up over the breadth of the earth, and encircled the encampment of the holy people, the beloved city. Then fire came down out of heaven from God and utterly consumed them. [10]The devil who led them astray was cast into the lake of fire and brimstone, where both the beast and false prophet [had been cast, see Rev. 19:20]; they will be tormented day and night forever and ever.

COMMENTARY

Satan Sealed

At this point, John sees an angel come down with the key to the abyss. This key locks the door to planet earth, meaning that Satan and his angels are confined to this planet alone, and all of the wicked dead are locked in their graves. It is in this sense that Satan is bound: he has been leading astray the billions of planet earth for approximately 6,000 years, and now he has 1,000 years in which he is powerless to tempt anyone. The only "pleasure" that he gets, that of deceiving and destroying, is withheld from him until He who has the key of David (see Rev. 3:7) shall once more open the graves for a "short time" at the end of the 1,000 years. Until such time, no one can unlock Satan's prison.

Satan has deceived the overwhelming majority of planet earth into receiving the mark of the beast and forfeiting the seal of the living God, the badge of which is keeping holy the Sabbath day. Now, as the crowning mark of his work, Satan himself is sealed! In what sense could *he* receive God's seal? By force of circumstances, he is now forced to cease his work of deception, hence keep Sabbath, as it were, for 1,000 years (recall that *shabbat* means "cessation"). The "short time" to follow will demonstrate that no reformation of character was accomplished for Satan during the 1,000 years.

The Righteous Judge for 1,000 Years

Next, John sees what transpires in heaven during the 1,000 years: judgment. Two specific groups are identified: those who had been beheaded on account of the testimony of Jesus and for the Word of God are the martyrs under the fifth seal who were so described. These had been granted white robes, just as the 24 elders who participated in judgment wore white garments (see Rev. 4:4). They were told to wait until the number of their brethren should be made up. Who are these brethren? The second group in Revelation 20:4: those who did not worship the beast or its image or take the mark.

Those in the first resurrection serve as priests and kings, and of course, biblical kings and priests are judges (see 2 Sam. 15:2; Deut. 19:17). Judgment was given *in favor of* the holy people at the conclusion of its pre-advent phase (see Dan. 7:22); now, judgment is committed *to* them in its post-advent phase.

The martyrs under the altar who had been slaughtered were told to wait "a time" in the grave before their blood would be vindicated during the pre-advent investigative judgment. In perfect irony, the wicked must now wait 1,000 years as *they* are judged.

The wicked *do not live* throughout the 1,000 years. This runs contrary to the belief popular in Protestant and Roman Catholic churches that the wicked have been burning in hell fire from the moment of death onward and will continue to do so for the ceaseless ages of eternity. The text is plain that they remain dead until they are resurrected by Him who has "the keys of death and the grave" (Rev. 1:18).

Magog Gathered for Final Destruction

At the close of the 1,000 years, Satan is loosed. It is clear that his prison time did not work a reformation of character. Upon the resurrection of the wicked at the voice of Jesus (see John 5:28, 29), Satan immediately goes forth to lead them astray one last time in a vain attempt to take the holy city.

Observe that the wicked multitudes are in the 4 corners of the earth; the angels who held back the winds of strife prior to the sealing of God's people were likewise in the 4 corners of the earth. With the 4 restraining angels no longer at their post, the wicked who stand in their place are continually buffeted by all that their chosen leader, Satan, throws their way.

Reference is made to Gog and Magog, a reference to Ezekiel 38 and 39. Gog, the chief prince of Meshech and Tubal, is from the land of Magog (see 38:2). In the Bible, land is equated with those who occupy the land (see Deut. 32:43; Ezek. 38:16; Mal. 3:12). Hence, Magog refers not to a land of unknown location, but to the entirety of the wicked nations in the 4 corners of the earth, and Gog is their chief prince, Satan himself. The number of the wicked is as "the sand of the sea." This is enormously ironic, for this same language is *also* used of those who partake of God's everlasting covenant (see Gen. 22:17; 32:12).

Satan leads the wicked astray once more, convincing them that due to their sheer numbers, they can easily overtake the city. God rains down fire and brimstone, utterly consuming them as He did wicked Sodom and Gomorrah (see Gen. 19:24). This is all the more fitting, as the land beast called fire down from heaven to deceive those who dwell upon the earth, fastening them in his ranks (see Rev. 13:13).

Revelation 20:9–10 soundly contradicts the teaching of an eternally burning hell. It harmonizes perfectly with the Old Testament, which describes the wicked as both stubble to be burned up and carcasses (see Mal. 4:1; Isa. 47:14; 66:24). It agrees also with the New Testament, which says they will be reduced to ashes (see 2 Peter 2:6; Jude 7). In fact, the wicked don't *begin* burning until 1,000 years *after* the second coming. Further, "utterly consumed" does not harmonize with burning for eternity. Our God is a consuming fire (see Deut. 4:24; 9:3; Heb. 12:29), and that means exactly what it says. When wicked King Ahaziah sent soldiers to fetch Elijah, he called down fire from heaven, and it consumed them (see 2 Kings 1:10, 12). Earlier, at the Mt. Carmel showdown between Elijah and the prophets of Baal, God's fire from heaven consumed not just the sacrifice and wood, but even the stones, dust, and water (see 1 Kings 18:38). We also cannot forget that Nadab and Abihu were consumed by the same fire that earlier had consumed the burnt offering and fat at the inauguration of the wilderness sanctuary (see Lev. 9:24–10:2). The text plainly indicates that these people, sacrifices, wood, stones, dust, and water were consumed on the spot. No one understands this to mean that they are burning to this day.

If God has eliminated sinners by fire in the past, what indication is there that in the final confrontation, He will let them undergo a slow burn for all of eternity? This is when God purifies creation once and for all, restoring everything to its original Edenic beauty. *Yahweh* will make a new earth (see Isa. 66:22; Rev. 21:1). If the earth is still seething as a lake of fire, how can it be said that He makes all things new and there will be no more death, mourning, wailing, or pain (see Rev. 21:4, 5)? Sinners cannot withstand God's flames for eternity, for Isaiah 33:14–17 makes it clear that those who will dwell with the consuming fire and everlasting burning are *the righteous*.

One might question the foregoing, since the end of Revelation 20:10 states that "they will be tormented day and night forever and ever." This may sound like the ceaseless ages of eternity, but that is because of our modern understanding of "forever." The Bible uses "forever" to mean the extent of something's existence. The Bible describes the 3 days and 3 nights that Jonah spent in the belly of the fish as "forever" (see Jonah 1:17; 2:6); Samuel's earthly lifetime was "forever" (see 1 Sam. 1:22, 28); a slave could choose to remain his master's servant forever (see Exod. 21:6).

Note also that the wicked burn "day and night." How ironic, since Satan accused God's chosen "day and night" (Rev. 12:10). On the other hand, the 4 livings beings cease not worshipping God "day and night," and the vast multitude serves Him "day and night" in His temple (see 4:8; 7:15).

The beloved city is referred to as an "encampment," military language indicating the locale of God's army, His people. This word first appears in Genesis 32:2 when Jacob sees the host of God encamped before and behind him. Later, during Israel's wilderness wanderings, God's people were referred to as His "camp" (see Exod. 14:19). Now, following the antitypical Exodus, those who stood stiffly for His truth are pictured as His army in their encampment.

PART 4B': THE KEY POINTS

REVELATION 17:1–20:10: JESUS

Jesus' voice pleads with people to come out of Babylon. He commences His reign once the subjects of His kingdom are fully made up, when the marriage of the Lamb has come. The spirit of prophecy is the testimony of Jesus, who is the Rider on the white horse, coming for His bride at the second coming. He is the Angel standing in the sun, issuing the call for the birds to feast on the wicked. The righteous reign with the Messiah as judges and priests for the 1,000 years.

REVELATION 19:17: JESUS STANDS FOR HIS BRIDE

For the seventh time, Jesus stands in the sun as the Bridegroom who comes forth from His chamber (see Ps. 19:4, 5; 89:36), ready to take His long-awaited bride home and pronounce doom on His enemies.

REVELATION 17:1–20:10: THE WEDDING THEME

The second commandment asserts that God is jealous. As the heavenly Bridegroom, He desires full fidelity on the part of His bride; she is not to worship any image or likeness of her design. The Bible refers to the papacy as the great whore because she encourages all manner of idolatry, and thus infidelity to Christ.

By His grace, God's bride will prepare herself and be clothed in fine linen, radiant and clean, the robe of Christ's righteousness woven in the loom of heaven—His perfect character. However, prior to the second coming, she will not be above being tempted and overcome, so she must cling to her Bridegroom continuously.

REVELATION 17:1–20:10: DECISION QUESTION

In Revelation 19:11–16, we read of the blessed hope to which Christians of all ages have looked forward: the return of Jesus as Bridegroom to receive His bride. At the same time, chapter 20 paints the second death in all of its horrific terror. How great is Jesus' love for His corporate bride, that His death satisfied the death penalty for her—our—violation of the law!

Is any known idol standing between you and the Bridegroom? If so, take it to Jesus immediately. Do not play with sin. What about *unknown* character defects? These must go as well, since Jesus is coming for a bride without "spot, or wrinkle, or any such thing," one who is "holy and without blemish" (Eph. 5:27, KJV). Are you resisting the Bridegroom's plea to join His church, the Seventh-day Adventist Church? Perhaps you are a member, but you don't take your membership seriously. He is coming for His bride, and that is His church—the *faithful* members of His church who continue to advance in character growth. What in this life even compares with such matchless love? Money, fashion, cultural norms (recall cross-dressing in comments on Revelation 17), positions of influence … are any of these things worth forfeiting eternity with Jesus?

Will you not take advantage of probationary time *now* to ensure a place at the soon coming marriage supper of the Lamb? Why not pray as David did: "Create in me a clean heart, O God; and renew a right spirit within me" (see Ps. 51:10, KJV).